Praise for
Nightmare of Ecstasy

"Delirious and horrifying — and All True!" — Richard
Corliss, *Time*

"Finally the Ed Wood story told in all its naked wonder.
Nightmare of Ecstasy is an hilarious but heart-breaking
portrayal of a brave, eccentric and sometimes insane film
director. I stayed up all night reading it with my mouth
hanging open." — John Waters

"The literary even of the year!" — Phantom of the Movies,
New York Daily News

Nightmare of Ecstasy

The Life and Art of Edward D. Wood, Jr.

by Rudolph Grey

FERAL HOUSE

Nightmare of Ecstasy: The Life and Art of Edward D. Wood, Jr. ©
1992, 1994 by Rudolph Grey

ISBN: 0-922915-24-5

For a free catalog of Feral House books, send SASE to:

Feral House
PO Box 3466
Portland, OR 97208

Dedicated to
Ed Wood

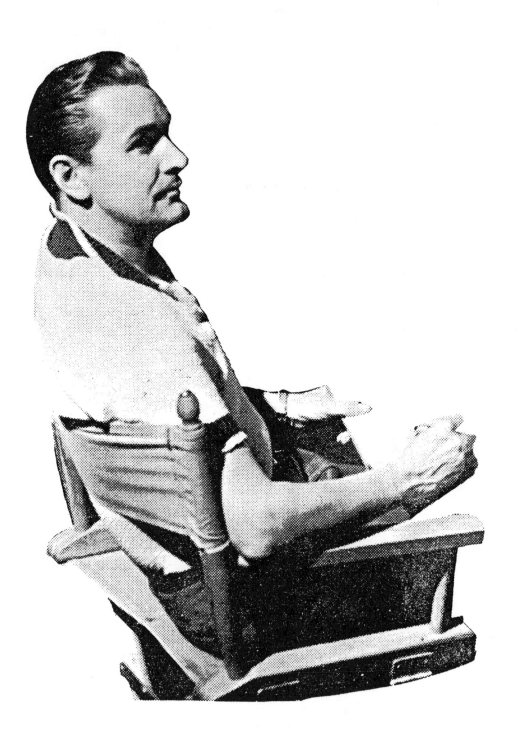

Introduction

"The imperfect is alive." — Carl Dreyer

A biography, under the most favorable of circumstances, is a slow and difficult undertaking. There were unusual problems in the case of Ed Wood, Jr., and the task of reconstructing his life and documenting his work was arduous and complicated.

In the world of low-budget exploitation filmmaking, producers were notorious for being literally "here today, gone tomorrow." Small corporations would vanish without a trace, and producers would often leave town — or even the country — posthaste. When these elusive individuals could be found, often they had kept no records of their own productions — no posters, no pressbooks, no stills ... and quite frequently ... no movies. Films listed as being in company vaults would, upon search, have inexplicably disappeared. The most diligent detective work would lead to a dead end.

The climate of sensationalism that followed Wood's death proved to be yet another obstacle. Former associates, such as the late Phil Tucker, director of *Robot Monster,* refused to discuss the past; others flatly denied ever knowing Ed Wood — or came down with a sudden case of amnesia.

Most of Ed Wood's own documentation of his career — scrapbooks, scripts, photos, films — were lost or sold throughout his three decades in Hollywood. At the end of his life, an old rawhide suitcase and what he could pack inside of it, was all that survived. The remainder of his personal effects had been consigned to dumpsters and garbage cans across Southern California.

The material in this volume is the result of ten years of research. Hundreds of interviews were involved, and many participants were contacted repeatedly over the years when new facts came to light. Obsession and perseverance have their rewards, and many one-of-a-kind photographs were rescued from certain oblivion. Particularly exciting was finally locating a print of one of Ed Wood's last feature films, *Take It Out In Trade* (1970), a surreal sex comedy that proved to be a major discovery.

* * *

This is an oral history by those who knew Wood intimately. As such, it is inevitably colored by the distortions of memory and vanity. I have sometimes chosen not to eliminate an individual's memory even if it contradicts another's account. Conflicting versions of biographical incident are often charged with meaning and moment. Discovering the objective "truth" of an individual's life may be impossible beyond a schematizing of life events: for the reader's reference, I have provided such a chronology for the "who-what-when-wheres" of Ed Wood's life. The mystery of the "why" is best revealed in the stories I have woven together in the main body of this book.

In 1957, Universal Pictures sold their classic '30's and '40's horror film library to television, where they were syndicated on many stations in a package called *Shock Theater.* Bela Lugosi, stage and screen artist of the first magnitude, had died just a year earlier. In his last years he was shamefully ignored by Hollywood, with the sole exception of his employment by Ed Wood. His classic *Dracula* was now being seen by millions. *Frankenstein, The Mummy, The Invisible Man, the Werewolf of London, The Wolf Man* were now being revived on television. On the rare occasions when I could stay up late, I would watch *Shock Theater* in rapt terror and awe. The genius of Karl Freund, James Whale, Tod Browning and Edgar Ulmer could not be resisted — I had been indoctrinated.

Movie houses across the USA were weekly invaded by double bills unleashing an onslaught of creepy things: Black Scorpions, Cat Girls, Saucer Men, She Devils, Teenage Werewolves and Frankensteins, Crawling Eyes, Vampires, Venusians, ambulatory tree trunks, zombies, giant insects — monsters of every conceivable persuasion. Monsters, along with rock and roll, became a national youth craze. They converged in early '58 with John Zacherle's "Dinner with Drac," a national hit 45 that shared the airwaves with Elvis, Eddie Cochran, and the Johnny Burnette Trio.

At the same time, a magazine hit the newsstands which capitalized on this youthful mania: *Famous Monsters of Filmland.* It proved popular and spawned imitations: *World Famous Creatures, Monster Parade, Monsters,* and *Things.*

The April, 1959 issue of *Famous Monsters* ran a four-page photo-illustrated article on the "Allied Artists release," *Night of the Ghouls:*

Night of the Ghouls opens in a cemetery. The camera takes us inside a vault, and from a casket Criswell the Seer rises and relates:

> For many years I have told the almost unbelievable, related the unreal and showed it to be more than fact. Now I tell a tale of the Threshold People, so astounding that some of you may faint. This is a story of those in the twilight time — once human, now monsters — in the void between the living and the dead ... Monsters to be pitied .... Monsters to be despised.

There was something about the claustrophobic story line, the starkly chiaroscuro photographs and the weird cartoon-like characters — Dr. Acula, The White Ghost, The Black Ghost, Lobo — which seemed to me completely unlike anything else around at the time, and it stuck in my mind. But this odd film was never released. File under Dimension X.

In 1961, WPIX-11, an independent New York television station bought a package of then-recent horror and science fiction movies. Included in this group were two by Edward D. Wood, Jr.: *Bride of the Monster* (1955) and *Plan 9 From Outer Space* (released 1959). For over five years these two films played about every seven weeks, and I would watch each telecast, religiously. For here was the immortal Bela Lugosi in his last speaking role in *Bride of the Monster,* as the "mad," supercilious Dr. Eric

Vornoff. In an old house surrounded by a reptile-infested marshland, he experiments with the aim of creating a new race of atomic superbeings. His goal: to rule the world! At his command is the hulking Tibetan mute, Lobo, and a giant killer octopus ... comic book elements that appealed to me on the same level as Stan Lee — Jack Kirby & Ayers monster comics of the early sixties — *Goom!, Googam, Son of Goom!, Fin Fang Foom!, Zzutak!, The Thing That Shouldn't Exist!!*, etc..

And what was a boy to make of the ultra-strangeness of Wood's low-budget spectacular, *Plan 9 From Outer Space?* The unsettling introductory ranting by Criswell set the tone:

> Greetings my friend ... We are all interested in the future — for that is where you and I are going to spend the rest of our lives ... and remember, my friend, future events such as these will affect you in the future! You are interested in the unknown, the mysterious, the unexplainable — that is why you are here. And now, for the first time, we are bringing you the full story of what happened ... on that fateful day.
>
> We are giving you all the evidence, based only on the secret testimony of the miserable souls who survived this terrifying ordeal.
>
> The incidents, the places, my friend, we cannot keep this a secret any longer. Let us punish the guilty; let us reward the innocent
>
> My friend, can your heart stand the shocking facts about ... *Grave Robbers From Outer Space!?"*

The atmospheric library music; Criswell's somber-pompous narration; the otherworldly ambience of Lugosi's silent footage; ghoul-doll Vampira; Tor Johnson rising from his grave; the ink-black graveyard; the wobbling plywood tombstones, and the jarring, idiosyncratic dialogue. I was fascinated.

In the '60's, I was intrigued to learn of other movies in Edward D. Wood's outré canon: *Glen or Glenda, The Hidden Face, The Sinister Urge.* But only the Wood-scripted *The Bride and the Beast* turned up on television. This unusual tale of reincarnation, a honeymooning couple in Africa, and their pet gorilla, Spanky, kept my interest in Wood running high.

In the fateful month of December, 1978, the Thalia theater in New York began Friday midnight screenings of the long-unseen *Glen or Glenda.*

Watching the 1953 *Glen or Glenda* in the sparsely occupied theater was a revelation. At the onset of the film, Bela Lugosi appears on screen as the "spirit-like god", delivering his lines with a remarkable intensity:

> Man's constant groping for things unknown ....drawing ... from the endless reaches of time ... brings to light ... many startling things ... startling ... because they seem new ... sudden. But most are not new ... to the signs of the ages...."

A coda of lightning and thunder. The spirit, who "controls all life," proceeds to mix smoking chemicals. In the laboratory of the gods, the spirit has created the elixir of life.

"A life is begun."

His face, superimposed over a busy city street, delivers an embittered, resigned diatribe of this pathetic race known as humans:

> People! All going somewhere. All with their own thoughts, their own ideas, all with their own ... personalities. One is wrong, because he does right. And one is right ... because he does wrong. Pull the string! Dance to that ... which one is created for!

Overwhelmed by this amazing film, I returned each weekend, bringing friends to share the experience.

At this time I began working with a colleague on a series of interviews for the San Francisco review, *Vacation.* After seeing *Glen or Glenda,* Wood was on a high priority list for future interviews. But time had run out.

On the morning of December 7, 1978, Ed Wood was evicted from his tiny Hollywood apartment on Yucca street. Destitute, he and his wife moved in with an actor friend. Three days later he died of a heart attack. He was 54 years old. The trade papers were not notified and there were no obituaries in any newspapers or magazines.

Ignored or reviled by critics when he was alive, Wood was the target of still more ridicule soon after his death. The jackals of bourgeois sensibility moved in. With an offensive smugness and condescension towards his movies and novels, they had a field day of derision over the revelation of his transvestism.

* * *

Ed Wood was a peculiarly American original, with a great passion for popular media: '30's and '40's B western and horror movies, pulp magazines, comic books and radio dramas. Wood, the all-American boy, idolized Buck Jones, became a Boy Scout, and enlisted in the Marines at the age of 17, six months after the attack on Pearl Harbor. He became a war hero and survivor after brutal conflicts with the Japanese in the South Pacific. All the while, he was a transvestite, an outsider to the mainstream of life.

Soon after the war he found work in a carnival, and his experiences in that bizarre and hermetic environment cannot be underestimated. These were some of the raw materials from which he shaped his unorthodox art.

Wood's art is a cultural mutation. He defies comparison — there is no one remotely like him. Displaced from time, his legend and reputation grows.

I remember the offhand comment of a Hollywood producer who was incredulous at Ed Wood's posthumous notoriety. In the last years of his life, Wood would come by the producer's office to use his typewriter. His comment keeps coming back to me:

> The really funny thing is that here is this alcoholic, this old bum that I really liked, and all the time I never knew that he was something special.

Rudolph Grey
New York City
October, 1991

CARL ANTHONY   If anyone ate, drank and dreamt motion pictures, it was Ed Wood. This was his whole life. Movies — 24 hours a day.

ROY REID   He used to call me every once in a while. He had some kind of wild idea.

GEORGE WEISS   Nothing can touch him, as many stones as they've thrown. Nothing can touch the fact that that man is an outstanding individual against all the others, when it came to, not only writing, but creativeness. In everything! Not only in the motion pictures — he was a stylist.

LORETTA KING   Ed Wood was absolutely one of the most handsome people...he was handsome in the way that we'll say, from a Fitzgerald novel like Gatsby or something like that ... from the 1920's. That type of look.

VALDA HANSEN   Ed said, "Do you think I care if i'm a millionaire? No, Valda. What hurts me is the cruelty toward me. The way they want to deride me. The way they want to put me down and scoff at me. I'm only trying to do the best at what I feel. All this garbage I see, they praise, and me, they seem to love to deride me."

DUDLEY MANLOVE   The poor guy sweat his balls off and then died ... and now somebody's getting rich off the fruits of his labor....

CONRAD BROOKS   A lot of times there was no food...rent money and booze came first ... because he didn't know whether he'd have rent money or not, so he drank. It was an escape for Ed Wood. So he wrote scripts, knocked them out, sold them for nothing practically. "Ed, we'll give you a couple of hundred..."

KATHY WOOD   I met Eddie when he was still young, and gauche, and happy, and he still wanted to do great things, and he still wanted to make the world his oyster....

HARRY THOMAS   It's pitiful, the way things ended, because he had so much faith in himself ... he was just elated with the things that he did. I'd go over and sit in his house and he'd run these old pictures over and over again...

LILLIAN WOOD   If Junior wasn't at school or work, we knew where to find him. He was at the movies ...

Ed Wood on his 17th birthday with his first movie camera,
a Kodak City Special, Poughkeepsie, New York

Ed Wood, Jr., Age 3

Age 6

13th Birthday

Childhood / The World Outside

LILLIAN WOOD   I was born July 5, 1903, and my husband, Edward Wood, Sr. was born on February 23, 1895. He died May 6, 1967. He had just retired from the post office. I'm from Jersey City — I'm not a Poughkeepsie girl. We were transported up here with the Kreske Company, in 1919, we opened the first Kreske store in Poughkeepsie. I worked as a jewelry buyer, my sister and I.

I met Ed Sr. here in Poughkeepsie, through one of the churches. We were married on the 28th of November, 1923. Junior was born October 10, 1924, at 115 Franklin Street, off the main highway. Yep.

FRED ROBERTSON   Edward Wood, Sr. worked for the U.S. post office, he was a maintenance man there. He was the post commander of V.F.W. 170...served in World War I. He was very nice, common type, down to earth, we're all blue collar workers, that's all we are. William Wood, his other son, was a career man in the service, he retired and passed away a few years ago. I never met Ed junior. His father was tall, white hair, tall and thin. He liked a few drinks like I did, he liked his beer.

Years ago I had some of Ed Jr.'s films, 100 foot, 16mm, that he took himself. Scenes of him playing G-man with cap pistols, black and white, the typical thing that a kid would have taken — a couple of guys playing cops and robbers, just clowning around, about four minutes.

KATHY WOOD   His dad bought him this movie camera ... and the Hindenburg was coming down the Hudson, on the course to where it crashed in New Jersey and went up in flames ... and Eddie filmed it, he said it was thrilling, exciting, he was so proud that he shot it before it crashed. He was always so proud of that. He had memories of his dad helping Franklin Delano Roosevelt lay the cornerstone for the post office at Poughkeepsie.

Eddie would stage plays in his backyard, all the neighborhood kids would join in, he would stage them, write little stories and then film them. He was always filming things ... and that's all he wanted to do, from the time he was four or five. He'd run around taking pictures. That's all he wanted to do....

LILLIAN WOOD   In school, Junior's best subjects were reading and spelling. He was a big book reader. Every time he'd go to the bathroom he had a book with him. Usually mystery stories. He also collected comic books. Eddie's boyhood friends were George Kesseck, Frank Wirsch and Eddie Seclas. They had a band, The Sunshine Mountaineers. Junior played drums. They also had ukelele and violin-cowboy music. They did high school dates, and they played in New York on Major Bowes. He had a steady girlfriend called Catherine Clark. She was very lovely...

KATHY WOOD   He was only a kid when he left to join the Marine Corps (at age 17). He was a theater usher then, a ticket taker. He had a singing group called Eddie Wood's Little Splinters. He always was great with names, that was before he went into the Marine Corps. I remember him telling me, I think he played guitar. It was a western singing group; they were on Major Bowes.

JOHN ANDREWS   When Flash Gordon first came out, what was that, '36? He was a little kid. His father was a mail carrier. And anyway, he and his little buddies from school would go every Saturday and see the latest chapter, and then on Sunday morning they would all get together after church, and replay the chapter they'd seen the day before. Alright. Everybody wanted to be Flash. Not Eddie. Eddie had no competition ... he wanted to be Dale!

LILLIAN WOOD   Junior and his brother, William, they always got along good, if anybody did anything to each other they were right there to tackle 'em. But...he was very jealous of Junior, I don't know why, because we did for both of them, we never did for one and not the other. Never.

KATHY WOOD   When he was a kid growing up in Poughkeepsie, he was always interested in the movies, especially the westerns, when he started working at the Bardavon Theater. He worked as an usher and was finally an assistant manager. And after the movies were over they'd throw away the stills, and he'd go and pick them out of the garbage cans out in the back of the theater. He had a good collection of the old movies.

His boyhood hero was Buck Jones. Too bad he never met him. I remember one time, this is long before he met Ken Maynard, Ken Maynard was on a tour up in Poughkeepsie, and he was riding his horse on the stage, and Eddie was watching from the wings, and the stage wasn't very steady...so the horse went right through the stage! Plunged right through, one of his legs. But when Ken was still alive, we used to go and visit him out in the Valley. And he lived in this trailer. And he and Eddie had a great time laughing about that.

KATHY WOOD   Eddie told me that his mother did dress him as a girl when he was two, three or four. So maybe she's responsible.

> ... Although it was known his mother had dressed him in frilly dresses
> until he was six, few ever thought anything about it. In fact most thought it
> was cute. After all he was cute ENOUGH TO HAVE BEEN A GIRL...
> — Edward D. Wood, Jr., *Sex, Shrouds, & Caskets*

SCOTT RAYE   Ed said his mother was punishing him. "They didn't know what the hell they were doing to me."

MONA McKINNON   He thought his mother wanted a girl ... instead of a boy. And that's about the only thing he had to say about it.

KATHY WOOD   He didn't embarrass me too much with it ... it was kind of a put-on half the time ... in those days, you know everything was camp. Like his tongue-in-cheek humour, it was the same way. And nobody took offense at it. Nobody at all. I mean, his mother must have known about it. She never admitted it; I never confronted her with it.

KATHY WOOD   Three kids from Poughkeepsie, Ed, George Kesseck and Frank Wirsch all went down to the Marine recruiting station. Only Ed winded up finally going- one didn't make it, one gave an excuse, Ed got asthma, or pneumonia — but only he made it in the Marines — he says he begged the commandant to stay in.

He didn't go out in the first wave, because he had pneumonia or something, the first wave of Marines were slaughtered completely, it was the second wave. He didn't ask to be held back, but he told me he wanted to go with his outfit, and he was always delicate. But for a delicate guy he lasted pretty long. But it kept him out of the first wave, luckily.

LILLIAN WOOD   Junior would send drawings during the war...scenes of soldiers, studies...

KATHY WOOD   Ed told me many horror stories of his experiences. They haunted him. But he was a brave man and I was proud of him. I wish I still had the medals- The Silver Star, Bronze Star, Oakleaf Cluster, Purple Heart, Sharpshooter's medal, and some I can't remember. We lost them while moving.

Eddie lived his lifetime during the war! He hated to kill, but ... he did....

He had nightmares about the first Jap he killed. Just after they had landed on the beach, and were advancing inland through Palm trees, Ed shot a sniper out of a tree. He saw a lot of action in the South Pacific, Nanumea, Tarawa, Marshall Islands...

He won his medals when most of the Marines were killed, and the Japanese were coming up a hill ... Eddie grabbed a machine gun, there was no one to feed it, he had to feed it by hand, and ... he wiped them out.

It had been a hot day. A very hot day. As Corporal of the Guard on the tiny South Pacific Island, it had been his duty to welcome the "Gentlemen of the Press", when they landed in their Navy Sea Plane, and escort them to the Colonel's quarters. Welcome them! Huh! The Marines had only been on this dangerous little speck of land for fifteen hours and already the press had come in. Jim remembered wondering who the Marine Corps press agent was. Jim then had the honor of escorting the "Gentlemen of the Press" back to their air place two hours later.

On the drive back from the tip of the island after seeing the "Gentlemen of the Press" off he felt himself feeling carefree. From the tip of the island where the landing field was to the spot where his headquarters was located was a good three mile trip. He took the first mile and a half singing at the top of his lungs. He waved joyously to the silver plane which rode in toward the island at fifteen thousand feet. But even as he waved a funny, unexplainable feeling of danger came over him. A frown upon his face. That wasn't the sea plane up there. It was a bomber.

Jim drove the jeep toward the nearest anti-aircraft barricade, jammed on the brakes and dove over the sand bags. As he hit the sand at the base of the gun the whole island shook with the explosion of the first load of bombs dropped by the Japanese bomber. The ack-ack crew jumped to life and their battle stations. Some one yelled for him to take over the fuse cutter. He hopped on the seat, checked the pointer arrow then looked quickly skyward. He could see five bombers in a group coming from the west, five from the east and five more from the north. The first plane dropped its load. "Those bombs look like drops of water coming through the sky," he remembered reflecting to himself at that time. Then they hit. A Sergeant fell forward on his face. The ack-ack spoke rapidly. Two planes fell in smoke, then Jim felt the burning in his side. He looked to the left where the gun Captain was staring in his direction. Jim looked down to his side. The blood had stained the right side of his shirt. Weakness overcame him and he fell from the fuse cutter's stool."

— Ed Wood, *Casual Company,* (unpublished novel) 1950

... He was alone in a fox hole. The night was dark, the enemy all around him. For nights the enemy had crept silently upon the unsuspecting Marines and just as silently slit their throats.

[He] had pledged it to himself that at all times, even if he couldn't see or hear, he was going to feel the presence of an adversary. He trained himself relentlessly in that one aim. His training paid off when two of the enemy crept silently toward his place of concealment. They reached it, but they had not come undetected. They would remain in the fox hole for the duration, perhaps for an eternity.

— Ed Wood, *Parisian Passions*

KATHY WOOD   Ed also was an excellent underwater swimmer, and he went on many secret missions in the South Pacific. He caught jungle rot in the South Pacific on his legs, and suffered through X-rays and treatments most of his life. He was also machine gunned up his entire leg, and had a lot of teeth knocked out by a rifle butt. He did a lot of hall and office work, and was the fastest typist in the Marines.

Eddie was in the G-2 in the Marine Corps. He was a hell of a good agent, in the South Pacific isles. When we had the pool, on Strohm street, he would show me how they would swim for hours underneath the water. He would jump in, and swim, very quietly, underneath the water without breathing. He would just come up and there were no ripples in the water. He used to tell me these were a couple of things they did, in the Marine Corps, when they had to make a surveillance on these different islands.

After the war, there were a lot of spies floating around, and he said he joined the Ice Capades as an ice skater, working undercover. The Ice Capades was on tour across the country. There were German or Russian spies, and Eddie was able to ferret them out. And they got rid of the spies.

Jr. at Graduation

With a friend, Honolulu

A gathering on Labor Day, 1942.
(l. to r.) Ed's maternal
grandmother, Jr., Lillian, Ed Sr.

Jr. and Buddies, World War II

Now Eddie, I don't know, I love him, he was such a bullshitter. But, it's possible. Eddie did the most impossible things which I later found out were true.

JOE ROBERTSON   We were both in the Marine corps, he was in the invasion of Tarawa. 4000 Marines went in ... 400 came out. He was one of the 400. He was wearing pink panties and a pink bra underneath his battle fatigues. And he said to me, "Thank God Joe I got out, because I wanted to be killed, I didn't want to be wounded, because I could never explain my pink panties and pink bra." He said, "If I'm wounded, I'm going to be in trouble, if I get killed, nobody gives a shit." And he told me that. And I laughed. In the Marine Corps, you don't do that stuff, you get 20 years. You go to Portsmouth, you know what I mean?

VALDA HANSEN   Ed said to me, "You have beautiful teeth. I've had mine knocked out, love, in the war. I said, "They knocked your teeth out?" "Well love, in the war, they take a bayonet, and then they knock your teeth out, and then they try to rip you between your legs." I was kind of innocent and young, I said, "Did they hurt you or something, Ed?" That's how innocent I was then, I was living with my mother and father. He said, "Well, lover", and he kind of laughed and looked at me, because I was innocent, "They hurt me ... we'll say that."

HENRY BEDERSKI   When he was in the war, when the Japanese guy knocked his teeth out, he battered Ed with the gun, and knocked his front teeth out ... and made Eddie so goddamn mad hat when Eddie killed him, Eddie said, "I kept on stabbing on him." He said, "That was so crazy, Henry, here I'm venting my anger, and the guy's dead." There's no doubt, he had some sadist in him.

KATHY WOOD   He told me he went to Northwestern University (in Chicago) after he got out of the Marine Corps. I'm pretty sure he took up acting, and I think writing. And that's when he told me he lived in an abandoned theater, or a theater that was dark most of the time, and that's where he got the inspiration for *Final Curtain*. He felt the vibes, as we say. He did travel with the carnival somewhere along the line.

Planks. Fresh lumber. Steel rods slammed to the ground and awaited usage. Trucks were hastily unloaded; the material almost immediately being carried away. Ground was broken. Frames began to take shape. Tents were unrolled; center poles were shoved underneath for raising. The ropes became secured. Iron and steel took the form of various rides. Circus type wagons took their places behind the tents. Flats and boards took the shape of ticket booths in front of the steadily shape taking rides and shows. Banners began to appear over the entrance of the girlie show; the snake show; the western show; the Hawaiian show. Wheels and spinners snapped into place in the concession booths. Multi-colored counters seemed to jump into position. Plaster dolls; trophies and other "schluck" materials were wrapped or unwrapped and placed on shelves in an alluring manner.

Then the layout of all the tent shows sprouted to finishing touches as the long Side Show banner was tied into place. The great banner boasted gigantic cartoons of what was to be found on the inside. The Fat Lady. The Tattooed Woman. The Indian Rubber Man. A Hindu spread out on nails. The Fire Eater; and an extra large poster of the Half-Man, Half-Woman, blow-off attraction.
— Ed Wood, *Killer In Drag* 1963

CHUCK LA BERGE In the theater, we had a bad night, we'd all sit around and share a bottle of gin. We'd get drunk and Ed would tell us all this weird stuff. He did the carnival. He wanted to be in show business, any phase of it. One of his stories was that he played the part of the half-man, hal woman. He had a beard. I said, "How in hell did you get boobs?" He'd explain that they'd put a needle in the nipple and blew it up. And he played the geek ...

JOHN THOMAS On the back of the script of *Crossroads of Laredo* there's an interesting clue as to where he went to school for his writing. This stationary, it says "Kingsmith School of the Creative Arts, courtyard, rear, 2118 Massachusetts, North West Washington, D.C." The Advisory Board of Artists at the bottom: Frank Lloyd Wright, Martha Graham, etc....

DOLORES FULLER Ed was a great admirer of Martha Graham. I believe that they wrote to each other, I know that he just spoke of her so often. He finally took lessons from her.

WOOD

Word has been received by the parents of Private First Class ED-WARD D. WOOD Jr., USMC, that he is in a naval hospital somewhere in the South Pacific. The extent of his injuries is not fully known. Private Wood enlisted in the service on May 18, 1942 and has served overseas for 13 months. He has two cousins, Lieutenant Joseph W. Mc-Donald and Air Cadet Thomas Mc-Donald, also in the service. The boys are the grandsons of Mrs. Fannie J Phillips, city.

"This is your ranking son and his new found love, Miss (Private) Shirlie Van Deusend"

Ed in his office at Sunset and Hillhurst during his
Streets of Laredo period, August, 1948

Sisters Win Roles in Stage Play

SUZI STEVENS

JEANNE STEVENS

Two sisters who have been serving doughnuts and coffee all summer long get their theatre "break" Oct. 25 when they open in a stage play at the Casual Company Player's theatre, 5271 Bakman ave.

The girls, Jeanne, 17, and Suzi, 16, both of 4353 Coldwater

Canyon blvd., worked in Mammy's Do Nut Shop, 12224 Ventura blvd. Jeanne is a senior at North Hollywood High school and Suzi is a junior.

The girls began a stage career several years ago in Denver as dancers and singers in a juvenile revue.

Last winter they performed in a musical show in Hollywood. They also have been on a television show.

The new play, titled "Casual Company," is a story of the Marine Corps. The girls' mother, Mrs. Alice Stevens, is the stage manager.

Out West — Hollywood

The blue sky started to deepen into a soft grey. The feeling of early evening took over the entire terrain; a cooler breeze; a quiet as if the world were suddenly silent except for the grinding of the train wheels. It was the twilight hour. And two of the twilight people sat in the same meditative silence. The world was standing, momentarily, still. But time and the train continued ever westward...

— Ed Wood, *It Takes One To Know One*

CONRAD BROOKS   I met Ed in a small family coffee shop in 1948. We used to have breakfast in there. He knew the people there very well, the waitress, her mom and dad owned the place. He was trying to promote that stage play of his, *The Casual Company,* had posters all around there.

ED WOOD   (Letter to parents)

29 October 1948

Dear Mom & Dad;

I was extremely happy to hear that you are both, at last, feeling good. Dad, I'm very happy that you pulled through your ulcer condition.

The show is going great guns. We have gotten only one bad write up, and that is herewith enclosed. The only reason it was bad because Mr. Bromfield, the drama editor was sick and the paper sent the copy boy. The copy boy thinks he will make good only by giving a bad report. The papers are retracting the story this week and everything will be alright.

We had a full house on Monday, but I guess due to the one bad write up, people won't come. We've had fair houses but aren't making any money yet. We've paid out about $600 so at least we've made enough to keep out of debt. Next week should be our profit week if all goes well.

Dad, a few weeks ago Ray Flin (Orson Welles' Camera Man) and I got together. He wanted me to write a story for the American Legion to be filmed for them. Its a story on the American Legion and it turned out to be very good. The story is copyrighted (air tight) in my name. Ray sent it to the A.L. Convention in Florida. That was three weeks ago. We haven't heard their answer. I wonder, if they haven't accepted it to be filmed, and with a few changes to make it the story of the V.F.W., if you could push it through to the V.F.W. convention when they have it. It is a good script and it will make a very interesting and enlightening film. And with Ray on camera you can bet the photography would be good. Ray, by the way is my big hope for an in to the pictures, or his wife. His wife's sister is Penny Singleton (Blondie of the Dagwood Bumstead series) I've had dinner with the "BUMSTEAD'S" several times.

I have a bottle of vermouth in front of me and I take a sip every once and a while so if my writing goes like ₜₕᵢₛ or like ᵗʰⁱˢ don't mind too much.

Speaking of the BUMSTEADS, really Arthur Lake and Penny Singleton, I have had dinner several times with Penny's folks, Mr. & Mrs. McNulty. Their son, Bernard is a close friend of mine, also Rays brother in law. Confusing isn't it. But half of the people [?] of the movies are related to the other half in one way or another.

Damn it, I'm running out of cigarettes. And it's too early in the morning to get any. Very soon I'm going to bed. Day light isn't far off, and due to some discussions of forth I have to be at the theatre by one-thirty. Yesterday I slept until nearly two in the afternoon.

I've got a whole file of clippings enclosed here, including a picture that was taken during the "Peg O' My Heart" show in May. I have more to them and will send in time. The small snaps were taken from the film "Crossroads of Larado", which I made last month. (By the way it still isn't sold).

Yes I think I received all the birthday cards. And by the way, I haven't gotten the pictures back yet that were taken at my birthday party. When I do I will send them on.

And I guess that's it for now.

Love,

Jr.

HENRY BEDERSKI Ed wasn't working. He had that office there, across the street from the Vista theatre, and he'd have gatherings there, and we'd carry on, a lot of talk, and that's about all, but we'd enjoy ourselves. Then Conrad got him into the Monogram studios, on Wednesday nights they'd have show nights for free, you could bring your friend. So we took Ed over with us. But Ed, in the meantime, had his mind on that play of his, *The Casual Company*. But the review was real bad. They captioned it "A ho-hum production."

CHUCK LA BERGE On *The Casual Company,* Ed absconded with all the money. I took over the financial end of it at the very last, but he had already spent all of the damn money, so that was the end of that. It must have lasted a week or so, it didn't last very long.

Ed had gotten hold of Joseph Cotten some way or another and invited him to come out. He came to visit us, and we did the play for him, personally, and then he evaluated us, individually. He praised quite a few of us in the play, said we had potential as far as staying in the theatre, or motion pictures. He said something to Ed that the play was interesting, he thought it would go.

JOHN CRAWFORD THOMAS Ed didn't have any footing in Hollywood...that's why he was on stage at the Gateway Theatre on Sunset Blvd., in *The Blackguard Returns*. He was just a down-to-earth individual with hopes and dreams like so many

Ed works for pretzels and beer as the villain in *The Blackguard Returns*

The clipping Jr. sent home to Ma

EVENT TOMORROW NIGHT—Members of the Kate Crutcher Players are presenting "Peg o' My Heart" tomorrow (Saturday) evening at the Ebell Theatre to aid the work of the Children's Hospital Convalescent Home. From left to right in the picture above are Mrs. Lombard Smith, Edward D. Wood, Mercedes R. Withers, Patricia Shea and Al Sears. Mr. Wood and Miss Shea are playing leading roles. Mrs. Withers is organist and Mr. Sears is directing.

others. We got to talking about producing a movie.

We rented Monogram's old offices, down on Sunset near Hillhurst by the old Vista Theatre. We had a sign on the outside that said "Wood-Thomas Productions."

Ed lived in my office for a while, but Monogram had another suite down the hall which I later picked up — 35 dollars a month. They were large offices. I rented that one for him, so he moved across the way.

On the script it was *Streets of Laredo,* I changed it to *Crossroads of Laredo*. It was shot in 16mm, Ed wrote and directed it, I produced. We were going to blow it up to 35 at the time. It was never dubbed, but it was finished. It took about two or three days. Ray Flin shot some of the better scenes, and Ed Wood just takes the camera and goes out and shoots, I don't know where he got the camera, but the film wasn't the best, it was war surplus film. We had a little western set at a ranch in Saugus. Cost us 60 dollars for a day.

Ed Wood — it was amazing how he would improvise. He was quite an ingenious individual. When we were shooting *Crossroads of Laredo,* we were supposed to have a coffin. I said, "Where are you gonna get the coffin?" Within an hour, he had one made out of cardboard, threw some water on it to make it look like it'd been laquered or painted — it was a foot short, but it didn't bother him! He just went right on — nothing stopped him!

CHUCK LA BERGE   On *The Streets of Laredo,* Ed was the villain, and I was the sheriff. And Ed couldn't ride a horse to save his soul. He was just a terrible horseback rider. And, in one scene, I was chasing myself! Because Ed couldn't ride. It was really a funny bit. But no one could actually tell by the film itself. I did a record of *The Streets of Laredo,* which was supposed to be dubbed into the film as the theme song. The guy who put up the money for that was a psycho case, he played the villain in *The Blackguard*. Nutty as a fruitcake. Of course, I realized he was on dope, later, but in those days, none of us did anything like that, we didn't do dope. He was doing marijuana or whatever ... God only knows.

JOHN CRAWFORD THOMAS   The movie wasn't going anyplace and I kind of went through the money I was receiving. The movie frankly did me in, and it was an embarrassment to my family. Ed left without saying goodbye ... and he had a habit of not paying his rent and leaving. That was a trademark of his. He'd run out of money — he's gone.

CHUCK LA BERGE   When Ed and I worked on *The Blackguard Returns,* a woman gave us a free beer and a bag of pretzels. To work. And sometimes that's all we'd have all day long. After the play was over, we'd go around picking up the pretzels that were left over. We starved — we were hungry. Pretzels and beer — that's about it. Ed was kind of camping out with people, and he'd already bunked with a lot of guys, and he stayed in my apartment a couple of times, and we drank a lot, partied a lot, chased broads.

Ed Wood on the set of
Streets of Laredo, 1948

Duke Moore in *Streets of Laredo*

Lyle Talbot, Bud Osborne, Kenne Duncan and Don Nagel in
Crossroad Avenger

GEORGE COOPER   The girl that did the mother in *The Blackguard* got sick one night and didn't show up, so Ed moved into the mother's part, from doing the father. He did the mother even with the mustache on. He was a riot at that. Everybody laughed their head off. He had the wig on, padding for breasts and the butt. He did scenes with Little Nell in their rundown broken-down shack.

KATHY WOOD   Eddie would tell me that when he first came to Hollywood, that the streets were safe, no one was afraid to go out at night ... the skies were clear, you could leave your doors open. The people you met, you knew you could trust them. Now it's worse than a jungle.

GEORGE COOPER   Let's say Ed and I were getting ready to cross the street at Hollywood and Vine, but an automobile stopped right on the crosswalk — well, we'd open the back door, walk through the back seat, open the door, get out, to get to the other side of the street. We used to get a kick out of doing different things like that.

Ed, Don Nagel and I used to drop by Redd Foxx's nightclub at Pico and Western and heckle the living hell out of him. After the show would be over, he would come to our table, and we'd give him suggestions on some of his stuff. Later on, we would see him do 'em. And old Scatman Crothers used to be there quite often to play the drunk, and he used to drop over and sit down and talk with us.

JOHN CRAWFORD THOMAS   Every woman was fair game to Ed. He had this one girl, Candy. He explained to me how she had never had a climax before — so evidently he knew the art pretty well.

There was another one, Gladys, she was a legitimate agent in Hollywood. I was able to observe things that went on, they had a kind of frosted glass on these doors, and I used to keep an eye on things, because I had invested money, I was involved. I can see her in this frosted glass. It was not a normal situation. She propositioned me, too, one time, so I deduced that they were having an affair together. He wanted to get ahead, and something like that would not stop Ed!

> Poughkeepsie, N.Y. Newpaper, Sept. 18, 1949
>
> Former City Man Enters Film Venture
>
> Edward D. Wood, Jr., former resident of Poughkeepsie, has just completed negotiations with Rene Lenoir of Switzerland, Robert Ganon, photographer of the Nazi war trials and Jack Ganon, sound technician, for the incorporation of "Story-Ad Films," in Hollywood, Calif.
>
> Mr. Wood, one quarter owner of the new firm, is the writer and director of all films produced by the establishment. He previously has done custom work for such national sponsors as the Dudley Steel Corp., The Aluminum Body Works, and the Crosley automobile manufacturers.

On the set of *The Sun Was Setting*, Ed Wood's first job as hired director
Ed (center) coaches actors Phyllis Coates and Tom Keene
Veteran cinematographer Ray Flin sits behind the Mitchell

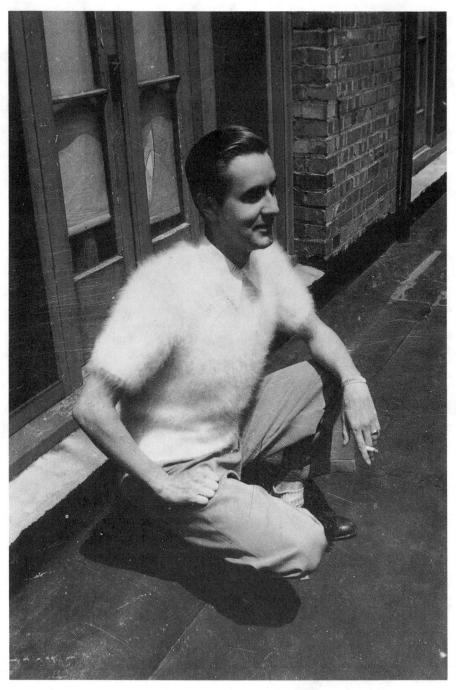

Ed Wood in angora outside his office, August, 1948,
in a snapshot he sent home to his mother

The Two in One

KATHY WOOD   Ed worked his way up into the story department at Universal. Eddie knew Tony Curtis very well, Tony liked to dress crazy sometimes, and when Eddie was at Universal, the same time that Tony was, they used to haunt the ... where the dressers were, and change, and try them on, they had a great time. Eddie was a good pal of his, and that was their little secret. That was one of the reasons that Janet Leigh couldn't take it much longer, 'cause Tony liked to wear those kind of clothes, too.

DOLORES FULLER   Ed knew Danny Kaye, who was also a transvestite.

DON NAGEL   He had his chance to be at Universal if he had wanted to. He blew it by not staying there when he was there. He was a night production coordinator. That's the guy that sets up the sheets for the following morning shoot. They used to go about three in the afternoon and set up everything for the following day and shoot whatever it might be. And he was working there for a while, about six months.

JOHN ANDREWS   He had worked at Universal, and he never recovered — to him it was a major event, like all the truckloads of sand, for *Abbott and Costello in the Foreign Legion* (1950), on a stage — that impressed Eddie till the day he died. The magnitude, because when you see the picture, you would think you were looking out over the desert in those long shots. But he was only there for a short time; he wanted to go out on his own.

PHIL CAMBRIDGE   Ed told me that he had been on the set with Lou Costello on a couple of films. Lou, unlike the personable little guy he was, was really a s.o.b. in person and hated Bud, along with everyone else. Ed said Lou had a chauffeur, and he would always humiliate the chauffeur whenever he was angry with someone — he would kick him, or hit him — whatever he felt like doing. One day he got the guy to come inside and he got a bar of soap and said, "Now you eat that." And the guy ate it. It was a bad business, bad business.

KATHY WOOD   Eddie did a few things as a female impersonator, and it was funny, strictly for laughs, this was when he was with Dolores. He would work shows, nightclubs, he would dance, I know he worked San Francisco at some club.

CHUCK LA BERGE   We were all sitting around, we were expecting a crowd one evening that had cancelled or something, we were all sitting around drinking in the theater. I didn't know that he was a transvestite, and he said something like, "I think I'll play Lily tonight," I said, "Well, go and put the gown on." Well, god, you know he went and put the gown on, put the wig on, he even shaved his mustache, and goddamn, he was beautiful! He really was. I said some smart-assed remark like, "Jesus Christ, I'd go for you myself!" When the cast came in, he's sitting there dressed as Lily, and people didn't even know who he was! They had no idea. "Who's the new Lily?"

KATHY WOOD Ed mentioned he did a stunt, falling off a stagecoach in *The Baron of Arizona* [1950, directed by Samuel Fuller], dressed in drag as a double for a female star. Vincent Price starred. When he was younger he told me he was mentioned as a look-alike for a young Errol Flynn.

CHUCK LA BERGE Son of a bitch had some beautiful wives. Uh! One wife was absolutely gorgeous. I recast the show, *The Blackguard,* later on in the fifties, and asked Ed to come out to play the sheriff — which he did. And he had a wife at the time, and she was a gorgeous blonde. And she played the part of Lily in *The Blackguard Returns,* and did a very good job.

DOLORES FULLER I had divorced the father of my two children after 14 years of marriage when I met Ed. He had a call for a movie, *Behind Locked Doors,* that he planned to direct. Prior to that, I had only done five or six small parts in movies, bit parts. I thought he was extremely handsome, and I was amazed at how young he was. I told him, "You're so young to be doing this." He took to me, and told me right then and there he was going to make me a star. Of course I probably didn't believe him. But it sounded nice.

We spent a lot of time together, he was writing his scripts, sitting at the typewriter, he'd bounce ideas off to me, we'd act out scenes lots of times to see how they would work. And he'd say he could write much better if he could wear my angora sweater. He would work for hours, sitting there, saying that it felt good.

He had his own place, but he was practically living in my home. I was kind of the breadwinner, putting groceries on the table, modeling, doing tv shows, *Queen for a Day.* I had a four-and-a-half size foot, so I modeled the slippers in a little short artist's smock.

EVELYN WOOD Alex had known me in New York, so ... we talked. We had a heart to heart talk. "Ed's not a homo, he just likes to wear women's clothes." So, that was okay by me, I could accept anything. I was very naive, but I still could accept things. I lived just back to back, across the alley, to Ed and Alex's apartment, we'd be sitting there, and Ed would say, "I'm hungry," so I'd say, "I'll go home and bake a pie." I could make a lemon pie in 15 minutes from scratch. Sometimes Dolores Fuller would be at their apartment, Ed and Alex, Bela, and me. We'd just sit around and shoot the bull. Ed would have on a blonde wig, a dress, high heeled shoes, silk hose, nothing that I ever wanted to beat him up and take away from him, and very frequently, an angora sweater. He loved boas and angora. As to Ed's dressing, Bela didn't care, I mean, you do your thing, I'll do mine kind of situation. Bela was very sophisticated. Suave, gracious, never offensive. We all treated it as if it was the most normal thing in the world. Ed would just smile and say, "That's the real me." But everything was just free and relaxed, and — it was just a fun place to go.

GEORGE COOPER   The minute he would get home, here in Burbank, his wife would have his clothes laid out on the bed — exactly like hers. And he would dress like her. But he didn't act feministic. He didn't act feminine in front of anybody, but the minute he would get home — chapow!

DOLORES FULLER   We made up a 3-D Christmas card where I was the Virgin Mary, we had some children around, Ed wanted to recreate the nativity scene. We sent those Christmas cards out with 3-D glasses. Ed played Jesus Christ.

PHILIP CHAMBERLIN   In a way, the Christmas cards are a kind of a parable. He was, no doubt, a martyr for his art.

KATHY WOOD   Eddie had this collection of comic books, Superman, Batman, he was just a kid when he left to go in the Marine Corps, and his mother got rid of all of them. He was so heartsick about them. It hurt him very much.

JOHN ANDREWS   Eddie bought comic books from time to time — Plastic Man, Mad, Huey, Duey, & Louie, anything bizarre, fantastic. Like Plastic Man — a guy turning himself into a service station pump. Eddie had a fixation with these things — anything that was far out. He loved *The Shadow, Chandu the Magician, Flash Gordon*. He told me his favorite film was *The Mummy* with Boris Karloff.

He had a real thing about *The Mummy*. In fact, he called me out to his house one day, he said, "Come out here to be sure that nobody cheats me." He wanted a casket built, a sarcophagus, so that he could float it in his swimming pool — and he wanted his garage painted like a pyramid. I mean it was a fetish about mummies and ancient Egypt. He had a thing about life after death — he was just enamored with that theme. He believed in life after death. Definitely.

CARL ANTHONY   Ed loved classical music. Beethoven, Liszt, Prokofiev.

KATHY WOOD   He liked classical music, opera, cowboy music, but not too much, thank god, to drive me crazy — bagpipe music.

MONA McKINNON   His conversation was all movies, actors, and books. Once he bought two albums of music: one was the Confederacy, and the other was the Union. He was quite a buff on the Civil War.

KATHY WOOD   Eddie was a hell of a good dancer. Oh god he was great! We had a lot of fun together. He liked swing music — forties jazz.

KATHY WOOD   We went to clubs like the Brown Derby, Ciro's, Mocambo, but not much ... we sort of stayed home and got drunk.

DUDLEY MANLOVE   We got together to play chess every now and then — he was a womanizer ... nutty about broads.

VALDA HANSEN   He was really handsome. I'm telling you. I remember one day he was cutting the film and he would stand there, smiling at me, and I was thinking, this

Was it the sweater, or was it the girl? Dolores Fuller in angora, early 1950's.
(Photos courtesy Dolores Fuller)

Ed Wood's 3-D Christmas Card, featuring Ed as the Jewish carpenter.
(Courtesy Dolores Fuller and Phil Chamberlin)

" . . . lo, I am with you always . . . "

guy is really good-looking. It's just that he had so much personality, you didn't think looks, you just thought of charisma, personality. Then all of a sudden it would hit you — that guy is a good looking guy, you know?

Ed had that quality of pixie charm, with genius combined ... and a touch of Errol Flynn. If you really saw Ed in person, he had green eyes, and chiseled features, chiseled chin, and he could have passed for his brother. And he had a lot of the haughtiness that Errol Flynn had.

> I love fuzzy, soft sweaters. I can't repeat enough ... they turn me on almost the moment I slip them on my body ... I can't wait to be had when I'm decked out like a cute little fuzzy bunny rabbit — remember the angoras in my wardrobe?
> — Ed Wood, *Diary of a Transvestite Hooker*

PAUL MARCO Ed was attracted to any beautiful girl. The first thing Ed would ask, "If you get the part in the picture, I want that sweater." Or, "I want to use that sweater and those pants." He always said that to them, and he always would giggle, and I would laugh, and I would say to myself, they don't know how true it is what he's saying. And they always thought he was kidding. And they would say, well, if I'm in it you can have it." But I've never seen him wholly in drag, it was always bits and pieces.

> ... He hugged his arms around his chest and let his hands move up and down the angora covering his arms. If he lived to be a hundred, the sensation of feeling the soft angora fur would always be a new thrill.
> — Ed Wood, *TV Lust*

PHIL CAMBRIDGE I asked him about angora, why not silk or satin? He said, "There's nothing more sensual than angora."

CHUCK LA BERGE He had a hell of a fetish. Angora. Oh God. He'd pick up on a girl just because she was wearing an angora sweater. And he'd get that sweater off of her, man, I don't know how he'd do it — but he had a trunk full of them. My piano player came to me one time, and she said, "Can you make Ed give me my sweaters back?" I said, "Oh no! Not you, too!" She said, "Yeah, he borrowed my sweaters, he said he needed them for a picture." I went up to his house one time and he had angora socks on ... angora shorts ... angora sweater.

JOHN ANDREWS He wanted to trade one of his sweaters, for one of Gwen's, who was my first wife, because it was angora. And she was going to give it to him, so I said, "Don't you understand, that when he puts on your sweater, he's fucking you. Vicariously. Don't you know that? Don't you get that through your head?"

VALDA HANSEN We were on this movie, *Revenge of the Dead,* and I wore this angora sweater. He acted like a man when he falls in love, you know, when I was in this sweater. I tell you, he went out of his mind, over that sweater. He said, "I love angora, please, lover, if you ever, ever give that sweater to anybody, please give it to me." He says, "I'll just take it home, and I'll put it in bed with me, and I'll cherish it, and I'll kiss it ... "

DOLORES FULLER   Edward would sit there with me, and write his scripts, and bounce ideas off of me, trying to work the scenes out. He'd go over the scenes with me while he was writing. And then pretty soon he'd ask me if he could wear my angora sweater. I went along with it, because it didn't seem like it was doing any harm, to sit there and do his typing wearing that. And so I asked him, "Why?" How did he ever get started on something like that? He said when he was a little boy, his aunt, or his mother, somebody put him into a snowsuit with rabbit fur in it. Or angora fur. And he said it felt so wonderful against his skin.

JOHN ANDREWS   Alex Gordon and Eddie were sharing an apartment. I think they were the original odd couple. Now Eddie was in full drag — in private. Later, he went into public drag. Alex would come in unexpectedly — and Eddie would be having a drag party! There would be a bunch of guys in drag, man! And they got their high heels, and their lipstick, and all this shit, and Eddie is their leader! He's conducting the whole goddamn orchestra — the whole soiree! He always used that phrase.

Alex told me when he was at Paramount, in his office, "well you know, I got scared!" So he moved out and left Eddie there. Now Eddie is shipwrecked, it was December, and he took up selling Christmas cards, door to door. He's driving down Melrose, he's a little under the influence, daytime, and he runs into a pedestrian. Knocks him down, backs up, puts the thing in park, goes over, and picks up the pedestrian. The pedestrian argued, he didn't want any help. Eddie says, "No, you have to have it." He gets him into the car, he says, "I insist on driving you home." They're driving along, and Eddie keeps staring at the guy. Finally, it hits Eddie who this man is. He says, "You're Tom Tyler." He says, "No, no." He denied it twice. Eddie says, "Oh, no, come on, come on, you're Tom Tyler." Finally he says, "Okay, I'm Tom Tyler, alright." It was Tom Tyler, who of course played Captain Marvel, The Phantom, and The Mummy in *The Mummy's Hand*.

DOLORES FULLER   He begged me to marry him. I loved him in a way, but I couldn't handle the transvestism. I'm a very normal person. It's hard for me to deviate! I wanted a man that was all man. I didn't need those quirks. It wasn't just the angora sweaters, but when he got into the whole bit, the high heels, and the whole drag....

Our relationship was pretty much like the movie, *Glen or Glenda*, I'm afraid to say. I went along with it for a time, but I had to accomplish much more in life than that had to offer.

After we broke up, Ed would stand outside my home, in Burbank, on Magnolia Street, we had a two bedroom home with a big guest / game room on the second floor. My father was living with me. And Ed would just stand outside and cry ... just scream and cry. "Let me in! I love you!"

What good would I have done if I had married him? We would have starved together. If I would have stayed, instead of running to New York. And writing 18 Elvis Presley hit songs, and doing summer stock, and going to college ... I bettered myself. I had to uplift myself.

Twenty minutes later Glenda adjusted her long auburn hair up under the red beret. Her face was made up to the expert degree which she had learned only through years of experiment and experience. She stood up from the vanity and walked to the mirror. Appraisingly she smoothed the long lined, long sleeved, red sweater down over her skirt. She made sure the seams of her stockings were straight and cut neatly into the red patent leather shoes. With a last adjustment to a flashy cheap costume jewelry bracelet on her left wrist she turned to face Rose who stood wide eyed in amazement behind her. There was nothing of Glen left. The nails were painted a deep scarlet, matching the lipstick. Glenda's musical voice said, "Do you approve?"

"Wow!" She had never seen Glenda dressed and made up to such perfection before. "I've seen pictures of guys dressed up in girls clothes before but you sure beat them all. I never seen any better nowhere- no place."

"There was a time my perfection in make up meant the difference between success and failure. Maybe someday I'll tell you about it." Glenda's voice came out full-rounded.

"You're absolutely beautiful. Get one of those operations like the boys have been doing in Europe and you'd be a real high priced hooker."

"I like things right where they are." Glenda took her in his arms again.

She snuggled into the soft wool of Glenda's sweater. "I'll miss you so much."

"Perhaps we won't be separated for long. I'll come, or send for you as soon as I can." Glenda kissed her, smearing the lipstick on both their lips.

Rose took a handkerchief and cleaned Glenda's lips. "We should both wear the non-smear kind."

"I'll remember that in the future."

— Ed Wood, *Black Lace Drag*

Glen or Glenda

&

Jailbait

Narrator: "Glen's problem is a deep one ... but he must tell her – soon. She's beginning to notice things ... his nails ... his eyes when he looks into a ladies store window ... so many of the little things that are hard to hide. Soon she will realize.

"Then there was the time Barbara was wearing the sweater Glen had always wanted to feel on his own body: it was becoming an obsession to him. He must have it..."

— Narration from *Glen or Glenda*

ED WOOD *Glen or Glenda* was a picture Georgie Weiss had slated for Christine Jorgensen. It was a sex change type of picture and there was no nudity ... purely clinical. We had a poem if you remember, the old one of "snips and snails and puppy dog tails, that's what little boys are made of, sugar and spice and everything nice..."

Well, Lugosi just turned the thing down flat. He didn't want to have anything to do with it. He didn't want to play in any B picture. He didn't want to go with the independents. He knew it was going to be about the Jorgensen thing. We could not get Chris [Jorgensen] because Christine wouldn't do any movies on that subject. Wouldn't even do a good lecture tour on that subject as long as the parents were alive. At least that's the story. She turned it down completely flat too.

I think that this is probably just before Alex [Gordon] and I started living together. We were at some hotel on Hollywood Boulevard ... I think we were close already. We used to see five and six movies on a weekend. We'd start on Friday night and never quit until Monday morning. So anyway it might have been three or four days later. It was very late at night; there was a knock at our apartment door. I think it was 1952, before the divorce. Knock on the door and there was Lugosi and Lillian and they talked and this time it was Lillian who did most of the talking. She said that if it was $1,000 ... now I have to contradict myself there. I think $500 was the offer that George (Weiss) made. Now I remember Lillian saying that it would be okay if it were to be $1,000. I'll have to check that out. We talked. And I had to see if George would go for it. He'd never had any kind of name with any of these pictures. He was making the early, early marijuana type pictures ... these girl wrestling pictures ... all this type of thing. It was the same with this one. It was called "taking the curse off" and making it. Even though it's an entertaining type of film you put the medical thing in it. I gave Lugosi the script at that point.

He was in good health, he was in really good health. Like many years later when he came out of the hospital, he had the fullness in the cheeks and looked really good, he always had legs that you could put your fingers around, but he was healthy and he wailed good and a booming voice and he could cuss up a storm as we all know ... never held back on any words.

So anyway I checked with George the next morning and he said go, just go. So we took the $1,000 offer. What he did in that picture. He played a spirit, a god, a lord, a puppeteer who is pulling the strings on everybody's life. The story is based on this guy who is going to change over to being a girl; he's got his own mind to think about it, but it is the puppeteer who is pulling the strings who is forcing him into this issue. We played very heavy on those two poems: Everything nice and sugar and spice that's what little girls are made of.

In this thing which is a cheap budget thing he and I were the only ones who made any money out of it. He tackled it just the same as he would have tackled *Dracula,* or any of his big movies. He's so completely serious. I don't care who he played he would put his whole thing into it. He would come across. He would do the absolute best he knew.

Bill Thompson, as well as being one of the most fantastic cameramen that I ever met, in his early days he had to grind his own lenses and things like that, well he was also a metal expert so he knew all these chemicals; things that would explode, things that would blow up and lightning that would go from rod to rod and you could put your hands through it, but don't touch something or the other. So I'm trying to explain to Lugosi about some of the electrical equipment and he says, screw you, I don't go near that, let it buzz, I'm over here. And the other one on the same thing is when he's pouring the liquid in order to make this transformation exact he has the proper ether in the air, the proper clouds or whatever you want to call it. So he watched Bill make the stuff and he took the little vial and poured it into the beaker and a puff of smoke came up and of course Lugosi jumped back as he always did with anything like this and I thought he was going to have some kind of fit; later with *Bride of the Monster* was when we really had almost the whole set explode. He wasn't even in that scene when it exploded. But anyway Bill says to him, now whatever you do when you pour this thing, stand a little away when it hits some of it's going to spill out and it will just burn right through your clothes and burn you. That's all he needed. You have never seen a more awkward pouring of this from the vial into the beaker and he says, I say, maybe we'd better try it from another angle, he says, if you want to go $5,000 and give me a ten foot pole, forget it. So one take was all we had on that thing.

I'm a young punk and here I'm working with the great master and I was fighting the fact that am I doing right by the man; am I doing right by the film? So I didn't look for the little niceties and the little humor bits and the things that came as I got closer and closer with the guy.

GEORGE WEISS I had a different idea about the picture, entirely. We were going to make a picture on the Christine Jorgensen deal. And then when Lugosi was cast as what he was it no longer became a documentary. Well, I didn't give a damn — I was

Bela Lugosi in *Glen or Glenda*

A *Glen or Glenda*
group shot.

Standing: Harry
Thomas, Tommy
Haines, Ed Wood,
unidentified tv

Seated: Conrad
Brooks, Henry
Bederski, Walter
Hajdwiecyz

(Photo courtesy
Conrad Brooks)

just interested in sales, I didn't want it to go on the shelf. I'm the only guy I can remember that used his own money and made pictures. So I had to watch it, it was my money, not someone else's. So, in the middle of the production I had to call San Francisco and sell the Western territories for enough money to continue the picture. And the guy only did because the strength of the fact that I was one who was continually making pictures, and if he didn't help me out, his source would have stopped. Because there weren't too many that were making that type of picture that could play the Main Street houses around the country. So I hocked the 11 western states for enough money to finish the picture. On *Glen or Glenda,* there were four days actually in the studio, on Larchmont. Lugosi's scenes were a day.

HARRY THOMAS Lugosi knew that *Glen or Glenda* was about transvestism — he always referred to it off camera as "medical science." He was not dumb. He was too smart of a man to go into it blindfolded.

EVELYN WOOD I talked to Ed about the film, Bela was there, I said, "Well now, I want no nudity, no sex scenes." They said, "Nothing like that. The man wears your clothing." I said, "Okay." I felt that was acceptable. I just assumed that Bela knew what the film was about, because we all sat and talked.

HARRY THOMAS When we were beginning to do *Glen or Glenda,* Ed said, "Harry, come over and pick up the script." So, he gave me the address, I went over there and knocked on the door. This beautifully dressed person comes to the door. Polished nails, hair all grown down. I said, "Oh, I beg your pardon, is your brother home?" "You mean Eddie?" "Yes, Eddie, is he home?" She says, "Oh, come in and have a cup of tea, he'll be here in a little while." I sat there, and she poured me a cup of tea, she was prancing around and changing garments, the ermine coat, all this, and I said, "I'm getting a little perturbed, I have a lot of appointments, do you think he'll be very much longer?" She says, "Oh, no, he'll be here soon." Suddenly, she comes out of a sliding door, and says, "I am Ed Wood." In all his glory. And I was shocked. I said, "Oh — you're not Ed's sister?" "No, I am really Ed. This is the way I want to look in *Glen or Glenda.*"

EVELYN WOOD I was given a script on the set, when I was in make-up, and frankly, I was so annoyed at the make-up man, he kept trying to kiss me, and telling me I had the greatest eyelashes in the world. I was trying to learn my lines, and I knew my time was limited. It was called then, *Transvestite.*

HARRY THOMAS Most of my pictures, especially in the fifties, were all science fiction, you see, once you get that reputation. And here I did Max Factor's beauty commercials, I did all these high-fashion models. *Glen or Glenda* was divorced completely from what I was doing. But it was fun.

GEORGE WEISS Lugosi was enjoying himself like a baby with a toy. There weren't four takes on anything. He went through like the trouper he was.

The film was made at the Larchmont Studio, on Larchmont Avenue. I wished I had sense enough to make a few horror pictures. Unfortunately, at that time, the only thing that the independent picture had was access to the state's rights market. I had a tough time selling this one. Because the burlesque type of house wouldn't want it because it was too highbrow. And it was enough of out of the closet to warrant a support. Even in New York, which it went into the wrong theater. But they did us a favor, only under pressure, two weeks before Christmas, when they don't do anything anyway. The picture didn't actually make any money. I couldn't even sell England. It was ahead of it's time.

Most of the cast, as far as I was concerned, I tried to be authentic, which was wrong. Because the criticism of *Glen or Glenda* was, why did I use such ugly people? Charlie Crafts [Note: In the film, drag queen Crafts gives Glen advice on his problem] was an orchestra leader down at the Million Dollar. Lyle Talbot, he was a pretty big star for Warner. Where Ed got him, I didn't know and didn't ask questions. Because he assembled a hell of a cast. Then there's "Tommy" Haines. I was criticized there again. Yet, Wood swore up and down that they were ... transvestites. So, look, for the 10 or 20 or 30 dollars that they got paid, I wasn't going to say no.

KATHY WOOD "Tommy" Haines, she-he-it, whatever it was, had a girl friend. We met them once out on the beach. I think she was a drummer in an orchestra.

HENRY BEDERSKI One of the transvestites in *Glen or Glenda* was a Polish fellow, he was a lieutenant in the Polish Army. He admitted to me that he was a homosexual, and he felt guilty about it.

GEORGE WEISS "The Devil" in *Glen or Glenda,* his name is Captain De Zita. He was my booking agent. De Zita booked strippers. In fact he booked in where Lenny Bruce worked a strip joint. So De Zita was living next door to where I had an office called the Harvey Hotel. And De Zita did everything from run the girls down to their dates, and then pick them up at two or three in the morning, to shaving them. So, he was what you call an agent hanger-on, because there were a couple of agents in that studio too. So, I pressed De Zita into playing the part of the Devil. He did a good job, and died shortly after.

HARRY THOMAS For *Glen or Glenda,* Ed didn't want to go too heavy on it, he wanted the make-up subtle, and I wanted to put the false lashes on him but he didn't want to go for that. He said, "You'll make me look too much like a girl, but I want to look like myself, my own identity."

JOHN ANDREWS Eddie tells Bill Thompson, "I want light right in his eyes, to make it look like he's staring out into the world...that effect." Bill says, "I don't know how to do it." Eddie: "Well it was in *White Zombie* ..." So Lillian [Lugosi] said, "Well I remember how it was done." She was married to him in '32, she was his secretary. She said, "Somebody get a cardboard box." There was a shoe store across the street. Somebody, a grip goes and gets a shoe box top, flattens it out, gives it to Lillian, and she takes a pin and pokes two little holes in it, tells Bill, "Now put a baby behind this,

Dolores Fuller, Captain De Zita (as the Devil), and Ed Wood in *Glen or Glenda*
(Photo courtesy of Dolores Fuller)

Ed's nightmare of the accusatory finger in *Glen or Glenda* (above) [Photo courtesy Conrad Brooks]
Resolves itself in reluctant compliance of Dolores Fuller (below) [Photo courtesy Tim Murphy]

a baby's a lamp, and you have your effect." Eddie told me that, if it wasn't for Lillian, they would never have got that shot.

HENRY BEDERSKI   Thompson was the one that was responsible many a time for the scenes to be static. He was worried about the shadows! Get movement in there! If Germany can do it and the others, so can Hollywood. Because Ed would direct the scene and then Thompson's telling him, "Place them over here, "Place them over there," to get the lights just right. "Don't move." Oh, that's a lot of crap! Ed even complained. He said, "Jesus Christ, I've got nothing but film." You see, Ed knew better, but he had to give in. Ed spoke to me, many a time, about filmmaking, he himself was definitely against stuff like that where you stand around. And yet, look, he made pictures like that!

EVELYN WOOD   Ed told me he wanted to do everything in two takes or less. In this one scene, I was to come out of the other room, into the living room, and find Ed in my clothing. Well, I looked surprised, but he said, "well, I think we can get a better look of surprise." I went behind the closed door, I waited. I waited. And I waited. I thought, they've gone to dinner. They've forgotten me. Finally, I heard Ed holler, "Roll 'em!" I came through the door, all the furniture had been removed. They had set it up as a kitchen. I was expecting to walk into a living room. Naturally, I looked surprised. Ed said, "Print it."

GEORGE WEISS   When you sell state's rights, each territory has the right, not only to change the title, but to exploit it in a title that's befitting: *Glen or Glenda* won't mean a dime in Texas. But when they put out *He or She?*, then they had a chance to survive. *I Changed My Sex*, that was the second title that came out, and that was because, if you didn't like *Glen or Glenda*, you could have this one. Everybody that was in exploitation did that. Because of the very fact that in New York, they bought a picture because of its title, they did that with *Test Tube Babies* too, they didn't even want to screen it. Just on the title alone. And certainly I wasn't going to submit *I Changed My Sex*, because sex wasn't allowed to be used in the title. And any time, if you're playing North Carolina, you'd better have a title that brings them in, and not *Glen or Glenda*. Or else they won't buy the territory.

The added footage in *Glen or Glenda* was because you had to have a picture that was at least 70 minutes. And in fact you couldn't sell foreign unless it was 90 minutes, because foreign didn't have a double feature. So, in order to be able to stretch out the footage, in up for 70 minutes of running time, we had to use every bit of the footage that was shot because film was precious. That was the type of deal that all independents found themselves in.

I tried to get others that had sex changes. Especially one from North Carolina. And I went up to Washington to meet with her, and she said she wouldn't want to go out on personal appearances, because Lugosi signified "horror" and any sex change, therefore, was horror. There were a lot of people who thought the same thing. What the hell did you need Lugosi for? Why didn't you stick to something straight? But then I used him for the name value.

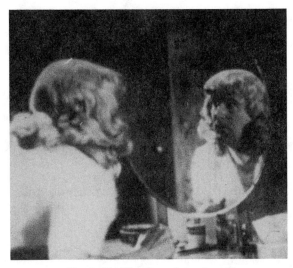

Glenda (Ed Wood) confronts herself
[Photo by Rudolph Grey]

Glen or Glenda advert.,
Taipei, China

Publicity Still for *Glen or Glenda* showing crew and principals
Back: Tim Farrell, Ed Wood, Lyle Talbot, William Thompson, Dolores Fuller, George Weiss
Front: Henry Bederski, Conrad Brooks, Scott McCloud, unidentified crew [photo: C. Brooks]

EVELYN WOOD   I went to the preview on Hollywood Boulevard. At that time, I was very naive, and, understanding this, the entire subject was verboten. I think Ed and Bela were there, and the audience seemed to like it.

HARRY THOMAS   Bela looked at the final print and said, "We didn't do that." I said, "no, that's from another picture." George Weiss took something from an older film [directed by Merle Connell]. One scene had a girl on a couch, and I put a beard on this guy, those two were a husband and wife team, they were legally married. But those scenes were from one of these girlie-type of mainstream things. Eddie didn't have anything to do with it, it was shot before *Glen or Glenda*.

HENRY BEDERSKI   In *Glen or Glenda,* I don't know why Ed had to become Daniel Davis. If a man worked as hard as he did, to place the name of Edward D. Wood, Jr. before the world, I don't see why in the hell he became Daniel Davis. You know what I would have told him? I would have said, "Look Ed, goddamn it, you're a big admirer of your Orson Welles, so you're Orson Welles, Jr. That's all." It was always, "Orson Welles, Orson Welles." He had a chance to become a minor Orson Welles, and he didn't do it. He would talk about Orson Welles, he looked up to the man, regarded him with affection, or admiration.

Jailbait

TIMOTHY FARRELL   In *Jailbait* I play a gangster and they change my face. The girl, Theodora Thurman, boy, they were watching her every move that she made. I couldn't hardly talk to her without somebody sliding right up to see what was going on. I guess they were afraid maybe a little hanky-panky or something. A hell of a good actress, by the way.

On that picture Ed Wood had posted a bond with the unions. And we were supposed to start shooting like next Monday. And we started this Monday. He gave them post-dated checks. And he didn't have the money to cover them. So we started shooting this Monday. And someplace around Tuesday or Wednesday, Jesus Christ! All of a sudden all these people came walking on the set — they were the business managers for all the IA locals, Screen Actors Guild [Lyle Talbot, at the time, served on the board of the Screen Actors Guild], and of course the guy from SAG was sort of upset to see him working there! And there was a big to-do on that picture. I don't know how Ed finally conned them into finishing the day's work, but he did. And the day's work took us to almost noon the next day. We just kept going, all night long. As long as he had the film he was going to get the goddamn thing done. Herbert Rawlinson was in it, and the next day Ed told me that Rawlinson had died that morning of lung cancer.

LYLE TALBOT   We worked at one place up on Sunset Boulevard, at a motel that had a swimming pool. We were shooting around the pool, and his cameraman and

lighting guy had the damnedest equipment — it was on just like, little wire things with tin cans, literally. I hear this voice, "Hey Talbot! What the hell are you doing down there?" It was Jimmy Cagney, he was up on the second floor, visiting some friends. I said, "We're making a movie — do you want to be in it?" He said, "Sure!" He wasn't drinking, Cagney didn't drink. About the time he was coming down, the motel manager appeared, "Get the hell out of here!" And he was threatening to call the cops, Eddie hadn't asked permission for it. Everybody just took off, and he'd go find another location. But Eddie was always stealing shots like that.

THEODORA THURMAN   Edward Wood was a very gentle, nice person. There were some rehearsals, nothing extensive. It was just a small set. Columbia Pictures offered me a starring role and I refused to come because I was new in New York, and I was working for *Vogue* and all these places like that as a fashion model. And New York excited me so much that I couldn't bear the thought of leaving, and I heard so many negative things about Hollywood that I couldn't chuck everything I had there, I was riding the crest of a wave. And I didn't want to cut it short, so I turned it down. And then a couple of studios after that offered me contracts. Same thing. I wouldn't leave. And then, I went to Europe, and worked for *Vogue* there. In Paris, mostly. And worked for the French *Vogue,* which was used in America too. And, I stayed a long time, so that when I got back I wanted to get into acting really seriously. Then I went with NBC. 'Cause that would take me to New York, instead of with the rest. So at NBC I was known as the sexy weather girl for Jack Paar.

MONA McKINNON   *Jailbait* was shot at my house in Alhambra, California. Anything that had to do with a street or a house, the exteriors.

DOLORES FULLER   We were shooting all night, and into the next day, and time just got away from me, and I didn't realize I was supposed to be on the set working as Dinah Shore's double on her show, *Chevy Theater.* I completely messed up my job, I was what they called a no-show, and I lost a job that I really loved. They said that I thought that I was a big star now and didn't need them.

That was Steve Reeves' first picture — it took him 27 takes to tie a tie. And he'd sit there with the girls, and eat his dried fruit and nuts. While we were waiting. And he just enjoyed girl talk. He enjoyed it like he was one of the gals. Big, handsome, beautiful hunk of man. And we had some kissing scenes, and there was no chemistry. Usually, when you get a hunk of man like that and you kiss him it goes right through you ... but with him it didn't!

STEVE REEVES   It was a pleasure to work with a director like Ed Wood. He was patient and understood how to make new and inexperienced actors feel at ease and get the best performance out of them.

GEORGE WEISS   They really took him on *Jailbait*. Howco. They were down in Texas. They were supposed to share the film in distribution profits, and he never got a quarter. I should think it was kind of his fault for not collecting. Because Joy Houck had about 80, 90 theatres throughout Texas and Louisiana, and I didn't think that they were kind of rooby-dooby, to use a N.Y. expression.

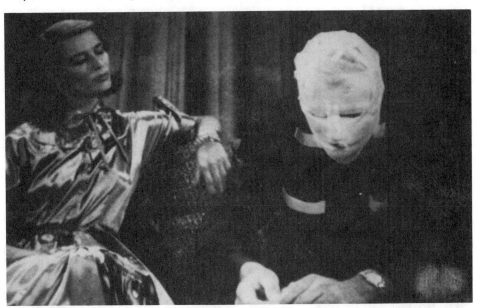

Two views from *Jailbait*. Above: Theodora Thurman and Tim Farrell.
Below: Theodora Thurman, Dolores Fuller, Tim Farrell (on couch), Herbert Rawlinson.

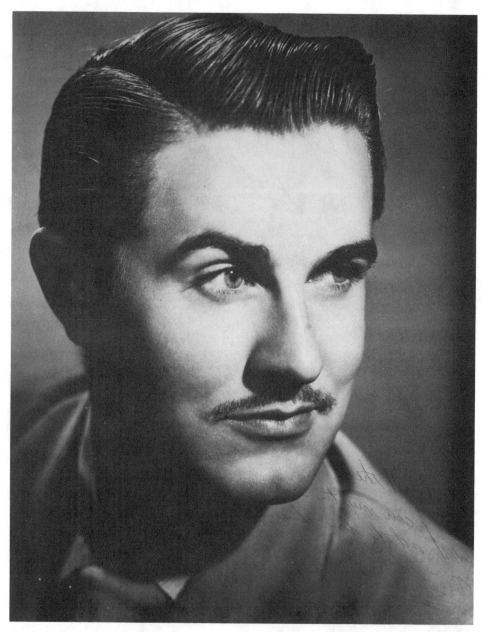

Early acting photo, inscribed by Ed Wood in ballpoint pen to Mona McKinnon: "With all the love I can muster — With all the love there Is — I love you, Ed." [photo courtesy Mona McKinnon]

The Method To His Madness

CONRAD BROOKS   Ed was always looking for independent money ... money off the streets ...

JOHN ANDREWS   Eddie paid Bela a thousand a day, five days, for *Bride*. Which took months to complete, because Eddie would keep running out of money! We were at the original Nickodell's one day ... Eddie was flat broke ... I mean, *broke,* broke. When he was broke, he was broke. So he tells the waitress, "I haven't been in here in years." Well what did she care? She didn't know him. She never heard of Ed Wood ... anyway, he says, "you see that room over there, it was a private dining room" — he says, "I used to rent that room, I'd invite a bunch of distributors and bring Bela with me, and on the strength of Bela's name I would get money for the next picture." And that's the way he did it.

CARL ANTHONY   There was one picture that did make money [most likely *Bride of the Monster]* of Ed's, if it had lost money, no problem. But the fact that it made money, people weren't getting the percentages they wanted. Then he found out he had over a hundred percent sold. As he was bringing in the last backers, promising this piece and that piece, not watching the books, because he's not a bookkeeper, and he just kept making the picture, giving percentages out, giving percentages out, and it got away from him! Then suddenly the backers bumped into each other, trying to collect, and found out Ed had sold more than 100% of the damn thing ... so he had a lot of pressure on that one. But he wasn't a businessman, the money wasn't important to him, he just wanted to get on with making movies, and he got carried away.

ED WOOD   One of the big things we all did was to promote for money. We had to all get out there and pitch in and Lugosi certainly did his share to promote with us. For example, the money for *Revenge of the Dead*. That was one case where we were selling strictly stock in the picture. Lugosi wasn't planned to have a speaking part. It would all be in mime. Anyway, for *Plan 9,* I promoted the money for these pictures. Sam Arkoff of A.I.P. was the attorney, by the way, for *Bride of the Monster* and *Plan 9*. For both of them I would get my stars, for instance, Lyle Talbot, Criswell, Bela, and the others, and I would have breakfasts on the set. We would take a large room at a restaurant or do it right on the stage if I thought that that would impress the potential backers more. I would make the pitch for the money, but I was always sure that the backers could see the stars that were going to be in the film.

MAILA NURMI   They used to have a lot of cocktail parties, trying to raise money, financing. Mainly Criswell, Paul Marco and those people. And they were trying to pretend to be Madison Avenue gentlemen of distinction. They'd all have dark suits on and everyone would stand with a glass, no one would sit, and I'd be the only woman. I always had to go to them, right? To help them try to raise money. And I would sit, and after a while everyone would have to look down on me, because I was the only one not standing, I was the only woman there. So then finally, ultimately, I'd have to stand too, and mingle with them. I thought it was so inane, they never did raise any money, I don't think, that way.

HENRY BEDERSKI   Ed was never exactly a confidence man, but he was the kind of guy, when he met with different people, he would inflate the whole damn thing. He'd always make it seem to these people that, look, we can't fail. I need your backing. And he convinced a lot of people. Yeah, he'd sit down and talk very calmly about it and sound like a lawyer. I remember he said, "Well Henry, I got to make a trip to New York today. I'm going on a plane, I'm shaking, but I got to go, to make that money."

DUDLEY MANLOVE   He had the burning desire to succeed and achieve. What he had in creativity he lacked in entrepreneurship. In many respects, Ed was a perfectionist. He startled me many times.

CARL ANTHONY   He was always looking at available stock footage from film libraries, to see what he could tie together. He would see enough stuff and then he would start writing a script where he could incorporate a lot of stuff and then he wouldn't have to spend the money shooting. His mind could probably take all sorts of loose ends and make some sort of continuity out of it. He'd be the kind of guy, if a picture was halfway through the shooting and somebody ran out of money and somebody else was a quarter of the way through their picture and ran out of money, and somebody else again, he could probably patch it all together and make something comprehensible out of it.

He was undoubtedly the fastest writer and the fastest director in Hollywood, always hoping that he would have a chance to slow down and attend to details, a lot of details had to be overlooked because of that. Like I recall Orson Welles one day setting up a scene to shoot a garbage dump, and every tin can in that dump had to be put in precisely the right place. He'd spend a whole day saying, "Move that ketchup bottle over here, turn it on its side, move this tin can over there, take the label off the beans," a whole day just to set up one garbage dump just to shoot one line.

JOHN ANDREWS   Eddie was a good editor. Eddie was a true, honest-to-god film maker. You have to know how to do everything. I've been a boom man and a camera grip on the same picture. And I know the shadows to watch for, and I know the mechanics of the fluid head, and this and that, and you have to. Or you're not going to make it.

DUDLEY MANLOVE   Ed was very precise in doing research on a picture, to get the exact phraseology if it were a technical thing. Then when he directed the picture, during rehearsals, he would go over it several times to make sure that everybody hit their mark, hit their spot, precisely. He left nothing to happenstance, he was very meticulous in his work. He and I played chess together, and a chess player takes that attitude.

KATHY WOOD   When Eddie was making a movie he was obsessed with it, from the beginning to the end, day in and day out. Sometimes he didn't even leave the set, he'd work all night, he'd just go until the actors practically dropped. But he loved it, the picture became a segment of his life.

TIMOTHY FARRELL   Ed wasn't a dictatorial director, he pretty much let you have your head. If he thought you were going off in the wrong direction, he would correct you, but in a quiet manner.

DON FELLMAN   "I'm a tyrant, I'm a tyrant," he said to me once, in this gleeful squeak. Then he went on to say that he used just the opposite approach back when he was directing. "And that's how I got the best from all my actors."

FLORENCE DOLDER   Eddie did not like this man on Hollywood Boulevard, who trained actors — Lee Strasberg. He hated him.

ANTHONY CARDOZA   Ed, I would say, was a pioneer, from scratch type of director-producer-writer. I mean, he had to do it all. He taught a lot of people, and I'm grateful for that. If they knew how he would make his own crosses for the graveyard, and hammer nails, scrap wood ... they're laughing at it, but that's a real producer, not a guy sitting on his ass. That's a guy that did it, man, did it all.

DOLORES FULLER   On the set, Ed would turn in one direction, tell somebody what to do, then turn in another direction and tell someone else what to do, and — he kept things moving, and didn't waste time, because ... time was money.

"It lasted days, minutes ... until he put on a goddamn nightgown."
Ed Wood marries Norma McCarty on the Sunset Sound Stage, 1956.
Celebrants include Paul Marco (third from left), and Hope and Bela Lugosi (left of cake).

Ed with Monster (left) and Valda Hansen [photo courtesy V. Hansen]

Marriage

VALDA HANSEN   The night he got married to Norma [McCarty] we all went to, supposedly a sound stage, and all of a sudden he said, "We're getting married." And we said, oh, sure, sure. But out comes a preacher and we said, now what's he up to? And we were all on the stage, Bela Lugosi, and Criswell, all of us. We thought we were just getting together for a cast party ... and Bela Lugosi was kissing my hands, and I was thinking of his movies, where he goes, "Oh my darling," And then Ed says, "Okay, shut up, everybody, cut it, cool it!" Oh, yeah, oh Ed. Okay, but we minded him. And we got quiet, And he said, "I'm getting married." Oh, come on, Ed. An the next thing you know, the preacher's there, and that's how he married them. And Bela Lugosi and I looked at each other and — "I guess he's married!"

PAUL MARCO   Ed forgot the cake, that's when he went down to Fairfax Avenue in this convertible and came out with this huge, gigantic wedding cake. Someone didn't get married and it was left over, and he made a deal with the bakery and brought it back to Sunset Stages.

KATHY WOOD   Norma wouldn't even take her clothes off in front of Eddie — the short time they were married — that's why the annulment came around. Eddie told me she used to go in a closet to get undressed. It only lasted for days, minutes ... as soon as he put on a goddamn nightgown.

PAUL MARCO   The marriage was very short. Norma McCarty threw him out of the house, if you believe that. His plain comment was "We just couldn't get along." She couldn't hack him wearing female clothes, because she was very, very straight-laced, very prim and proper. And she didn't drink drink-for-drink with him, and that sort of stuff.

I think she had something to do with putting some money into *Plan 9 From Outer Space.* I think she was an actress, like so many of Ed's stock company, that put money into the film. I don't think she was ready for seeing him early in the morning with high heel shoes and a nightgown. But he wasn't really broken up about it; he didn't act like it when he stayed with me, he just said, "Well you know Norma." And I said, "Yeah."

PAUL MARCO   One day, when I came home, he was all dressed up, and he said, "I've got someone I want you to meet. And that's when I met Kathy, and she came over, all dressed up, and — gorgeous! I can see her right now, a gorgeous blonde, with a big fur coat. And she was a secretary. And then she kept coming over. I don't know how long it was that he was staying with me — a few days with him seemed like months. He had no place to go, and when he left he went with Kathy.

KATHY WOOD   I met Ed 3 or 4 times for the first time. I met him once at the Wiltern theater, the Church of Religious Science. They had the Sunday holdings there, and up in the balcony, of course it was dark, and about 3 seats away from me was this handsome profile. And he passed the collection plate, and the next Sunday he was there, too. And I never saw him again, just sitting there, 3 rows away from him. And I kept thinking about him.

One night, I was going out with my boy friend, from Pacific Pipelines, and we went to the Cameo Room. He had to go to San Francisco, and after he left, I thought, well, I'm going to have one more drink. I only lived a block away. And all of a sudden he comes in, the same guy with Bela Lugosi. Lugosi was a little bit under the weather. So Lugosi left, and Ed sat at the end of the bar, drinking, and tears were coming down his face. I'm always a sucker for someone who's upset , so I said, kind of loudly, "Is that poor man crying?" He looked over at me and said, "No, but I'll tell you my story." There was a whole bunch of us sitting around, drinking, and he said, "I wasn't crying, I just have a cold." And that was the third, and fatal time, we were together after that forever.

I fell in love instantly. I kind of hope Eddie did. I don't know what relationships Eddie had with other women, but I know we held hands, looked at each other, had the same experiences apart, cried together, fought fiercely, were two together.

He didn't even take me to bed the first night. I was awed by him before he screwed me. We sat and drank coffee all night, looking at his scrapbooks.

Ed had an old yellow convertible, he used to drive me to work in downtown L.A. We had to stop every two miles or so on Sunset going downtown to buy brake fluid. We bought a maroon Custom Royal Lancer through trading in Ed's yellow convertible and my entire bank account. My company moved to San Francisco and I stayed here to be with Ed. We drove to Las Vegas and got married between poker and craps and went on to Salt Lake City in a blizzard, eating canned sardines and crackers, living dangerously and crazy happily, missing cows, deer, rabbits on the road.

While we were having prime ribs in Salt Lake City, Ed got an awful toothache. The jukebox was playing "The Poor People of Paris." Saturday night in Salt Lake City! Ed took me to the movie *The Man with the Golden Arm* and *Robinson Crusoe*. He went to the police, they found a dentist. We went to the Mormon Tabernacle and Huge Copper Mine, Salt Lake. We made friends with the managers at the motel. Nice people those mormons. Snow, snow, we loved it.

CARL ANTHONY Kathy was a very sweet woman, very, very dedicated — she really loved that guy.

KATHY WOOD Eddie and I used to go to Ciro's ... and a particular night we were there there was a bunch of jugglers, and they asked for someone from the audience, and of course, who volunteers but Eddie. He was a little bit drunk — they had him between them, he's supposed to stand still, and he was kind of weaving back and forth — he almost got clipped. We went to Mocambo's, Ciro's, they were a lot of fun in the late fifties, there was another club that had jazz combos — Julie London was married to Bobby Troup — he had a club. We got around, Sunset Strip, Earl Carroll's, but we just liked to go out — when we had the money. I remember the night we went to Earl Carroll's. Eddie had bought me this beautiful zip-down Chinese dress ... white silk. He also bought me this white fox stole. I'll tell you I looked pretty damned good. Of course Eddie was really dressed up, he looked like a million dollars. What he could do to a tux ... believe me. Eddie, being like he was, could sort of put himself in two places at once, he was so in tune with women, and with men.

VALDA HANSEN He loved women, but he'd like to wear eyelashes sometime and lipstick, too, when he put those gowns on. It's like he loves women so much he's taking on the persona and becoming, having this woman wrapped around him, and in him.

Kathy Wood, in a photo taken by
Ed Wood, circa 1964

Publicity shot of Dolores Fuller for
Bride of the Monster, March, 1955

Bride of the Monster

PROFESSOR: I have searched for you everywhere — everywhere I heard stories of monsters — and now I am here- sent to bring you home...

VORNOFF: Home ... I have no home- Hunted ... despised ... living like an animal — the jungle is my home! But I will show the world that I can be its master. I shall perfect my own race of people — a race of atomic supermen that will conquer the world!

PROFESSOR: Ahhh, yes- a really great master race. As I convinced my superiors only you could create. One with which our country can rule the world without debate...

VORNOFF: You misunderstand me, Strowski. I do not intend to return to your country. My plans are for myself ... alone....

PROFESSOR: Are you mad, Vornoff?

VORNOFF: One is always considered mad when one perfects something that others cannot grasp....

— from the screenplay *Bride of the Atom* by Edw. D. Wood, Jr.

ALEX GORDON   *Bride of the Atom* was a title Eddie thought up. My title was *The Atomic Monster.* Later on the script was completely rewritten.

Sam Arkoff was a lawyer who helped me get out of the problems with *The Lawless Rider,* and we didn't have any money to pay him at the time, so what he would do was, before he went to his office, he would often come to the apartment I was sharing with Eddie, and get himself a free breakfast, instead. So Arkoff came to the door, and, at that time, I couldn't even boil a couple of eggs, Eddie would do all the cooking. So when Arkoff came to breakfast, I said, "Well, Eddie's still asleep, I'll get him and I'll have him make you a couple of eggs." So we both went to Eddie's bedroom door, and banged on it, and opened it up, and there he was with Dolores. So this shook me of course, and I don't think Arkoff ever forgave me for that. I didn't know that Dolores was in there, because I never would have tolerated it.

GEORGE WEISS   Now, I had nothing to do with it, and I can't even verify it, but Ed Wood helped to start American Pictures, which later became American-International, a guy by the name of Arkoff. Nicholson was a theater man. He owned the Picfair, I think. But that doesn't change — they stole all Ed's brain, and froze him out. In fact the dope let everybody read his scripts. That's how trusting he was.

DOLORES FULLER   We had *Bride of the Monster* all finished, and we had a date in a theater to premiere it, but we didn't have enough money for the lab costs. We were so concerned with all the publicity out, and everybody coming to the premiere, and not being able to pick up the film, that we made a deal with Sam Arkoff, who had a little one room office in the Nickodell restaurant building. I guess the deal he made was pretty stiff because with these two pictures that he bought from Edward, he started his whole empire of American-International pictures.

KATHY WOOD   All through his life, Eddie condemned Arkoff. He really hated him, and he was bitterly unhappy about what happened. Eddie gave them a script on approval, and they changed the characters, they changed it a little bit around. Eddie had written it for Lugosi, it was about this old horror actor that couldn't get work anymore, so he took his vengeance out on the studio. The idea they took, from Eddie's idea, was about a make-up man who takes revenge on a studio.

SAM ARKOFF   *How to Make a Monster* was Herman Cohen's picture for us and his writer [Kenneth Langtry and Herman Cohen]. Let me ask a question. Where did Ed get his idea? You see, here's the whole thing with everything: Ed probably saw a picture before *How to Make a Monster,* so he got the same idea, and he changed it around. That's the way everything's done in this town, anyway, for Christ's sake.

Alex Gordon brought Ed to me to get him out of some legal problems of various kinds. Alex used to bring me in clients generally that I didn't want. American International Pictures started in 1954, and I kept up my law practice until '56. So I was really doing both at the same time. And Alex knew every one-lung producer ... and that's about what you would consider Ed Wood. There was something about Ed Wood that was likable. I didn't pay too much attention to him, basically, because I must say that Ed was a loser, in my book. There wasn't anything in his pictures. Fundamentally, there were just too many things deficient. He wasn't worth the kind of time that it took. I hate to put it on that basis, but I really wasn't getting paid as I remember, and kind of as a favor to Alex, getting him out of problems every now and then.

I'm not saying that I didn't get anything, I don't think I ever got as much as a cigar out of Ed Wood. I don't remember ever getting a buck out of it.

One of the problems that these one lung producers used to have, used to be the fact that they had to use whatever money they had, so they never had the withholding money ... they withheld the money from the actors or whoever it was, but they never paid it to the government. That was always one of the things that all of them did, and Ed was the kind of guy that had to live from hand to mouth. All I can say is, if you had clients like Ed Wood, you'd have to feel like a street cleaner following an errant horse ... that's about the size of it.

ED WOOD   The money for *Bride of the Monster* took me almost a year to raise. I shot three days on that thing. I shot the police station and that particular sequence and where Bela walked into the hall with the creaky stairs and where Tor came in and where the cops came into the building and where it caught on fire and where they came in with the fire place. That's all I shot in those three days. A couple of the actors took me to the labor commissioner on it because I had to have a three week lay off to try to promote the rest of the money. I called Joy Houck in Louisiana. I said, "Joy you like the script" and I said, "Now I need the money. I have three days of

Lugosi in the can." And he said, "Why the hell don't you let him out?" Anyway we laid off at first for three weeks and it suddenly got into six weeks and then it got into nine weeks and then all they are just fighting away. Lugosi was the only one who didn't fight me about it.

And finally when I got the money which was by old man McCoy. Tony McCoy played the lead in it. I was the sole producer on that thing until they came in on it and Tony took over the reigns on it. And not knowing how to handle unions he ran it up and he said anything they wanted to say would go and it went until it was over $89,000. On that speech I worked a long time mainly because I wanted it to be without saying it's Russia, but we had to get the old man out and he's very serious about making these giant monsters and as I say in there ... it's not so original ... there are so many things. It's just a rewrite of a thousand times. But I had to get him away and when Strowski says, "I've come to take you home," the only thing he could say is, "Home, I have no home," that type of thing.

That came from the spot I saw over in Griffith Park although it wouldn't photograph the way I wanted with the two boys standing in the dirt by the police car, by the way, we took that scene 17 times, McCoy just couldn't come across with dialogue. He was the worst I ever had. I was in too far and I couldn't let him go and, besides the father had the money. Loretta [King] was a horror character in herself. She could take no liquids of any kind. Her skin — you would touch it here and it would stay there. She was solid white. Any liquid she would immediately throw up. She was becoming completely dehydrated. I almost married her by the way for her money. She had a million dollars. Anyway Lugosi would tell her she was going to look like the mummy and he says, I would never have played the mummy because I don't want my skin to look like that.

The kitchen thing was the funniest thing that happened. Tor walks across to Loretta King who is on the couch and he's got this angora beret which is a fetish. Here's this giant, Tor ... this thing is glaring at Loretta. Now Lugosi comes in with a whip. Right away he sizes up the situation: Tor with the girl. Tor wasn't going to hurt the girl. You always had to have the sympathetic monster. That's what made *Frankenstein* so great. So Lugosi starts beating the hell out of this giant with this felt whip. So he's smashing the giant and gets him out of the laboratory and Tor is screaming and Lugosi is saying, "Get out, get, get out of here, leave her alone." Now after he gets him out he slams the door and Lugosi comes back winding the whip as he crosses very slowly. Had to have him really slow. Notice the camera. Always lets him lead the camera instead of the camera coming down on him. Since the studio wasn't that wide.

An elephant knocked the wall in two days after we were shooting, by the way. It was called the Sunset Stages. He was pulling the camera. He's winding this whip up and now we pick up Loretta and she's up against the wall and she's all shaken and frightened and Lugosi as he's walking he has that beautiful little snickering laugh of his, heh, heh, heh — which is not a laugh, it's almost a piece of dialogue. Nobody

Tony McCoy, Tor Johnson, Ed Wood, Bill Thompson, unidentified script girl, Don Nagel
on location at Griffith Park for *Bride of the Monster*
[photo courtesy Don Nagel]

Conrad Brooks and Ed Wood during a break on *Bride of the Monster*
[photo courtesy Henry Bederski]

"Don't be afraid of Lobo, he's as gentle as a kitchen."
Loretta King, Bela Lugosi and Tor Johnson in *Bride of the Monster*

else could do it. Karloff, Lorre, Greenstreet, it was his, and I would get that in every picture. He says, "Heh, heh, heh, don't be afraid of Lobo, he's as gentle as a kitchen!" That's how the word *kitchen* came in!

On that big speech Lugosi came to me, when he read that he called me and he said, "Eddie, that's just too much lines, I can't remember that lines, I'm not young anymore, I can't remember those lines."

TED ALLAN KFWB took over the studio where *Bride of the Monster* was filmed, after I left it. It was at Yucca and Argyle, back of the Pantages Theater, right next to Capitol Records. That was Ted Allan Studios, where *Bride of the Monster* was done and finished. It was a 110 X 110 foot stage and 110 X 80 foot stage. I had two stages, and the basement had all the editing equipment, and there were a dozen offices up on the corner.

SCOTT ZIMMERMAN Ed said, "The house in *Bride of the Monster* was a real house. A canvas tarp was rigged up behind it to serve as a gray sky, because I didn't want the other houses in the background to show."

LORETTA KING The way *Bride of the Monster* was filmed was, we worked a few days, and then there was no money. So it was shut down, and then I went on down to Laguna and was in stock, Keenan Wynn and *Petrified Forest,* and all those things, and when I came back I had forgotten about the movie, I just thought, he'll never finish it. I had gone over to Arizona, just for a week. While I was there I received a call from him, frantically, "Get back," and this was on a Saturday. Because on Monday morning at 6:30 we're starting to shoot. So I drove all that day, and I got the script, looked at the script all night, I just didn't go to bed, and I was there at 6:30 and he starts shooting it right away! Well, that was just Ed Wood!

JOHN ANDREWS Eddie stole the octopus. I mean he physically picked it up and stole it! From Republic Studios.

ED WOOD The octopus was used in *Wake of the Red Witch,* by the way. They had it in Republic's attics up in the top; it was up on the ceiling for years and we lost one leg as we took it down. That baby was heavy. I think it weighed about 150 pounds. When Tor comes up and he does his thing and Lugosi says, "Lobo, you hear? They think *you* are the monster!" — that was the scene shot at the end of the film when Bela was very, very ill. He went off the set after that scene and probably laid down for hours. Bela might have worked eight days. Anyway, he wanted more money. It was $750.00 we agreed on, now he wanted $1,000.00. He actually walked out on me. It was strictly a union picture. McCoy and the others were going out of their minds. I was, too. We went to the Guild and Jack Stewart happened to be the President at the time. He said, "I'm sorry, the man says he's sick. There's nothing that you can do about it. Anyway, we agreed to give him the extra $250.00 and then shooting resumed.

We went out to Griffith Park looking like an MGM studio. We had four or five fire engines around for the scenes we shot there. They had guard gates set up and the whole bit. Bela was right down on the set the next day even though there was no doubt in my mind that he was very, very, very ill. It was March and it was colder than a son of a bitch. While I'm shooting on the other side of the mountain, my prop man was supposed to be creating a lake. We got over there and they didn't have a lake. No lake. So we dammed up the little river that runs through Griffith Park and created a lake that was about three or four feet deep. The octopus had to be covered so that the broken tentacle wouldn't show. When we shot that scene, the fire chief was really adamant about us getting rid of all that water that had backed up. I told the prop man to bang a hole in the dam and the water rushed out of there like a tidal wave. It completely flooded the golf course that was just on the other side of the road. It was the worst flood they had ever seen. Lugosi had to do one scene in that freezing cold water and he was freezing. When he got through with the scene, he drank up a whole bottle of Jack Daniels just to get warm.

The prop man was collecting $20.00 a bottle for the booze. Lugosi's double for the film [Eddie Parker] was a bit too tall for the part and we had to do quite a number of takes before we could match their heights. On one scene, I took two takes, because the first didn't match, but it slipped by me in editing so you can see one scene where the two just don't match at all. It's the scene where Lugosi becomes the giant.

JOHN ANDREWS When they were shooting *Bride of the Monster* up in Griffith Park, and he dug out that lagoon of a thing, for the octopus, somebody, I think it was Art Manikin, camera grip, didn't want to get in the water, it was cold, and Jesus, midnight, and, it was stolen, it was a sneak, I've done that many, many times, I've stolen shots at the airport. Anyway, Bud Osborne says, "I'll get in the water." And he did. And Bela was drunk, and stoned, and loaded out of his mind, took off his shoes and socks, pulled up his pants and *he* got in the water! So, it was pretty wild times, and fun times, it was good times, making pictures. That's the only thing that counts is getting the thing on film. That's all that matters. No matter what you have to do.

ALEX GORDON Eddie rewrote the script *The Atomic Monster* and made a very low budget picture vaguely based on it..

ED WOOD I wrote *Bride of the Monster* for Lugosi. I wrote every line in that. I gave Alex Gordon a credit because he gave me an an idea.

DOLORES FULLER He was 60 thousand dollars short for *Bride of the Monster*. And this girl comes in with the money — Loretta King. And I remember, we were talking business with her, and we were in a bar, a night club. And she refused to ever drink water. And I asked her, how she could go through life, because you have to flush yourself out, you know, to be healthy. She said, "I never drink water, because it puts weight on." But anyway, she came in with 60 thousand dollars, so he gave her my part. That he had written for me. And I was heartbroken. And that sort of disgusted me, after the whole thing, everything I was doing to help support him and all, and bringing in the money, and bringing in the costumes, from my modeling jobs, and all the clothes. His values, it didn't set right with me. Loyalties should mean more. We could have raised the money some other way. So I took a lesser part, I just had a few lines in the picture, instead of the lead like I was supposed to have. Ed just told me, "There will be other pictures, you'll star in other pictures."

LORETTA KING   Before *Bride of the Monster* I was on *Camay Theater,* and I was working, and I just didn't have any reason to put up the money for the film, nor did I have it at the time. I just didn't have the money at the time! So, he never once approached me for anything like that. He never asked me nor did anyone representing him. I said to Dolores, I've gone on many interviews where I didn't get anything. I had no idea I was going to get this part. But then I guess he had to tell her that I put up the money! Ed Wood wanted somebody — and this I admired him for- he wanted somebody that he wasn't involved with. And as far as money was concerned Tony McCoy's dad did that.

MARGE USHER   I was on the set of *Bride of the Monster, Plan 9 from Outer Space,* and *Revenge of the Dead.* I was right there all the time, sometimes he had me get a bottle for him or something. I couldn't care less, it wasn't my life, it was his he was ruining. He'd drink anything. When he directed, well, he'd disappear, I don't know where he'd keep it, it was none of my business, but he always kept a bottle around, you could always tell when he'd perk up after he was tired, and then he'd perk up away. You could always tell when he just had a slug.

HARRY THOMAS   I have never seen Ed drink on the set. Never. In all the pictures that I was on, he never took one drink on the set. When he was working, he never took a drink.

LORETTA KING   There was a scene where I was strapped to this table, and Tor had to come in and rescue me and take the manacles off of me...I thought he was going to break my arm every time! But he tried to be gentle.

JOHN ANDREWS   While he's doing *Bride of the Monster,* Eddie didn't have a car. He's writing, producing and directing a picture and he doesn't have a car! But he always had a ride. So they're driving along, someplace, and Bill Thompson said, "Tell me when the light's red." Bill Thompson, director of photography, was color blind!

LORETTA KING   They were shooting what was supposed to be a night scene in Griffith Park, but actually it was the daytime and then they made it a night scene. For special effects, Ed Wood was on top of the car, it was a big storm, and I was driving it, and he had a watering can, and had the water come down on the windshield! And it was things like that, you had to admire the way he would do these things. I mean there he was with the watering can, strapped to the top of the car.

TED ALLAN   Bela Lugosi was in pain during the shooting of *Bride of the Monster.* And he would relax every once in a while, but we just thought maybe he was taking aspirin or something a little stronger. He would get sort of a glow, and then he would be very relaxed. A pain killer, I guess a good strong pain killer of some sort. Then he would be more attentive. Ed Wood wasn't a martinet or anything but he was trying to produce, direct and write the whole thing, so he was kind of short with him on occasions, in his directing, when he couldn't remember his lines. But Bela just went on his way, and took it in stride. He probably figured, well, he had the painkillers, went on his way, and did his job, and went home.

FRED OLEN RAY   Ed told me that he borrowed hand movement for Lugosi from *White Zombie*. I said, had any of Lugosi's previous work influenced you, and he said, "Perhaps the hand scarf scene from *White Zombie*."

BEN FROMMER   In *Bride of the Monster* I was a suspect, in the police station. I used Larry Tierney's dialogue from *Dillinger*. "No tank town jail can hold me, I'll be out of this here rat trap in 24 hours." I asked Ed, "Can I use Tierney's dialogue, when they put him in jail, in Dillinger?" "Yeah."

JOHN ANDREWS   Eddie hated, loathed, despised, wanted murdered, I'm not overdoin' it, man, I'm telling you straight — George Becwar. George plays this foreign agent Strowski, whatever he is, in *Bride of the Monster*. And he goes to the swamp to visit Bela. He's trying to get Bela to go back to Hungary or wherever it is. Which the Hungarian communists actually tried to get Bela to do. They actually sent for him, to come back to Hungary to be Minister of Culture. Plays, museums, stuff like that. And he told Eddie that he was afraid to go over there, that they'd send him to a gulag.

George Becwar was dissatisfied with the amount of pay. First he agrees to the amount of pay. Shit, he only worked a day. Then he calls Screen Actors Guild and complains about Eddie, and they shot down the production, and caused Eddie a lot of trouble with his backers. Anyway, Eddie lost his ownership, he lost everything. And he hated George Becwar to the day he deceased. I mean with a passion!

Another guy he hated that bad was the manager of the theater where *Bride* opened, it's Huntington Park, I don't know the name of the theater. He told Eddie what he thought of the picture: "Stinks." Eddie gave me a group shot, 8 X 10, of Dolores, Eddie, I think Tor was there, Marco, and when he gave me the photo, he said, "Wai-wai-wai-wai-wai-wait-" And he takes a pair of scissors, and he cuts this guy off. He was on the end. He folds it up, and he throws it in the wastebasket. And I said, "Who was that?" He says, "Well, he's not there anymore, so it doesn't matter." He wouldn't even talk about it.

HENRY BEDERSKI   You know how Tony McCoy came to play the lead? His old man put up the money. Tony McCoy appeared in one picture after this, and then I never heard of him again. He had all those cans of film there, sitting beside him, and it looked like something overwhelmed him. He was Mr. Gloom himself. There was something going on between him and Ed. Things just weren't right.

DENNIS RODRIGUEZ   Tony McCoy's father [Donald], who owned a meat packing plant [Packing Service Corp.], he demanded that, in exchange for the financing, not only was his kid going to be in the movie, but that they had to end it with an atomic explosion.

MARGE USHER   The thing I had against Ed though, was, it kind of sticks in my craw, was that he left me holding the bag for quite a little bit of money, and other people I know, too. And clients of mine. It's one thing I didn't like, leaving me holding the bag with my actors. We had several meetings with Ed and all, and I was a little skeptical about him the more he talked. So Tony's father put up some of the money for the picture, and with all the promises in the world, and then it didn't get finished, and then his father had to go back in to salvage the thing and practically went broke putting up the money for Ed's picture. Ed never had a sober day all the time he was doing it. He could have done so much better if he'd just laid off of it. He'd get blotto by the end of the day, and then they'd shoot at night, he was just bombed out all the time.

ROBERT CREMER   Ed never started with a budget, he raised a certain amount of money, and then went into production. He'd get this far, and then he'd buy six more cans of film, and pay off Lugosi a little bit, so he could go down to see his chiropodist and pick up his drugs, and then they'd work for a while, and then he'd run around and get some more money to just keep everybody happy, while he kept trying to finish the film. So, by the time he got finished with the film, he couldn't remember how many bits and pieces of money he got, to pay off who, to buy how much film when, and it was sort of deficit financing.

ALEX GORDON   What was funny was the sneak preview, which was at the Paramount Theater on Hollywood Boulevard. They sneaked it with, of all things, *The End of the Affair,* with Deborah Kerr, based on the Graham Greene story. Sam Arkoff and I went to see it, and, strangely enough, he thought it was quite good for the money.

MAILA NURMI   Ed Wood gave an affair at the Paramount Theater, a benefit for Bela. It was advertised, and they sent invitations to everyone that said, all the money goes to Bela, he's sick and he needs it. Nobody came. Nobody.

MILDRED WORTH   Frank and I attended the preview in a Hollywood theater, and the audience just guffawed at the end. They thought it was the silliest thing they ever saw. And I think Ed was kind of chagrined about it.

ED WOOD   Bela and I were walking on Hollywood Boulevard. We had to wait for a red light on the corner of Hollywood and Vine. He just stopped dead. All of a sudden in this big, booming voice, the likes of which I hadn't heard in years, he suddenly goes into the speech and says: "Home ... I have no home. Hunted — despised — living like an animal — the jungle is my home! But I will show the world that I can be its master. I will perfect my own race of people — a race of atomic supermen which will conquer the world!" And he did the whole thing on the corner. A crowd gathered and they applauded him at the end. He did the whole thing. And

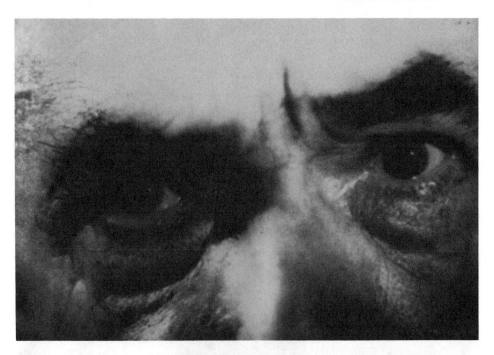

Top Photo:
Bela Lugosi's
eyes in
*Bride of the
Monster*

Right:
Lugosi on the
set of *Bride of
the Monster*
[photo courtesy
Richard Bojarski]

when he was finished he walked right across the street. And the people that had heard all of this nonsense who were going in the same direction, had a double hemorrhage when they saw him turn into the mortuary. He was just going in to see one of his friends, but they didn't know that.

Bela was in the hospital when *Bride of the Monster* was released, but I took him to see it after he was released, at the UA theater in L.A. and he liked it. He really liked that speech. He met an old man when he came out of the theater. And this old man just latched on to him, grabbed his wallet out and got a piece of paper for an autograph. We had left the theater to go out so that he could smoke his cigar. When he was really hard up for money, he would buy the rope cigars, really long ones that he could cut in half. And they stank. Oh, did they stink. This old man said to him, "Well, I'm 62 years old. I feel very old." Well, Lugosi brought his chest way out and he said, "I'm 71, but the brain, the brain, it never feels that you're old. Only the body looks old, but never the brain. The brain is young, then the body is still young, like a young man."

Ed Wood and Maila Nurmi (Vampira) at the "Testimonial Benefit" for Bela Lugosi [photo courtesy Paul Marco]

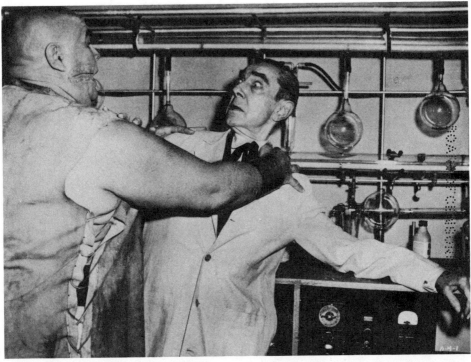

Two views of Tor in action from *Bride of the Monster*. [bottom photo courtesy David J. Hogan]

Saucer flies in Plan 9 From Outer Space

Tor Johnson rises from the grave, with Vampira. [photo courtesy Eric Caidin]

Plan 9

RULER: What plan will you follow now?

EROS: Plan nine — It has been impossible to work through these earth creatures — Their soul is too controlled.

RULER: Plan nine — (takes up paper reports) Ah, yes ... Plan nine deals with the resurrection of the dead. Long distant electrodes shot into the pineal and pituitary gland of recent dead. Have you attempted any of this plan as yet?

EROS: Yes ...

RULER: How successful has it been?

EROS: We have risen two so far— We will be just as successful on more ...

RULER: The living — They have not become suspicious of your movements ... ?

EROS: We were forced to dispose of one policeman — However, none of the risen have been seen — at least not by anyone who still remains alive ...

    — from the script of *Plan 9 From Outer Space* by Ed Wood

CARL ANTHONY Before he started shooting *Plan 9*, we were both bachelors. And since we were more or less working together day and night raising money, Ed and I just decided to live together. It was just for the duration of the picture, more or less. That was when Kathy met him. We were right in the heart of Hollywood, somewhere on Bronson Street. His hours were always irregular, but he was drinking, and that was the problem.

REVEREND LYN LEMON J. Edward Reynolds was a highly respected man among southern Baptist churches in the area. He did a lot of evangelistic singing in the churches. He asked me to ride with him one day on his route for an electronics firm. In the course of the day he told me he had *The Billy Sunday Story* and Ma Sunday's permission to develop it and produce it on film. He wanted to do that very badly, but didn't have the capital to produce it. He hit upon this idea that we would produce his friend Ed Wood's script, which was a science fiction thing, and we'd form a corporation, and we'd pool our resources, develop, produce that film, sell it, take the profits from it, put them back into the corporation, and produce *The Billy Sunday Story*. And thereafter we'd produce nothing but religious films. So he wanted to know if I would like to come in on it — it sounded good to me, so I borrowed some money on my life insurance, and put $500 into it.

KATHY WOOD When we moved into the Mariposa Apartments, Edward Reynolds was the manager, he was also one of the leaders of the Baptist Church of Beverly

Hills. When Reynolds put some money up for the film, one of the conditions was that the cast was to be baptized before filming. Eddie was baptized in a Jewish swimming pool in Beverly Hills. Tor and Eddie both, they wanted me to go in but I said, "No way."

ED WOOD   We finally did get the money out of the Baptists except that they insisted that we all become Baptists to get it. Tor Johnson was watching everyone getting in it and being dunked three times while the minister read prayers. Well, just when it was his time to get into the pool, he whispered to me, "Watch what happens when he dunks me the third time." So this skinny old reverend father dunks Tor for the third time and Tor stayed on the bottom. The Reverend was screaming, "He's drowning! Help! Help!" running around like a madman trying to get someone to help him get that huge wrestler out of the pool. They came across with a lot of money.

REVEREND LYN LEMON   Ed Reynolds came back, later, he said he and Ed Wood had talked about it and they wanted to know if I would do a funeral scene in the film. Ed told me to step up there and go at it, they got me into position, and when they called "Action!", why, I started. "The bell has rung on his great career ... it's hard to say the proper words about a friend, and Inspector Clay was my friend, a close friend." And I used the scripture passage, "Greater love have no man than to lay his life down for a friend." Coincidentally, we buried Tor out in Eternal Valley Memorial Park in '71.

DUDLEY MANLOVE   Tor Johnson had such warmth! He was so cooperative — just a lovely man. Always on time, always knew his lines. As you know, he was a former wrestler, but it was just a put-on. He would go and have drinks with his opponents after a wrestling match.

PAUL MARCO   Ed did most of the talking with all of the Baptists, and I sort of sat in the sidelines. The baptists didn't put the money up for the whole thing, partly it came from various small investors. That's why Ed wrote J. Edward Reynolds and Hugh Thomas into the beginning of the picture, as the gravediggers, because they all wanted to be in it. Ed could convince you to buy the Brooklyn bridge. They fought like crazy over the title *Grave Robbers from Outer Space*. Ed loved that title, and, right to the end, when they changed it, he said, "I don't like the title, I fought with him and fought with him, but I didn't win."

Lugosi was very despondent that Ed couldn't deliver to do a picture right away after *Bride of the Monster*. When we submitted *The Ghoul Goes West,* that was the picture he was going to do. That's how the scenes of Bela came about which were used in *Plan 9,* because he wasn't strong enough to be on a horse. *The Vampire's Tomb* scenes were shot instead, a graveyard, Bela in his cape. Ed wrote the story of *Plan 9* around the people I introduced him to, like Vampira, Bunny Breckinridge, who was my house guest at the time, and he made him an outer-space man, and David de Mering was his secretary, and he made him one of the pilots.

MAILA NURMI   Oh, I was incensed when I found out that Ed Wood wanted me. There was a column in the old *Los Angeles Times,* and it said that Ed Wood was doing a new film, and he aspired to use Vampira. Oh, I read it and I was livid, because at that time every major studio wanted, they were all bidding for me to do a major film, and I was holding off wondering which one shall I select. But I got blacklisted and Ed Wood got me. If someone had said, "You're gonna work for him," I would've said, "You're mad, never in a million years ... " So, there I was, starving, trying to live on 13 dollars a week, and someone came to me and said Ed Wood is doing a movie. He's got film clips of the *Sincerely Yours* premiere, with Liberace, the fans outside, he's got film clips of flying saucers, he's got stock footage of jeeps and Army stuff, and he's got some old discards of Bela Lugosi movies, cut-outs from his other films, he's gonna put it all together, and he's written a script around it, and he's sending it to you. And I said, "Oh, that's swell," because no one else was sending me anything. And so then I got this script. They said it was 200 dollars a day, that was the union minimum back then. And you'll work one day, so it'll be 200 bucks. I said, "I'll tell you what, allow me to do it as a mute, as a zombie, non-speaking, and I'll do it." I rode on the bus in full costume to get to the studio, on Santa Monica Boulevard, right in the shadow of the Hollywood Presbyterian cemetery.

Ed stood behind the camera, and because I didn't talk, he would just say, "come out of here," and "go in there," and "roll 'em" and so forth, and at one point I screamed. When I finished screaming those jaded old Hollywood roués applauded, because I made a sound at last. It was difficult to walk in that costume, and the flooring was not very steady there, there were lots of rocks and wrinkled fake greenery and stuff on the ground. I didn't have a decent costume for *Plan 9.* I didn't know where my costumes were, either I had thrown them away or lost them. What I wore was old, worn out. It looks like I had a hole in the crotch of the dress, if you notice. A hole in the crotch and I thought, oh well, nobody's ever gonna see this movie, it doesn't matter.

GREGORY WALCOTT   Ed's films are another category. Three rungs below B movies — dingy, third-rate fringe type films....

Ed had poor taste and was undisciplined. He had no taste. If he had 10 million dollars it *[Plan 9]* would have been a piece of tasteless shit. I liked Ed Wood, but I could discern no genius there. His main concern was making his next film.

For the cockpit scene, the set decorator took a piece of masonite board, bent it, and hung a shower curtain behind it, and called it a cockpit. That was the last scene we filmed.

The producer, Reynolds, said Wood is going to use pretty good special effects. I thought that would be the salvation of the film. It looked like they shot the thing in a kitchen. I told my wife when I got home, "Honey, this has got to be the worst film of all time." Thirty years later, it's come back to haunt me.

ED WOOD   Bela was to have a much larger part in the picture. When he told me that he needed the money, I had the script already. It was just a matter getting the

$800 promotion money to be used for the day's shooting we did with him in the graveyard. He was to be Vampira's husband. The doctor who doubled for him after he died was a chiropodist named Thomas R. Mason and he had the same skull structure as Lugosi. You can see where we used him in the scene where the vampire enters the house. Bela Jr. saw it and said that it was a hell of a double. I had to kill Bela off much earlier than I planned when he actually died. He would have been the grandfather of the two young people living in Tor Johnson's house. After Lugosi died, then the vampire had to become an incidental character to the plot. If we had had imitators like Rich Little around at the time, we could have dubbed the voice and used the double to carry the full weight of Bela's part.

In cutting this thing after Lugosi is killed by the automobile, it was so phony. He leaves the house and picks up the flower that his wife has planted. He is going to the cemetery to see his deceased wife's grave. His daughter and son-in-law live in the house on the outskirts of the cemetery. This would have been the part where Lugosi explains that he believes in flying saucers and the like while visiting his daughter and son-in-law, who is a pilot. As Bela walks off scene, you can hear the phony scream. He would have been picked up going to the cemetery, but instead we had to stage a car accident. The phony scream was thrown in and so was the screech of car tires.

The filming of *Plan 9* started just over a month before Lugosi died. We shot in a cemetery in Sacramento. Tor's son Karl was lieutenant of police at the time. Every one of the police cars that we used were borrowed from him. Now he weighs probably as much as his father did. He said, "You know that cemetery thing you want to do, they are tearing up a graveyard out here for a building project and it would be a perfect place to shoot." I thought that would be perfect, but I didn't want to close the deal until I made sure that Lugosi wanted the job. I called Lugosi and he told me that he needed dough at the time. His words were barely intelligible. But I called Karl and told him that I would bring out Lugosi the next day. I asked if we could use his house. He said, "Sure," We gave him $100. So here we go into this graveyard, an old Mexican graveyard that went way back to before the turn of the century. They wanted to build a complex of apartment buildings there and were ready to put up this high-rise there. We thought that the bodies had already been removed from the plots but later we found out that they hadn't. Karl Johnson and Carl Anthony went out with us to work on the set. All of the tombstones were turned over and some were cracked. The angles were bad for shooting because they had already begun excavating on the edge of the graveyard and I could never shoot to the left. And I couldn't go too far to the right, either, because there was a road right there. So, you can see in the picture that the shots are all front shots with hardly any angles. The tombstones on the edges had to be rearranged. Karl and Carl were helping me drag tombstones all around. Bela could not really help, but he was there laying a hand on the tombstone so that he looked as if he were helping. Karl sprained his back with one that must have weighed half a ton. I paid a few $25 mourners and used some reflectors to shoot the scene. Headlines in the San Fernando newspaper, "Ghouls Invade Cemetery." The editor had no idea in the world who invaded the cemetery

Top: Lugosi as he appears in Plan 9
Bottom: Lugosi's double, Tom Mason, in Plan 9. Similar ears?

and changed the tombstones around. The article went on to say that relatives of long deceased persons have been searching through this graveyard trying to find their relatives. We had the biggest laugh over that one.

GREGORY WALCOTT   I was a member of the same church Eddie Reynolds was attending. He financed *Plan 9* under the condition that I would star in it. The production schedule was four days, a lot of the stuff that they used was shot with a hand-held camera out of a car window, and a lot of stock footage. I had just finished working on a big film at Warner Brothers where I was under contract. They spent about 10 weeks working on a film and here was Ed Wood spending four days on a film, so it was kind of beyond my understanding, ability, and adaptability to be able to do something like that. But he was pretty remarkable. He'd go off at lunch to look at the rushes ... and he'd come back two hours later. You'd think he'd be back even earlier than most people. But there was one line he would say all the time, "I know my script, I know my script." He didn't direct the actors too much, he was mainly concerned about camera angles, and getting it done.

MONA McKINNON   We had fun on the set. On *Plan 9* Tor Johnson was chasing me across the graveyard set, and the grass was cloth or something, and it had the gravestones on it. Well, I tripped and fell, and the whole graveyard just slid with me. So we had to reset up and reshoot that.

LYLE TALBOT   I got a call from Ed Wood at a time when I wasn't doing too well, so I was going to take any job, and I said, "Fine." We didn't sign contracts of any kind. Eddie paid me off in cash, and sometimes it was a lot of singles, like somebody had handed it to him in a wad, and he just stuck it in his pocket. A couple of times he'd come pay me in the morning before we shot. I remember him saying to me, "Lyle, I won't give you a check, because I don't want it to bounce or anything ... "

HARRY THOMAS   When visitors came on the set to watch, Ed'd come over and talk to them while he was shooting. He'd get 'em a chair, have them sit down. He was very gracious. And he always had a laugh, he always had a smile for somebody. And that was when he was sober. He was elated when he was drinking.

DUDLEY MANLOVE   I've always had a very good memory, I'm a very quick study, and there was one particular scene where it was rather lengthy, a long speech, and Ed said, "Boy, if you could go through this whole thing, without having to intercut, it would save me a lot of money." I said, "Well, don't worry about, I'll do it." And I did it. And it saved him a buck or two without having to intercut or retake. I don't think I retaked a scene in the whole thing.

KATHY WOOD   I had a hand in writing a little bit of *Plan 9*. One afternoon on Mariposa Avenue, we were trying to figure out how to make this particular scene credible, and I came up with the word "Solar," Eddie came up with the "Solaronite bomb." And the rays from the sun, and that's a hell of a speech, and I remember we got the bible out, and we were talking about it, we were talking scientifically and everything, and he didn't think it was corny, he believed in it.

MAILA NURMI   John (Bunny) Breckinridge was playing himself in *Plan 9*. He was a black sheep of a very wealthy social family and was born and bred in the manner — he was just one of those eccentrics that lost his money. He was delightful, I loved John, and I love him in the movie. And they laugh at him, it's so campy, but that's the way he was, he wasn't acting.

HARRY THOMAS   Eddie said, "Treat Bunny Breckinridge real nice, he's a good friend, he's brought in some money." I did treat him nice, I treated all of those people nice, they were a bunch of weirdos!

JACK RANDALL   Bunny had gone down to Mexico to have a sex-change operation, and he had an accident on the way, and the kid he had with him was killed. And then Buddy did some time in the hospital, and then he stopped off here on his way back. And David [De Mering] met him in a gay bar, and immediately became his secretary. He moved in with Bunny, and I think he used to dope him at night to put him asleep.

Bunny's next door neighbor was an alcoholic female with two kids. I think they were 11 and 13. Boys. And Bunny told her one day that he was going down to L.A. and then over to Las Vegas. She said, "Why don't you take the boys with you?" So he did. They stayed in a motel on Sunset Boulevard, and I remember I went over to pick Bunny up one day to take him over to my house for dinner. Anyway, I went up to the room and one of the kids propositioned me. Which sort of raised my eyebrows, shall we say. Bunny had to go out of town someplace, so he turned the kids over to somebody here in L.A. to look after them for a few days. The guy was awaiting trial on a molestation charge. The kids' father was a high-ranking Naval officer in Washington and he got wind of what was going on, and tipped off the F.B.I. or somebody. Anyway, Bunny was arrested. There was a big court case with television coverage. Bunny adjusting his makeup in front of the television camera. He went to Atascadero for a couple of years. Atascadero is an institute for the criminally insane. Usually sex-connected. He spent a couple of years there, where he became "queen of the laundry."

JOHN "BUNNY" BRECKINRIDGE   About my movie *[Plan 9 From Outer Space]*, I thought it was alright, but I think I made a big mistake in doing it. Because it was a lot of rubbish. After all, I was a well known star in Paris. For six years I danced and sang in revues. I played on the stage under a French name, Jacques Solange. It's a French name for girl. I knew people like Puccini, Massenet, Mary Garden, all this crowd, because we had a lovely house in Paris and entertained a great deal, and all that, so I've enjoyed myself, I've always enjoyed myself. I always look on the bright side of everything — I'm never depressed. And if I don't like somebody, I just don't see them. Period.

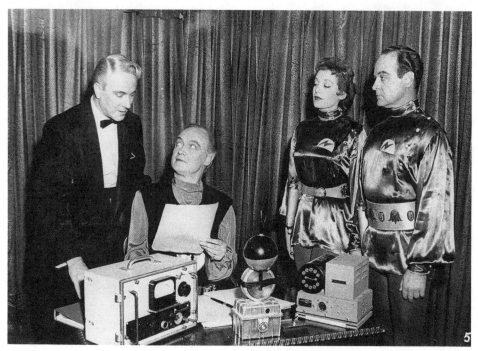

Two Views from *Plan 9*
Top: Criswell, John "Bunny" Breckinridge, Joanna Lee, Dudley Manlove [photo courtesy Dudley Manlove] Bottom: Carl Anthony, Duke Moore, Ben Frommer, Tor Johnson, Paul Marco, Conrad Brooks [photo courtesy Conrad Brooks]

KATHY WOOD   Tom Mason [who doubled for Lugosi in *Plan 9]* was a chiropractor and hypnotist. We always called him Dr. Tom. Eddie got valuable information from him on therapeutic hypnotism for *Bride and the Beast*. Tom and I found out I was a perfect hypnotic subject, and it got to where he could hypnotize me on the phone. Just with his voice. One time while I was hypnotized, I had my hands out to both sides, and Tor Johnson put his full weight on them trying to force my hands down to my sides, but he couldn't do it.

MARGARET MASON   Kathy was always trying to pull a stunt — she was going to put a spell on you if you didn't do what she said. Which didn't impress me in the least.

CARL ANTHONY   The musical director, Gordon Zahler, was a paraplegic. He scored films all off of records, library music.

ED WOOD   None of us knew what a spaceship looked like. Tommy Kemp was my construction engineer on that. Again, of course, Bill Thompson was the cameraman, had to read his light meter by candlelight. It was solid union on the picture. And this stinking little studio with sacks across the ceiling. It was about 150 feet long by about three or four feet wide.

Everything was there on the set except the airplane. We didn't even have a mock-up of the airplane, because we didn't have any more money. Everybody was hocking their insurance policies to keep everything going. We shot the square flying saucer back in Karl Johnson's garden. I said, "Well, we're not going to see the round top of it. All we're going to see is a blimp." Those were my exact words to Tommy Kemp. I went down to the hobby store and bought three model kits of flying saucers and they had these flat bottoms on them. That was why the bottom was square. The special effects were going to be shot later by the cameraman, myself, and the electrician and grip. We built again with cardboard houses and everything. We built an entire town on this long table and with piano wire we brought the round models in over this make-believe town. They were made of balsa wood, and we put a little gasoline on them to get some smoke coming out behind it. But every time that we lit the back of the flying saucer, the damn piano wire would break and down went the flying saucer and every time that happened, we lost two or three little houses on the table.

We had to figure out something else. That ended the square gondola on the bottom of the round saucer, even though I've already shot the film of the square gondola for the interior shots. Every time that the flying saucer went down it cost me another $20.00 to replace the part of the set that it damaged. I went to a special effect company, Ray Mercer's and I said to Ray, "I don't know what the hell I'm going to do with that set. How can I get around the problem?" He said, "Well, if you want to shoot those same flying saucers, we can put them on piano wire and shoot them against black velvet and then superimpose them on footage of Hollywood." I went to Reginald Denny's hobby shop and they didn't have any more models. We just couldn't find any anywhere in Hollywood or anywhere else for that matter. Kids were buying them up as if they were going out of style next week. Ray Mercer had another idea that he thought would work just as well. He wanted to use old Cadillac hubcaps. And that was what turned out to be our flying saucer. They didn't have any Gondola on the bottom of them, but it worked. Bill Thompson said the hubcaps were bright silver and too hard to light so he just painted them all green for the camera. He painted them the shittiest color green I have ever seen. Well, my eyes were looking at them in color rather than black and white. I know now. I told him to paint them beige while Thompson was gone and when he came back about an hour later, he was screaming and yelling, "I don't like that." So finally, I exerted my authority, and it was one of the few times that I ever played the big cheese director and I said, "Those goddam flying saucers are always talked about as being silver. You make them silver and just shut your mouth because that's the way we're going to shoot them." They kicked up a fuss. Well, it turned out that he was right, because they practically glowed on the screen, but we didn't have the money to correct them in the labs.

HARRY THOMAS   I begged Wood to let me change the costumes on the space people and make their faces different. I said, these people talk like they're from Southern California University. I wanted to put colored wigs on them ... green ... and make their faces green. A Frankenstein green. And I wanted to change the eyes. I had the eyes made — they were opaque — I was going to put the slits in the pupil the other way, like cat's eyes. And each one of them I had made chin pieces, extend the chin to give them a long, narrow face. And I had 'em already made! All I had to do was tack 'em on with surgical adhesive. I figure 15 or 20 minutes on each one of those guys. I thought he'd go through with it, because I said, "Wood, these people look too normal. They look like people on this planet. Their voice has to be changed," "Well how am I gonna do that?" I said, "Talk into this glass." I picked up a glass and talked into it. He wouldn't buy it. Instead of the military costumes they had, I sketched a few faces and I said, "Wood, let's make them illuminated, and with shrouds." And all they had to do was put them on, and we could spray them with illuminated paint. "And it won't cost you a dime." And he wouldn't do it. He said, "We don't have the time." This is why I refused to put my name on the credits, and had Tom Bartholomew, my helper, put his name on it. I was really mad at Wood.

KATHY WOOD   At the preview for *Plan 9 From Outer Space* It was raining like hell. We had this Cadillac convertible, and couldn't get the top up! I said, "Eddie, you go down there, to hell with it, I'm not going. It's raining outside, and we can't get the top up!" Poor Eddie! Poor, darling Eddie! Anyway, Eddie gets in the car and he looks so sharp. And here it is, Eddie's driving along, trying to look nonchalant, the rain is pouring, he's all dressed up in this suit, he's going over the top of Barham Boulevard, and everybody's looking at him! He's crazy! And he's trying to be nonchalant. Even though the car was starting to fill up!

BOB BURNS   At the premiere of *Plan 9* Tor Johnson seemed to get a great kick out of the whole thing. He was laughing at himself when he was on the screen. Criswell introduced the whole thing, said what a great film it was, and then one by one, the people who were in the film got up. Tom Mason, the chiropractor got up to thank the "late, great Bela Lugosi" for giving him this chance to have his debut in this film. Even the cameraman, Bill Thompson spoke about how he enjoyed doing the movie. Dudley Manlove, the head alien, got up; Paul Marco also talked. Then Ed Wood got on stage and said, "I'd like to dedicate this film to my great friend Bela Lugosi." The excitement of the night was very up, everybody was very very up about it. There were a few laughs here and there about some of the bad effects and some of the acting stuff.

GREGORY WALCOTT   I remember the preview night; I sat next to Ed Reynolds and I felt so sorry for the poor guy. Reynolds tried to sell it to the distributors. Nobody would buy it, nobody would touch the darn thing. Hal Roach had a company back in New York, D.C.A., they decided to release it for him. I don't think anybody got a dime out of it. It was such a heartbreak for Mr. Reynolds. He died a few years later.

DAVID FRIEDMAN   My close friend Don Davis, who passed away a few years ago, edited *Plan 9 from Outer Space,* and also was in it. He played a drunk in an alley who sees saucers flying overhead and it was prophetic, he drank himself to death.

KATHY WOOD   Over on Mariposa, Reynolds and Eddie got into a big fight ...

PAUL MARCO   Reynolds would threaten Ed, things about how he should cool his dress, be more on the man side, because it wasn't good for the church. Ed had to go through a lot of changes for the money to finish the picture. Ed told me that the Baptists were taking over, and that I would have to relinquish my executive position.

KATHY WOOD   ... and Eddie and Paul had a big argument, and Eddie knocked Paul down the stairs, and we had a big to-do about it, and then I fell asleep on the sofa with a cigarette in my hand, and burned down the couch. One thing led to another, and Edward Reynolds kicked us out. He was one of those guys who professed to be religious and sanctimonious, but he was really a damn crook. Which was all found out later.

The day we left, we had rented a truck, we had our furniture loaded, and as we were pulling away from the building, I was cursing Reynolds from the back of the truck. "You're never going to make any money on this movie, you're going to end up a drunk...." Reynolds came over one day to our new apartment, still pretending to be Eddie's friend. I kept saying to Eddie, "Don't trust him, there's something screwy." As I was coming into the apartment, I heard Reynolds say, "Here's a dollar, and for other considerations," ... and I grabbed the dollar out of his hand and said, "What the hell's going on?" And Eddie grabbed the dollar back from me and said, "It's okay, don't worry." In that particular instance, Reynolds had taken over the control of *Plan 9.* For one dollar.

MAILA NURMI   Criswell told me that *Plan 9* opened in N.Y on 41st Street, in a tiny little theater, and that it played there for a year and a half. Tiny theater, but it filled it. He said it made a ton of money. Not for Ed Wood, for Criswell. 'Cause he had money invested.

PAUL MARCO   *Plan 9* never played Hollywood, and that I know for a fact, I think the closest place it played was San Diego. So I don't think it played in very many theatres until it hit television. And then it was on all the time.

PHIL CAMBRIDGE   He was very, very proud, he said, *"Plan 9* is my pride and joy ... if you want to know me, see *Glen or Glenda,* that's me, that's my story. No question. But *Plan 9* is my pride and joy ... we used Cadillac hubcaps for flying saucers in that." So I saw the movie, I guess it was on late night television. There's a speech, I guess it was towards the so-called climax of the film, in which the head alien, standing in the cabin of the ship, makes a speech, which I guess was Ed's equivalent of *The Day the Earth Stood Still* when Michael Rennie makes a little speech. That speech was incomprehensible to me, it just came off like gibberish. I thought, that's pretty damn funny, this guy says all this stuff and he hasn't said a word. And I went in to laugh with Ed about it, and he said, "What did you think of the speech?" I started to smile and laugh, and he said, "Wasn't it great? I never worked on anything so hard as I worked on that speech. Did you really like it?" So then I had to tell him I did.

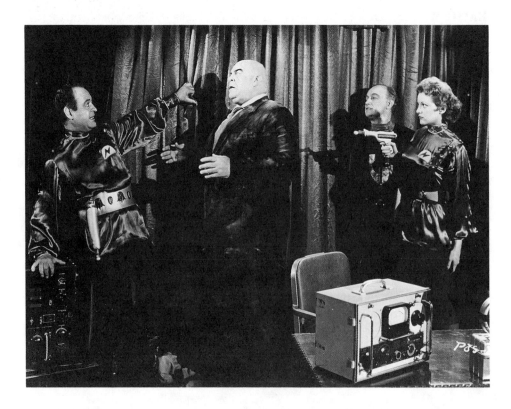

Left: Dudley Manlove, Tor Johnson, John Breckinridge and Joanna Lee in *Plan 9*
Above: Set materials are revealed in this shot of Vampira in *Plan 9*

Criswell climbs out of his coffin to deliver the opening monologue in *Night of the Ghouls*

Ed Wood directs Kenne Duncan, Tor Johnson and Duke Moore in *Night of the Ghouls*

Night of the Ghouls
&
The Sinister Urge

1. EXT. CEMETERY — MEDIUM SHOT — PAN — NIGHT

The CAMERA PANS an old cemetery; crosses; headstones; markers; monuments; etc; ending the PAN on an ancient crypt or vault.

DISSOLVE TO:

2. INT. VAULT — MEDIUM WIDE — DOLLY TO MEDIUM SHOT — DOLLY TO CLOSE — NIGHT

We are centered on an ancient, weather worn casket in the vault. The CAMERA DOLLIES in, to a MEDIUM SHOT; the entire casket fills the screen. After a moment of establishing, the lid begins to rise until the entire screen is blacked out — then —

SUPERIMPOSE MAIN TITLE AND CREDITS

The CREDITS DISSOLVE OUT — Slowly the casket lid begins to lower. Standing straight and stiff behind the lid, with weird lighting behind him, we see CRISWELL.

CRISWELL: I am CRISWELL...

The CAMERA moves in to an EXTREME CLOSE — as CRISWELL continues.

CRISWELL: (cont'd) For many years I have told the almost unbelievable — related the unreal and showed it to be more than fact — Now I tell a tale of the Threshold people so astounding some of you may faint. This is a story of those in the twilight time — Once human — Now monsters — In a void between the living and the dead — Monsters to be pitied — Monsters to be despised — The Night of the Ghouls —

— from the screenplay, *Night of the Ghouls,* by Ed Wood

TONY CARDOZA   I first met Ed in August of 1957 through a friend of mine who was a Fuller Brush man, believe it or not. He had run into Ed Wood, and they partied, and then when I got out here, he told Ed about me, that I was going to invest in a duplex apartment house. Instead, they talked me into investing in this movie!

KATHY WOOD   One morning Ed's taking a bath, and the Fuller Brush man comes to the door. His name was George Cilly. He started talking with Ed and forgot all about selling brushes. He wound up staying all afternoon, playing with Ed's unloaded gun.

VALDA HANSEN   Ed had known me before *Night of the Ghouls,* he had seen me as an ingenue, and he said, "I want to do a movie called *The Night the Banshee Cried,*" and I said, "Would you like me to read something for you and record it?" And he said, yes, and he gave me this long speech, and I acted it on a tape. I'm the Banshee, and I come out and I go, "It's been so long ago ... I lived on this Earth..." I'm dispossessed and I moan, and everything.

That was it. He said, "She's the White Ghost, she's Sheila." He came up to me — I was wearing all black — tight skirt, tight sweater, and gold belt, high heels — he said, "How tall are you?" I said, 5' 6" .... he said, "You're perfect!" Then he smiled, a twinkling smile, half pixie, half coy, and said, "Are you my lover?"

You know "the fingers" in *Night of the Ghouls,* the scene with my hands and long white silver finger nails? Everyone says, god, how did you train your fingers to move like snakes like that? Funny, Ed Wood told me to do that- and he loved it! He triggered emotions into future expression that aren't fully understood at the time it's shot!

Kenne Duncan kept whispering obscene things in my ear, over and over between takes — "Do you like tongues" over and over. And Ed was frazzled, hadn't shaved, tired, worn out, he'd work way into the night — it was all on his shoulders, money was scarce. He was worried, tense, but always courteous, optimistic inside, but none the less, beat. Well, Kenne kept on whispering what he'd like to do to me, a virgin, and all of a sudden, the shy girl had finally had enough of this old wolf, so I screamed over the mikes, everything on the set, "Oh shut up!" and everyone cracked up, and was ready to burst, but most of all, Eddie — he laughed, he cried, he kicked his legs on the floor!

On the set, Ed would sometimes get very dramatic when he was directing us, but you never had the feeling that he was hurting you, or maligning you... Ed had a way that...he could go into a tirade — "Didn't I tell you, this is not going to work, why do you keep it up?" and he'll blow ... and then all of a sudden we'd all start laughing ... and then he's just like a sweet child, and he'd say, "You know I love you."

PAUL MARCO   I was knocked out, because I got too close to Tor, and they put a full load in the damn gun, and sparks hit his big arm, and he knocked me out because of the fire on his arm. He picked me up like a peanut, put me in the casket, closed the damn lid, and there I laid, until they were yelling, "Where the hell is he?" and then they remembered I was in the damn casket.

KATHY WOOD   One day, Bunny was at our place, our humble little apartment on Mariposa Street, the old Jean Harlow apartment. And he had this great big beautiful Panama hat with a red ribbon around it, and Eddie and Bunny decided on the way down to the set, to sit in the back seat of the car with a skeleton. Everybody was looking around and laughing, and waving, and Bunny was having a ball.

VALDA HANSEN   While filming *Night of the Ghouls,* I was in my White Ghost dress, mist all around us, and the willow trees, between takes the men began to "howl" at me, teasing me with wolf cries and sexy motions, and trying to embarrass

Kenne "Horsecock" Duncan and Valda Hansen in *Night of the Ghouls*
[photo courtesy Valda Hansen]

me a little, because I was 16, sweet 16 and innocent. I went off by myself in the mist, and I found a moth on my shoulder, clinging to me with little silver wings. I began to stroke his little wings. No one pursued me, they had all gone away, and there I was in the mist, alone. I felt a presence — I looked up: there was Ed Wood, looking intently, scintillating green eyes, looking at me, and then he turned away.

We were on this earth, but not of it. We both knew each other. That moment said it all....

RONNIE ASHCROFT I met Eddie Wood at the home of my good friend Kenne Duncan. Kenne had been under contract to Republic Pictures for years and was known and billed as "the meanest man in the movies." He always played the heavies. So I was over Kenne's house one day and a knock came to the door and in walked Eddie Wood. Kenne introduced us, and Eddie looked at me and, with a pause said, "Ron, maybe this meeting will solve a problem." Kenne looked at Eddie and said, "Hell, don't tell me we have more problems! What is it now?" Eddie explained that his assistant director had just quit, and he had to replace him by six o'clock that night. Kenne's mouth popped open. There was a long pause. I said, "I'm available!" Eddie laughed. "Ron, you're a mind reader." I said, "No, I'm broke." Eddie explained the set-up. "I'm shooting at Picture Recorders, the dubbing company, I'm using the small stage they have next door, and I have three sets ready to go. We will shoot from 6 p.m. to midnight. The dubbing room closes at six, but one of the mixers will stay on to record the scenes.

I remembered Picture Recorders, I dubbed a couple of pictures there. So I said, "Hell, Eddie, that stage is not much bigger than a phone booth." Eddie cut in, "Hey Ron, listen to this: I got the stage for 20 bucks a night. And you know what Tommy Kemp can do when it comes to saving a buck on low budget sets." Well that was true, but I thought a moment and I said, "Eddie, for chrissake, the juice bill, 20 dollars won't even cover that. The cost of the lights." Eddie put up his hand and said, "Hey Ron, not to worry, I'll have time, the damn electric company bills every two months. I said, "Eddie, you make Roger Corman look like a big time spender." Eddie laughed and said, "I'll give you a list of the scenes, and you grab the actors and get em to work out their lines and give them their action and so on, so that when I'm ready they come on and they're already rehearsed and I can get it in one or maybe two takes. Is that alright with you?" "Fine." So at 5 o'clock that night Eddie, Kenne Duncan, Bill Thompson, and a couple others go to College Inn. Eddie right away starts ordering martinis, telling funny stories, at one point he pulled a damn big roll of bills out of his pocket, I don't know how many hundreds, knowing Eddie it couldn't be a thousand. Little did I know that the deal he had with his people was to pay them up front in greenbacks before they'd work.

We all sat around having a good time until I look at my watch and say, "Eddie, it's past six, we'd better get on down there." "Oh, well, let's just have one more drink." He started to get pretty well-oiled and I was getting worried. He had another round and he whipped the roll out and started paying, and Jesus, that roll really diminished.

So we go on down to the set, and as usual there's a lot of standing around, screwing around, and time wasting, and finally they got a scene in the can. Eddie says, "Go on down and run Tor's lines with him." So I went down and introduced myself to Tor. He says, "Mr. Ashcroft, before I come out of this door, I want to see the money." I took off and cornered Eddie. Eddie says, "Well, screw it, I just blew quite a bit at the College Inn and so Tor's just going to have to wait. You go back there, don't get too tough..." I said, "Hey, I wouldn't even think of getting tough with that guy." "You just tell him that I'll have to pay him later."

So I went back, knocked on the door — "Mr. Johnson, I talked with Mr. Wood, and he says that..." And he says, "Come on, tell me, don't give me your version, tell me exactly what he said." "Okay. Eddie Wood said that he doesn't have the money, that you'll have to come on out and do the scenes, and he'll pay you later." He gets up, and with one hand he grabbed that latex make-up on his face and he just ripped it off, threw it on the floor, quickly got into his regular street clothes, and said, "Mr. Ashcroft, I'm saying goodnight." And he walked out.

So I told Eddie, and he says, "Ah, shit. I thought he'd come out and do it. Well you'd better start running lines with Kenne and Valda." I couldn't find Kenne, I saw Valda Hansen, and said, Eddie Wood wants me to run the lines with you and Kenne." She said, "Just a minute, Mr. Ashcroft, I'm getting paid to work in this picture, but I'm not going to get into any extra time with Mr. Duncan."

I saw Kenne strutting around and I said, "Hey, Eddie wants me to run this scene." He said, "Well, I'm ready, let's go." I said, "Well, there's a problem, Miss Hansen says she's not coming out to run her scenes, she'll only come out when he's ready to roll the film." Kenne says, "Well I'll be damned. When I met her, all I said to her was, 'Gee, I'd like to chew on your tits!'"

The whole damn evening went this way. The next night went that way. Then Eddie called me up and said, "Ron, I gotta tell you that the assistant's back...would you get mad at me if I say that I'll just give you the hundred..." I said, "Eddie, that's just fine with me."

SAM KOPETZKY   I was the boom man on the picture. It was a two week shoot, and the general impression I had was that it moved slowly. He had trouble with Tor, Tor did a number on him. All of a sudden we couldn't shoot because Tor wouldn't come out of his dressing room. Wood's walking around, "Son of a bitch wants more money."

VALDA HANSEN   I stood one night in the rain with him. He was crying in the rain, in Westwood. I'll never forget that night. The tears were streaming, and so was the rain. He said, "They're going to do me a *Plan 9*, all over again, and I'm not going to take it, Valda." He said, "I love this movie so much, it's almost like part of me. And they're not going to do it to me this time. This movie is my baby — they're not going to take it away from me." It was so sad. He was so sober in those moments ... so deep, so tragic. Few knew or saw that side of Ed Wood.

PAUL MARCO The first preview was a big old R.K.O. theater with balcony after balcony, one of the old vaudeville theatres. We were up there, and the place was packed, it was mobbed. And *Imitation of Life,* with Lana Turner had played with it.

Afterwards, all the black kids came over and Eddie kept on saying, "That's Kelton — that's him!" He was so proud of it, they screamed when Tor Johnson was coming after me down the hall. They screamed for what seemed like minutes, "Watch out! Watch out! Turn around, turn around!"

ED WOOD Letter to Anthony Cardoza:

2 August 1959

My Dear Tony

Just a few lines to let you know my new address:

Do me a favor — don't give this address to anyone who doesn't already have it — because I want rid of the idiots who have been hanging around the place— a couple you know well, plus many others.

I think over here I can get things done because it's very quiet. We have a small house — much cheaper in rent of course — you know they kicked me out of the other place — but at least I was able to leave with the few possessions I have.

Am seeing Corridine at KTTV again tomorrow about the picture *[Night of the Ghouls]*. He has been talking for over a week — but nothing definite as yet. He's got the cash if he decides to go ahead — he also has a picture which this one would go with for a double bill.

Don't dishearten — I never let anyone down yet — and I'm not about to now.

Ed

Letter to Anthony Cardoza, 22 Sept. 1959:

Dear Tony:

Haven't heard from you in some time so thought I'd better write and see if you're dead and buried — or just working too hard — and to hope the family is all well.

As to our picture it is being shown again tonight — and always I hope. I have heard there is quite a few films available up until the holidays, but after that there will be the worst shortage in history up until the summer of 1960.

However — I am doing several things to aid it — I want to add some Lugosi footage at the beginning-ending-and middle instead of the Criswell stuff we now have — and also take out the junk in the first reel — and possible change the title — this should do it — because the rest of the picture is not bad.

George Weiss in New York has the Lugosi footage and has advanced

Top: Criswell, Tor Johnson, Valda Hansen and Paul Marco at the Preview for *Night of the Ghouls*
[photo courtesy Valda Hansen]
Bottom: Valda Hansen, Criswell, Kenne Duncan in *Night of the Ghouls*
[photo courtesy Valda Hansen]

the fact he will let me have it on a pay later basis. This is good because so many of you have to be paid off first.

Also I plan to do a sex film for another outfit in the next couple of weeks and can throw several days work to you if you want to be an actor in it. Sex in so far as it will be legal and play the regular motion picture theatres — nothing dirty — but enough to get a good sale and bring it in cheap for the outfit.

I'm anxious to hear from you — so write or come by soon. Still don't have a telephone — can't make the scene for the deposit.

Ed

Headliner producer Roy Reid in front of marquis for the Ed Wood scripted *The Violent Years*. Reid also produced Wood's *The Sinister Urge*

The Sinister Urge

Johnny hesitates a moment. Dirk raises his knife menacingly. Dirk, it is apparent, has sensed Johnny's mood.

DIRK: Don't try it, Daddy-O. You can't take me as long as I got this shiv. Maybe some other time — but not when I got this fixed at you.

Johnny sinks into the couch. Dirk snaps a look out of the curtained window.

DIRK: That's it — Play it cool, man — Play it cool...

JOHNNY: What's with you?

DIRK: You creeps figured you were real smart puttin' me in that fixed car. Only I don't dig the Angel bit.

JOHNNY: What are you talking about?

DIRK: You and the broad take all the big gold and leave me with the crumbs — Only now I decide I run the show. I'm gonna put both of you out of circulation.

JOHNNY: Look — Dirk — I didn't want to put you in that car. It was all Gloria's idea ... The whole thing was her plan — The car — The brakes — everything...

DIRK: Sure, man — Sure.

— from Ed Wood's script, *The Sinister Urge*

CONRAD BROOKS The original working title for *The Sinister Urge* was *Hellborn*. George Weiss started the film, one day's shooting we did on location. So the thing was laying around for about six months. And Weiss evidently couldn't raise the money to complete the film. So, I raised the money to buy the film from George Weiss, but I couldn't come up with any more money to finish the film. So then Ed made a deal with Roy Reid, who bought the footage from me. Weiss originally wanted me to play the [Dino] Fantini role. Roy Reid made a lot of changes in the script, and I guess he decided to use one of his players. So I just was in the fight sequence with Ed in *The Sinister Urge*.

ROY REID Ed wrote the story, and he wanted to direct it, so I let him. I was sitting there watching him, and he behaved alright. We cast the film in an acting school on Sunset Boulevard. It was one of those low, low budgets, as things were in those days. Dino Fantini, who played the young hood, was only 18. He had no experience previous to this in movies.

MICHAEL "DINO" FANTINI I was in Harry Keatan's acting school, a workshop, and Roy Reid and Ed Wood came in and auditioned a bunch of us. Ed Wood said, "I want *him* for the part."

CARL ANTHONY Later I heard Dino Fantini went into a Kentucky Fried business.

He was really a dedicated actor, this guy worked at it, tried to make it.

ROY REID   Jean Fontaine we found in L.A. We picked her up after seeing her nightclub act, singing and dancing. She was recommended by friends of Bill Thompson. The clothes she wore in the film were clothes from her act.

CARL ANTHONY   Jean Fontaine was married to a medical doctor in Beverly Hills, so she played around with acting as a hobby, as some of them do. He worked long hours.

ROY REID   Ed knew what he was doing. Oh, yes, he was capable. Of course, I've always maintained pre-production preparation. We crowded everything into 8 hours. I set up 5 sets at Rocket Studios, a small independent studio. We just went from one to the other. Instead of a 10 day schedule, maybe we'd have a six or seven actual shooting schedule. The cost of picture making is in the actual shooting. It's the time element. It's who you've got on the payroll, and how many, and how fast you can move. That's it.

ED WOOD

MY PLANS FOR SHOOTING ARRANGEMENT AND WHY

I have Matt's office scenes set for the first day as the first day is usually very hectic — the crew getting to know each other — the actors for the first time meeting each other — thus it seems by the board that the Matt's office is the easiest thing to shoot since the major portion of the day will be taken up with Matt and Randy. Around noon things will settle down, thus I will bring in the Inspector and Romain — Romain being very important to the whole plot I want to be able to use as much time on his scenes as possible. Scene totals for first day is 26.

The second day we start the morning easy with Mary and Francy because the confusion of having the major portion of our actors on stage during the day, later on, will give us cause to shoot an easy scene — then a tough one — then an easy - and so on — as long as the set is the same. Thus as Johnny's office ends we start again on an easy shot of the Photo studio where Mary is being photographed. She has had many dress changes during the day — and much dialogue so here she simply sits — then the others follow easily saving the raid to last because we may have to break up the set a bit and can spend much of the remainder of the day on it. The INT. PIZZA Joint is a simple one line pick up that if is not shot that day — although I'm sure it will — can be done the previous day or the next day. All our leads are on Weekly anyway — so I'll have this boy Dirk standing near at hand. Total scenes for second day is 21.

Gloria's apartment or living room and patio scenes speak mostly for themselves. Shooting it in continuity as it is a good idea because of Gloria's many costume changes. She should be able to change quickly as the camera is changing set ups. I have saved the police arrival for last so as to take no chances in wrong positions happening during the Dirk and Johnny scene. Total scenes ... 30.

For the third and fourth day we must figure for outside. There is an excellent possibility of bringing this picture in in four actual shooting days and one pre-production by doing this.

We have 50 silent scenes that can be shot with little or no crew — cars driving in and out — Mary out of house — Dirk alone kills two girls in the park — all silent. There are 15 scenes in which dialogue is used. This of course will go the fourth day — then shooting anything that has not been shot on that one pre-production day ... Again I emphasize — Our major actors are on Weekly salary — and the others are one day bits — No loss.

Stock shots are not included in board breakdown but all else is.

ROY REID   Bill Thompson was on camera. I think that was the last thing that he did. 'Cause he was losing his sight. And vision. His vision was getting bad. Ed had to check his lighting. We both had to check his lighting. He did some pretty big things, one of the top cameramen in the old silent days. Big Bill Thompson.

MICHAEL "DINO" FANTINI   We went up to Harry Keatan's ranch in Palmdale and did a lot of shooting up there, we'd spend the weekend, sleeping in bunks ... Ed used his house in Glendale for exterior shots. The shot with the girl and the cigarette was in Griffith Park.

The scenes I was in were done first take, I never had to do 'em over. Mostly the interior stuff they had to shoot a lot of takes. Once we went through a rehearsal on the exterior stuff, I knew what I had to do, usually it went in one, maybe two takes. For the interiors, we got the lines down, went over them together, went through a rehearsal, and that was it — shoot it.

> *Sinister Urge — Headliner Production #112 —* Budget Breakdown
> Mimeographing: $87.00
> Direction: $2,600.00
> Cast: $3,020.00
> Studio Rental (3 days): $750.00
> Sets (6 sets) — fully constructed: $750.00
> Set Dressing & Props: $550.00
> Camera Crew & Equipment: $2,835.00
> Sound Crew & Equipment: $660.00
>   Laboratory:
> Raw Stock: $1,000.00
> Developing & Print: $2,750.00
> Dubbing: $750.00

Title & Ending, Insert & Dissolves: $600.00
Music Score: $750.00
Editing: $900.00
Audit: $250.00
Insurance, Taxes, Legal: $400.00
Production Supervision Expenses: $1,500.00
TOTAL: $20,152.00

MICHAEL "DINO" FANTINI   I remember when *The Sinister Urge* opened, in Palmdale, California, a little town in the desert. They had a bunch of kids there, at the matinee, and we had to sign autographs for them. I don't remember *The Sinister Urge* playing anywhere in L.A., but I saw the film on 42nd Street in New York. It played there for 13 weeks.

Dino Fantini
and
Betty Boatner
in
lobby display
for
The Sinister Urge

A quartet from *The Sinister Urge*

Upper Left: Henry Kekoanui

Upper Right: Jean Fontaine

Left: Ad mat from Headliner Films

Below: Bondage scene, and an initiation for Ed Wood into the world of sexploitation

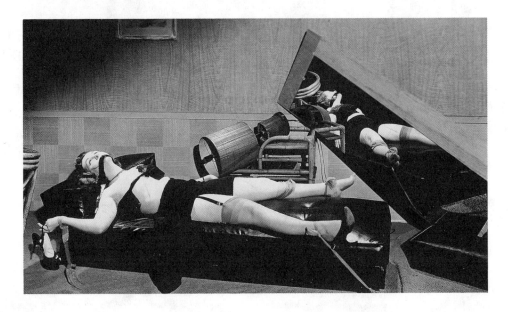

The Wood Spooks
(Bela, Vampira, Criswell,
Tor, "Bunny," & Kenne)

ED WOOD   I can remember the first time Vampira was on channel 5 in L.A., they were showing *White Zombie*. Lugosi and I watched it together. He said he would like to make a movie with her. He said *White Zombie* was his greatest film, he liked that even better than *Dracula*.

MAILA NURMI   I first bumped into Bela Lugosi on Hollywood Boulevard, with a beret and roller skates, he came around the corner, Las Palmas and Hollywood Boulevard, and bumped into me.

We first worked together on *The Red Skelton Show* in about June of '54. I don't remember the script. I know I lay in a coffin, the kind of mausoleum they have where the caskets roll in and out of the wall? Red Skelton pulls the thing out of the wall. He thought he was opening an oven, and instead this corpse was in there, resting in peace.

Bela stayed in his dressing room alone. We took a curtain call together. He took my arm and we walked, quite some length, to the curtain. He got his arms out from under his cape, and took my arm in the good old Victorian or European manner, and made me feel like such a lady. He was so genteel and so elegant and so regal. Oh, he was magnificent. He made me feel like a noblewoman, that's what. And here I was, this Hollywood tramp.

JOHN ANDREWS   When Bela was on *The Red Skelton Show*, he had Eddie come over. "Eddie, they don't know how to write for me. You write. You write."

ED WOOD   I was Lugosi's dialogue consultant. There were certain words which had to be changed because he couldn't form them properly.

HARRY THOMAS   Bela was very generous and always sweet talking to me. I'd ask him a lot of things about his private life. He'd say, "You know, life is not so easy." I said, "Yes, it's fragile." He shook his head and agreed with me.

ROBERT CREMER   No one else was lining up to help Lugosi. He was just closed out of the marketplace altogether. The fact is, Ed always felt that he was the sole individual concerned about Lugosi in his later years, and the only one who came forward and tried to help him.

PAUL MARCO   I always used to see Ed tickle Bela's chin, and Bela would just shake and smile ... and it would just bring Bela to life again. Just like a little kid. "Eddie! How 'bout our next picture? When are we going to do it?" That's all Bela wanted to do — work.

Ed would tease Bela about his wife, "How'd you get that young blonde?" Ed used to tease him about that and made him feel like a stud. He liked that, at his age.

HARRY THOMAS   Bela used to smoke these terrific black cigars. And he'd say, hello, have a cigar, have a cigar. I would take the cigar, you know, to be friendly, and he'd light it, and in a few minutes, the room was going around, but I didn't want to let him know that I wasn't man enough to take these things. He'd say, "Good cigar." I'd say, "W-wonderful." He liked his hair slicked down. Factor made a substance called Bandoline at that time, it was kind of greaseless, and I'd slick his hair down, trim it for him, and he says, "I like you, you trim hair, and I don't have to go to the barber." And I say, "Another thing, Bela, it's free."

JOHN ANDREWS   Bela loved dogs. He had two favorites: one was a Doberman named Dracula who would run up and grab his ankles. Bela Junior told me that Bela had scars on his ankles to the day he died from that dog. And he had a white German Shepherd, Bodri.

Now Eddie gets this dog and he takes it to visit Bela, Bela's in his rocking chair, loaded, and the dog goes up on his lap. And Bela says, "This is a cute little monster." And so Eddie names the dog Monster.

ED WOOD   The kids loved Lugosi and there were no Halloweens that I know of that he didn't appear in his doorway in his Dracula outfit with witches yellow and brown candy for them.

JOHN ANDREWS   Bela got WAY far out, man. Those parts really affected him. They became part of his psyche. Hope and Bela were married at Manly Palmer Hall Home. Bela calls Eddie a few days later, They wanted to go on their honeymoon. "Would you drive us?" "Yes, sure." So they went down to another county, someplace, to a motel. And Bela was insanely jealous. They check in, get two rooms — one for the couple and one for Eddie. Eddie wakes up, it's 2 a.m, it's dark. And Bela's standing there, gesturing, he's doing his Dracula bit with his hands — he thought he could hypnotize you — "Eddie ... what ... do you want ... with Hope?" "I don't want anything to do with Hope," "Eddie—" And he keeps doing all these hand gestures from *White Zombie*. The next morning, Bela had no recollection of the incident whatsoever.

CARL ANTHONY   Bela mentioned how sometimes Universal would take two days to do a single scene, and he marvelled at the way Ed could shoot, if necessary, 20-30 scenes in a day. He marvelled that the man could put together something even remotely coherent with the speed with which he was sometimes compelled to work with, to stay within the budget. Bela appreciated Ed as an artist, — there was a deep mutual respect there.

JOHN ANDREWS   One time — Eddie told me this — we were drinking — which is very unusual ... ohhhhh! I'll burn in hell for that! This was when he was with that blonde — Dolores. So ... it was a Sunday morning, and Eddie said, "Let's go to the

Upper Left: Beer commercial? Bela chats up unidentified actress (left) and Dolores Fuller.
[photo courtesy Dolores Fuller.

Upper Right: Ed and Bela Lugosi at Paul Marco's Christmas party, 1954.
[photo courtesy Paul Marco]

Below: L.A. newsclip on Bela's self-imposed stay in a hospital for heroin addiction.

'Dracula' in Dramatic Appeal to Break Drug Habit

—Herald-Express Photo by Ed Phillips

Actor Bela Lugosi, broken and weak after an admitted 20-year struggle against drugs, sits on bed in psychopathic ward of General Hospital here today after giving himself up and asking for aid to break the habit. Picture was taken during bedside hearing on the movie "Dracula's" petition for voluntary self-commitment. At left is Superior Judge Wallace L. Ware who said to Lugosi, "it was a commendable thing for you to do." Right: Deputy Counsellor J. Langos.

beach." She was bored. He was bored. And half loaded. He had that Buick convertible at that time. Bela was always ready to go anyplace — he was so bored to death, man, and neglected ... forgotten — broke.

So they get down there in Malibu. Eddie and Dolores strip down, jump in the surf. Bela rolls up his pants around his knees, kicks off his shoes and socks, and he would go out to the edge of the surf line. He was scared to death of the water. Dracula! Jesus! Later they go to the Albatross Inn. So now they're really getting it, I mean, high! They've been drinking all fucking day, and now they're drinking inside! Bela got in a bad mood — "Fuck this place! I don't like this place! Eddie! Why did you bring me here? This place-" And he's banging on the table! "It is stupid, this place!" And the maitre'd comes over and says, "Mr. Lugosi, it's a great pleasure to have you here. May I shake your hand?" "Certainly." And he takes the guy's hand and says, "Fuck you!" Anyway, do you know they went ahead and served them? Eddie told me that no one ever had Bela arrested. No matter what he did. He was just too big. Who's going to have Dracula arrested?

DON FELLMAN   It was too clumsy to ask what Wood was putting into his book on Bela Lugosi but luckily he tossed out a few tidbits on his own. One thing he told me was that Lugosi would go crazy in restaurants! He'd throw women's expensive fox fur pieces out into the street — and Ed had to pay for them! He almost made it sound like he enjoyed this stuff. I asked him why Lugosi did these things and he said, "No reason! That's the beauty of the man!"

MONA McKINNON   I've been to Bela Lugosi's apartment and it was really weird. He had more strange stuff around ... skulls, and different voodoo things ... all kinds of weird stuff.

VALDA HANSEN   Bela and Ed went to a cemetery one night, and they had a ball! Ed said that Bela Lugosi got his old black cape out, and he would go "whooo" like a bat, and he was flying all over. They crawled over the full gates of the entrance, and they were running around in the moonlight. Bela was saying, "I am Dracula ... I am the bat!" And Ed said, "I tell you, lover, I never have been so turned on in my whole life!"

ED WOOD   One night he called me at Burbank and he didn't have anything. He didn't have any scotch at that time ... he just had his unemployment to keep him going. He asked me to come down to his place with a bottle of scotch. It was 3 a.m. He came out from behind the two curtains where he always went when he was going to take his needle. He closed the curtain when I was there, because he knew that I didn't like that. He's got a gun. He pointed it at me, he's shaking like a leaf and he's crying. I think it was because he didn't have any money for his stuff, his drugs. And he's just shaking all over. Well, it stopped me dead. He's got the gun pointed at me and he said, "Eddie, I'm going to die tonight. I want to take you with me." Well, I couldn't believe my eyes. So, not being one to panic since I was attacked by a shark in the South Pacific, I tried to calm him and I said, "Well, I've got your scotch here."

He walked over with the gun in his hand. I said, "Why don't we have a few drinks first?" He just walked over to the refrigerator and pulled a can of warm beer off the top — never drank it cold — and walked back over to me still carrying the gun. I gave him the bottle and he didn't even use a shot glass this time. He drank boiler-makers. Finally he put the gun down and when I thought that he was cooled off, I took the gun and put it back in the drawer. That was the only time that I ever saw him suicidal, because Lugosi was afraid of death.

JOHN ANDREWS   One time, when Bela was still with Lillian, they were living on Rodeo Drive, not in Beverly Hills, way down there, but I mean way down, half way to Inglewood, practically. One day Eddie was over there, and Bela couldn't hit it. And Eddie said something to the effect, "Oh, poor Bela, he can't get it," and blah blah blah. Lillian turned to Eddie with the kit and said, "If you love him so much, you do it. I'm sick of it." But Eddie didn't know how to do it, he was scared to death.

ED WOOD   I didn't know he was going to the hospital. He called me from the hospital to let me know he was there. He wasn't committed. He just went in because he knew he could get his help there. And he did not tell me that he did not have any money. I visited him almost every day and as soon as he started getting the thing he'd scream to the nurse and say, "You have to fix me, you have to fix me!"

He told me that they kicked him out at about midnight because he couldn't pay the hospital bills. About how he was put in with these alcoholics and druggies and they were trying to kiss him. His words were, "They shit all over me, they piss all over me. I can't stand it." He was starting to put paraldahyde in his room temperature beer with the scotch. This stuff would stink up the whole house. You know what ether smells like. They took him off the same way as they would take alcoholics off. He learned to like it. It was a quick high.

JOHN ANDREWS   After Bela shot *The Black Sleep,* with Tor Johnson, John Carradine, Lon Chaney, they went all the way up into Washington promoting the thing. Tor and Bela stayed in the same room every night. For the first two nights, Bela would say, "I'm going to jump out the window! I'm jumping! You can't stop me!" So finally Tor had so much of it, he said, "Go ahead and jump. Just JUMP! Get it over with!" And Bela, "Well, I go back to bed now."

MAILA NURMI   Let me tell you about the personal appearance tour we went on. A group of Wood spooks, right? Oh, it was great. Just three weeks before Bela died. They rented a limousine, an antique hearse. In the front seat was Tor Johnson. Bald, with the white cataracts. And in the back there were two little seats for Bela Lugosi and my flunky named Excelsior. He had on a black velvet drinking gown backwards, so that it was like a mandarin collar. He carried an antique violin case with a foot sticking out. And he wore a great poison ring; he looked very ominous, like a mad scientist. I'm lying in the coffin in the back, as Vampira.

We were tub-thumping *Bride of the Monster.* We pull up at the Pic Theater, and

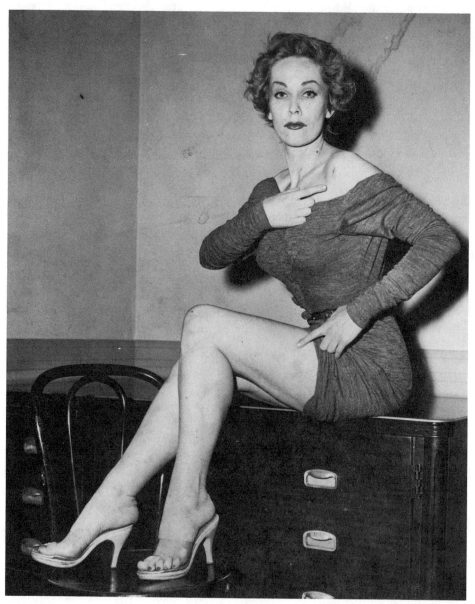

Maila Nurmi (Vampira) demonstrates to members of the New York press in January, 1956, bruise marks on leg and shoulder that were inflicted by a would-be rapist.

[photo by Louis Liotta, courtesy of Miriam Linna]

there was a bit of paparazzi, not much, but a bit, and they opened the side of the hearse. They wheel this coffin out, and I'm dead, right? I came out feet first, and the cameras shot up between my legs. Later they spread photographs saying they saw a black spot up there, saying it was beaver. But that was my black girdle. I hate to disappoint 10 million fans, but that's what it was. Anyway, we went in the theater, and I had to guide Tor down the aisle because he couldn't see with those white contact lenses. Bela was staggering, and Tor couldn't see. People were throwing popcorn, they were so disrespectful and angry, and one woman yelled, "The blind leading the blind!" They hated Bela, he had so much bad publicity about being a drug addict, and they were vicious.

Bela got out of his death bed to make this appearance that night. He was staggering because he was dying. And the woman saying, "The blind leading the blind!" He was such a sweet man, one of the sweetest people I've ever met. After we left the Pic we drove to Inglewood, where *Bride of the Monster* was playing. After we came out they told us that some teenagers messed up the hearse while we were in the theater. So we were stranded in Inglewood and we had to get a taxi. In those days, there was just one dark highway going over the mountains, winding through those dark mountains. La Brea. And the oil wells pumping — very spooky. So there we were in the taxi, all four of us crowded in. These teenage thugs followed us, and pulled us to the side of the road in the deepest, darkest part of this oily abyss. The cab driver was radioing the police, and Tor Johnson said, "Let me talk to them." He said, "Poys, caw home. Pee caw poys." You know how he talked, the Swedish accent, "Pee caw poys, caw home." And they did. They went home.

KATHY WOOD   Eddie gave the *Final Curtain* script, which he had written, to Bela, and Bela loved it. Bela was sitting in his apartment on Harold Way and was reading the script when he died. It sounds like a stage play, but that's what happened. When Hope came home, she saw the script lying on his lap.

ED WOOD   I was his front pallbearer. I touched his hand and the large ring of Count Dracula as he lay in the coffin, he was buried in the full Dracula costume, full dress suit, cape and crest. I said, "Goodbye dear friend Bela."

* * *

MAILA NURMI   After my show at KHJ, I went across the street to the Ranch Market for a hot dog. I was in full drag. That's how I met Criswell. He said, "Oh, my, you're, you're Vampira, you're Miss Vampira. I have a friend who would love to meet you. She'd be so delighted. I'm referring to Miss West, Mae West...." I said, "She would be delighted to meet *me?*" He said, "Yes. She's a great fan of yours." I said, "Well, she's already met me, she fired me from *Catherine the Great.*" After that he was our go-between. She loved to cook, and when she thought she'd done something really nice, she'd send it over in her limousine with her chauffeur to Criswell. And then he'd call me up, 'cause I was starving, and he'd say, "Miss West sent us some Swedish meatballs." So I'd go over and we'd eat them.

BUDDY HYDE   Criswell and I, after doing his tv show, a half dozen of us would all get together and have a cocktail at the Brown Derby. We'd go over the show and hash it out, what we did wrong, etc. And Cris and I started what we called the Brown Derby Friday Night Club. And this thing grew into about 125 or 150 people. For something like 10 or 12 years.

Ed showed up one time, at the time, I thought he was kind of nuts, if you didn't know him, you'd say he's gotta be nuts. And then you'd find out that half of it was kidding, the other half was actually based on fact.

VALDA HANSEN   Criswell and Ed were very close, and they had a lot of capers together, they had a lot of fun times together.

MONA McKINNON   Eddie told me that Criswell liked to sleep in a casket....

BUDDY HYDE   Criswell had a very interesting life, born in the back room of a mortuary in Indiana and all that business. His full name was Charles Jeron Criswell King. In his back room, he had a coffin — white silk and satin lined — he would crawl in there and take a nap.... The way he became a predictor was, he was a newscaster in New York. And the station all of a sudden gave him the signal that for 15 minutes he had to ad lib. And so he'd say, "Since we don't have any more news, I predict that what's going to happen tomorrow is this," and he predicted a piece of news that did happen, and the damn station was flooded with calls. About the situation, he'd say, "What the hell, I've found a gold mine!"

HARRY THOMAS   Criswell invited me up to his place off of Hollywood Boulevard and he showed me a lot of coffins and he was telling me how comfortable they were. That Ed sure knows how to find 'em.

JOHN ANDREWS   I'm sitting up at Criswell's and we're drinking, and he says, "Do you know, these idiots are actually buying my book? They actually believe I can predict the future. Shit, I couldn't look out the window and tell you what the weather's like."

* * *

KARL JOHNSON   Ed and my father were real close. We used to go fishing down in Mexico together, Ensenada mostly. Ed liked to shoot, being an ex-Marine. I used to invite him over to fire a few rounds with us.

KATHY WOOD   Tor's wife Greta made the most beautiful Swedish dinners. One time we went over to her place on Easter — what a table, oh god!

HENRY BEDERSKI   Tor spent a few nights at my place. So he's lying in bed there, and I said, "Tor, if you don't lose that weight, you know it's going to kill you." Words to that effect. When I got through, he sat up and said, "Man, you've frightened me." And I could see he meant it.

Top: Ed Wood, John Andrews, Criswell, Shelley and Steve Apostolof gather for the opening of Apostolof's theater on Santa Monica Boulevard, 1968.

[photo courtesy Steve Apostolof]

Ed's daughter, Kathy,
on her 17th birthday, May 23, 1963

Kenne Duncan and Ed Wood, April 1962

HARRY THOMAS Tor took me over to his house in the Valley, we were sitting around, a hot summer day, and he says, "The little woman will be home soon." And I hear a thump-thump-thump-thump. He opens the door, and it's a *big* woman. I say to myself, my god, that's little? They start bringing the food on, cakes and hams. Tor says, "Little Karl is coming to eat with us." I hear the thump-thump-thump in the hallway, there was Karl — big, seven foot guy. "This is my little boy." These people were like the three big bears.

Then they started eating, and they had special chairs to sit on, because they'd break an ordinary chair. Anyway, they'd say, "Eat, eat. Eat. You want to be big and strong." They could really eat — they had spoons that looked like small shovels! For dessert we each got several boxes of ice cream, and this shovel of a spoon. "Eat — the little woman made it." I said, Geez, this is so much — strawberries, bananas, coconuts, with whip cream, how am I going to eat all this? Then Tor says, "We're gonna have a little watermelon in a little while. Eat up, eat up." I was groaning. I was in pain. I said, "I'd rather take the watermelon after the food digests." They brought the watermelon out — each one of them had a half a melon a piece. "We're gonna have some more food after we have a little snooze." I said, "No, no, please, I gotta go home!"

KATHY WOOD We were all drinking together, Eddie and Tor were playing a scene from *Bride of the Monster,* ordering Tor around, pretending to be Lugosi. It was just playing around, but he picked me up by the neck, and it bruised — Eddie told Tor, "Down Lobo! Down! Down!" So, he put me down.

TONY CARDOZA One time, Tor got plastered, drank a full *gallon* of wine, at my house. And he just went down on the floor, just rolled over, and it took six of us to put him in the back of a pick-up truck, to get him home.

JOHN ANDREWS When Eddie lived in Glendale, about '62, '63, Tor goes out there, and he brings a case of beer. That's 24 cans. Eddie didn't drink beer, Kathy didn't drink beer. Out of courtesy, they each had one. That left 22 cans. Tor drank 'em all! By nightfall, he gets up, opens the door, and collapses. He's dead to the world, and they can't pick him up! They can't pull him back in!! And they spent the night with the door wide open, Tor crashed out in the doorway.

TONY CARDOZA He was in New Dehli to wrestle a guy named King Kong. The promoter said, I'll give you three thousand and a round trip ticket because we don't get a lot of money here," and this and that. In the ring, Tor sees that the promoter's packed 80,000 people in the stadium, and he says, "You son-of-a-bitch, you going to pay me only three thousand dollars, and all these goddamn fucking Indians. I'm going to kill you!!" He chased him around the ring and everything, and Tor got his money.

Jack LaRue threw us out of his restaurant on Ventura Boulevard because Tor would ask the waitresses for some "T.P." The waitress would say, "What's that?" Tor said, "Table Pussy." So Jack threw us out. Tor said, "Jack, you're my friend, what do you mean we go out?" "Sorry, Tor, but you've got to get the fuck out of here." He was funny, though, old Tor, God love him. He used to steal toilet seats out of hotels, because he broke so many of them. He would take them home, put them in a suitcase.

DON FELLMAN   Ed was talking about some traffic accident Tor once had. Tor's car was apparently one of those midget foreign things, and not much bigger than he was. The story was that he got a buzz on and went for a nice little drive. From Ed's voice he seemed to have a twinkle in his eye, I could tell he really got off on it — the whole picture: big Tor in this tiny car, driving around like a happy idiot. Kathy didn't think Ed should be telling these type of stories. "He's dead," Ed shouted back, as if to erase all other considerations. "The man is dead."

HENRY BEDERSKI   Tor had sad memories of India. Tor was being chauffeured somewhere, and a little boy jumped on the car, asked for some pennies, and this chauffeur pushed that kid, while the car was going. Tor said, "Christ, that little kid fell in the street, bumped his head and nobody cared."

TONY CARDOZA   In India they sent a 13 year old girl up to Tor's hotel room. So he's sucking her breast and it tastes kind of bad, and so he turns on the light, and finds that she was dirty, not dark-skinned! And her tit was white where he was sucking it.

* * *

"Well-Known Visitor Flies in Fluttering

Bunny Like Christine? Heavens, No, My Dear!"

Wearing a pink ribbon in his hat, women's shoes and a quart of cloying perfume, John Cabell Breckinridge — known to his intimates as Bunny — is in town today to film the first half of a movie that could make history.

Bunny, a 50 year old grandfather with $8,000,000, expects to complete the movie as a woman after some hocus-pocus surgery in Mexico City.

But the he-would-be-a-she resents any comparison to Christine Jorgensen, late of Copenhagen.

"Christine is a fake ... a phony ... nothing but an altered man, my dears," Bunny twittered to the press after flying here from his San Francisco home.

"I want to be a wife."

He said he plans to change his sex at the insistence of his secretary — who happens to be a 26 year old man.

"We will be married in Mexico after the operation and after his wife — a woman — divorces him. His name is Jamie and he's sweet and good looking." Breckinridge said, displaying "their" wedding ring on the proper finger.

He said the planned movie is called "Magic Moment," the moment or the magic being his hoped-for change of sex.

Breckinridge said his daughter, the Contesse de Bruchard of Cannes, France, thought it was "fine" he was going through with the operation he has wanted since he was 15 — long before she was born.

His arrival at Lockheed Air Terminal aboard a United Airliner caused quite some consternation.

Two dozen redfaced businessmen scampered for cover when they spotted photographers at the plane door.

"Not me," each protested as they ran down the landing ramp, "He's coming." Only one or two inquired who their odd fellow passenger was.

A few minutes later Bunny, powdered to the eyebrows and waving gaily, left the plane.

A stewardess confided he had paused to dab some "My Sin" perfume behind his ears.

— *The Mirror,* Friday May 14, 1954

* * *

CHARLES ANDERSON   Kenne Duncan was always the notorious bad man of the B westerns. Sometimes with *Lone Ranger* you'd see Kenne as the bad man. He always had this sneering quality, he was very good. And he never progressed beyond the bad man and the B westerns.

KATHY WOOD   When Ed and I were out with Kenne Duncan on his boat "Oil Ken," a 36 footer, we had a ball.

Every time we went out through the breakwater, Kenne would be navigating, and when he saw the sailboats coming at him, he would scream, "Here come the ragboats! Watch out!"

When he was docked at Marina Del Ray, Ed and I would go down and spend weekends. I would be the galley slave and Ed and Ken would work on the "Oil Ken." One time, Kenne was bringing the boat up from storage to the dock, they were drinking it up like mad, and ran right into the dock. Roy Barcroft fell overboard. It was real crazy...

HARRY THOMAS   Kenne was a ladies man. He had parties, risqué parties. Being a lover of the female gender he had all he could. There were naked people floating around ... typical Hollywood party. He said, "Stick around, you'll have some fun." I was looking at Kenne ... and, you know, all men are not created equal.

ANTHONY CARDOZA   Kenne Duncan's nickname was "horsecock."

RONNIE ASHCROFT   Kenne had a book, and it was quite thick, of the women that he had in bed. He said there was over a thousand in there. A thousand women.

He darned near worked in every picture I made — *The Astounding She Monster, The Outlaw Queen,* he was a very good friend of mine. When he committed suicide, I couldn't believe it. He was tired of living. Just like George Sanders — he had seen everything, done everything. All he did was sit around and watch television.

CHARLES ANDERSON When Kenne died, Wood was named executor of the estate. He staged a memorial funeral. It was held around the swimming pool of Ed's Strohm Street house. And he, and Kathy, and various friends all gathered around the swimming pool, and each one would take turns walking out onto the diving board to say a few words about Kenne Duncan.

* * *

CONRAD BROOKS Ed met his daughter in around '67 when she was in her late teens. The daughter was living in the town of Lancaster and had traced her father's whereabouts. She stayed over for a day or two, Ed was either driving a cab at the time or working for Sam Yorty, writing campaign speeches. Not much was said about it after that ... apparently they didn't hit it off ... Evidently the mother was a girl he met while he was in the Marines.

BOB DERTENO Once he was leaving for New York. I understood that he was going to his daughter's wedding. Later on, somebody told me, "Ed Wood's a grandfather."

LILLIAN WOOD She was 17 when she sent me her picture. She was born in '46, I know that. We sent her a watch when she was going to graduate, and we never heard if she got it.

KATHY WOOD I met the self-professed daughter. There was never any proof, only the woman's statement on a birth certificate. Ed used to tell me about 20 or so of his buddies lining up, waiting for her services in the Marine corps, he being among them. So it could have been anyone. There was only her accusation.

VALDA HANSEN I met Ed's daughter at his house in the Valley. She looked just like him. Beautiful, delicate. Green eyes, dark chocolate brown hair, she was very sweet.

JOHN ANDREWS When his daughter came down and was sleeping on the sofa, Kathy kicked her out! The next day Eddie was getting roaring drunk, he said, 'Oh, you kicked out my daughter! You kicked her out!" She says, "Oh, she's not your daughter, that bitch lied to you." Blah blah blah.

KATHY WOOD When Eddie's brother Bill was sent to Vietnam, he came over to our house on the way over. It was around Christmas, I put out all the best silver and cooked a big dinner ... we sat there drinking the whole bunch of us, and it ended up in a big fight. I had given Bill a little brass statue of Buddha a newscaster gave Ed. I said to him, "Take this with you for luck." From what I understand he fell off the back of a transport truck in Japan and ended up in the hospital — never did get to

Vietnam! Bill was always a little bit jealous of Eddie, and I think his wife was the same way. They were jealous of his success.

KATHY WOOD His mother was a martinet, a strict disciplinarian.

LILLIAN WOOD He would call every three weeks, always at two or three in the morning. He'd send me money, $100, without his wife knowing.

KATHY WOOD The worst thing that happened was when Eddie's mother came out and I had to sleep with her. Oh god I hated that! She didn't like me and I didn't like her and that's all there was to it.

Bela's funeral. Ed Wood is pallbearer, center, right, face partially obscured.

Weird Scenes
with the
Pied Piper

KATHY WOOD   There were people always hanging around Eddie, like a planet going through space, all sorts of things attach themselves to it. Spinning around Eddie. There were all sorts of people that wanted something from him, or had something to give him, and it became sort of a drag, if you'll pardon the expression.

JOHN ANDREWS   Eddie had a left side and a right side ... and you would never know where he was coming from. He could change that fast. One time I went in to his kitchen and he had a cigarette in each hand! One for each personality! Eddie would present himself as a moralist, that he was perfect, and that most of the rest of the world was evil, sinful, but he was divine. Bela was the type, very passionate. Eddie, the same. They either liked you, or they fucking hated you, and I mean hate, hate.

   Eddie, he couldn't stand to see anybody get ahead. He wanted to be number one, he wanted to be the lord or the mistress of the whole damn scene, and he really resented anyone who was more successful than him.

HENRY BEDERSKI   Goddamn, Ed had no money, but he sure lived fancy. I said, I have some money and I live poor. But I knew Ed needed a front, and he had the guts to do what he did. I couldn't move into a place and say, alright, 500 a month, I'll pay it, then after a month, I haven't got it, Ed figured, ah, what the hell, the world won't collapse, because you didn't get your goddamn rent.

PAUL MARCO   Every time he or Kathy would have a little argument, and she'd nag him, "Don't drink so much, save some for me!", that type of thing, he'd turn around and tell her, "Oh keep quiet!" — then he'd take out his teeth and grin, and she'd burst out laughing, and everything would be forgotten in two seconds.

KATHY WOOD   Whenever the Good Humor man came by, Ed treated all the kids on the street to ice cream. He was like the pied piper. All kids loved him because he never talked down to them, and treated them as equals.

HENRY BEDERSKI   There's one thing that I noticed about Eddie. If anybody did anything wrong, it was always, "The idiots, idiots." That was his favorite word. "Idiots, idiots. They're all idiots. He's an idiot." Idiots!

MONA McKINNON   We used to have some pretty wild parties ... I don't mean sex or anything. But just cutting up and having a good time. We'd dance and tell jokes, that was the big thing. And the latest gossip. And we'd all get very drunk, and collapse, and sometimes we'd be there the next day. Eddie would like to have Halloween parties and dress up as Hitler. He was funny, strutting around as Hitler. He looked just like him.

FRANCINE HANSEN   But I could always remember one afternoon we went over there, to his house, he was such a nut, really. All of a sudden he found that Kathy had wedgie shoes. He put on her wedgies and made a fool of himself ... with his crazy shoes.

VALDA HANSEN   Then he started doing bumps and grinds like a drag queen. We were all hysterical.

HARRY THOMAS   He was one person that would always call me every other day, and it was always a joy to hear from him. I knew it was him, nobody else would call me that late or that early. "Got somethin' for ya!" — this is the way he used to talk — "I got somethin' to show ya — I want ya to come over — I got a new idea!"

HENRY BEDERSKI   One time he says, "Well, Henry, we're going to the A & P. And I'm treating." Well, he starts throwing all kinds of stuff into the basket. A steak, this, that, and I get stuck with the bill! He said, "Goddamnit Henry, you ought to be glad you're helping out a movie director." What the hell, I had a lot of fun with Ed!

KATHY WOOD   If we had the money we could have been going night and day with parties, just having a ball. But we all got older ... and poorer.

> We had another martini, standing very close to each other, and I felt the first opportunity to let my hand brush across her ample bosom. It happened as I replaced my empty glass to the stand. I had to reach across her front, and the firm mounds, heaving heavily, brushed lightly across the back of my hand. The thrill went through my body like an electric shock. And I could sense a sudden tensing in Gloria's body. It had been such a brief incident, but so electrically charged. She did not pull back, and there was still the twinkle in her eyes. I knew she wanted me as much as I wanted her, but I couldn't bring myself to the final point of making it a reality.
>
> — *Suburbia Confidential,* Ed Wood

KATHY WOOD   Eddie once had a black Cadillac convertible sitting in our backyard. The garbageman had his eye on it. So he paid Eddie $50 for it and said, "Hey, I'll throw in my pet monkey!" Eddie said, "Oh, I don't know, let's see him." He brought it over, and it jumped on Eddie's head and immediately shit on his face!

One night, I think it was around 1970 or something, the next door neighbors were growing their own marijuana, and Eddie, very daring, went over and smoked a number. And he said, "Oh, I did it, I did it!" He became all silly and goofy, like he went behind the barn and smoked a cigarette.

We met the Hell's Angels, '64, '65, that era. The nicest people you could ever meet, they were selling little model prairie schooners, covered wagons, so we bought a couple of them. They were proud of being Hell's Angels. They took us over to see some of their friends in North Hollywood. They especially liked Eddie. He could fit into any place, anywhere, anytime. They'd take Eddie on their Harley Davidson motorcycles to an appointment someplace and get splashed when they'd go through a mud puddle. And here's Eddie, all dressed up in his suit and tie.

DAVID WARD   Me and my friend Jimmy Whiton, who wrote *The Abominable Dr. Phibes,* were visiting Eddie, around '73, his place on Tiara Street in North Hollywood, and Eddie had the flu or something, Kathy was drunk, and this transvestite was keeping Eddie company. It had had the operation, I guess, so Eddie said to this person, "Show 'em your tits!" So the thing pulled up its blouse. I think I said, "That's nice, yeah, real nice, well, we gotta go now Eddie..."

BOB BURNS   A couple of guys brought some Ed Wood films up to CBS once and we were looking at it during lunch hour. There was some color 16mm footage of Ed walking into the frame, in drag, almost like a fashion show, two or three different outfits. He had a blonde wig on, and what looked like women's dress suits. One was a pink-tangerine color.

PAUL MARCO   Criswell always had an open house, or a picnic out. Ed and Cris liked Italian food, especially spaghetti. Cris would make a big pot of meat sauce, which was his specialty. Criswell would always have a potluck thing, everybody would bring something out on the porch every Sunday, his very large apartment, huge living rooms, with the dining room combined. But mainly our social life was having people over to the Hollywood Brown Derby. Every Friday night.

JOHN ANDREWS   With Eddie, every day was New Year's Eve ... shit! In the old days, I mean old days, Criswell worked with Mae West. If you knew her you called her Miss West, and he worked with her, on the stage. So they remained friends through the years. She called him one day, "Have you got a dollar?" "Oh my gawd, you need a dollar?" "Yes, I need a dollar Cris, come down to my attorney's ... blah blah blah." So he got down there by cab, because he didn't drive. So she says, "Do you have that dollar?" "Yeah." "Well, give it to my attorney." So he hands over the dollar, and the attorney hands him the pink slip on her Cadillac limousine. It was a '54. She was buying a new one, and just gave it to Cris for the title!

So Eddie, Cris, I would be in the back seat, and Cris would have his latest stooge, whoever it might be, chauffeur us around ... and, you talk about some wild fuckin' rides, man! Eddie's drink was Imperial, which was a cheap blended whisky. And Cris had to have a Beefeater martini, extra dry. And I would drink whatever I could consume. We would drive wherever we felt like, up the Strip, go bug Herb Jeffries for a while. Eddie tried to promote a picture starring Herb Jeffries [a swing-style jazz singer], but he couldn't get it off the ground, unfortunately. That thing would be priceless.

STEVE APOSTOLOF   We would go into a place and have a hamburger, he used to love hamburgers and french fries, that's alright. But he would take the ketchup, and he'd pour the whole goddamn bottle on it. I said, "Eddie, goddamn it, the waiters are giving us dirty looks." He'd pour the whole goddamn bottle and smile.

KATHY WOOD   Eddie was so proud of this color tv set. It was real hot one night, and he was sleeping in the front bedroom. I was smoking, and somehow the couch caught on fire, it spread to the blinds, I woke up, heard the fire engines coming. I kept screaming for Eddie to wake up. Firemen were downstairs, breaking in the door, just about the time they're coming up the stairs, Eddie runs in front of the tv., stark ass naked, and he's saying to the firemen with their axes, "Don't hurt my tv! Don't hurt my tv!"

PAUL MARCO   He was a fanatic cowboy movie buff. He'd look at the *TV Guide* and circle everything. He'd watch Buck Jones at 3 in the morning. The television was never turned off. I don't know when he slept, the lights and the television would be on all night long.

JOHN ANDREWS   Eddie calls me and says, "John-John, can you give me anything on B-u-c-k J-o-n-e-s?" He would elongate these words, it's one syllable but he would get two or three syllables out of it, see? And I said, Yeah. What do you want?" "Did you ever h-e-a-r of Big Little Books?" I said, "Well, sure man." "Ya have any?" I said, "Well, yeah. I got one on Chandu the Magician —" "Ohhh! Ohhh! With Bela?" "Yeah." "How much do you want for it?" I said, "It's not for sale, Eddie, they're too hard to find. How am I going to find another one? I'm keeping this. I've got The Lost City —" "Which Lost City?! Which one?" "The one with Kane Richmond." "Ohhh!" And I mean, he's coming, man. I said, "That's not for sale, either, Eddie, these things are priceless, man, we're talking about 1935." "Well, can you give me any Buck J-o-n-e-sss?" "Maybe. I'll call you in a couple of days."

Well, we talked every day, frankly. But I knew it wouldn't be easy to find. So I went up to Cherokee Books. Upstairs, they had a whole section of Big Little Books. Shirley Temple and all kinds of things. So I find three titles, all from serials, they were a dollar each. Later I called Eddie, I said, Hey man, I've got this, I've got that, three titles." They were all illustrated with stills, the original production stuff. Anyway I sold them to Eddie for two dollars each. And he was so grateful. And then, about a week later, Criswell called, he says, "My gawd, is Ed mad at you!" "Why?" "He says you're paying 10 cents each for books and selling them to him for two dollars. Is that true, John?" "No, that's not true. That's way off. And besides, I did the research, I'm burning up gas, I have to get something."

I was working the Beverly Hills Health Club, I was an instructor. I met this guy with a bookstore. He had bought a bunch of photos, one of them was a five by seven of Buck Jones, in the full wardrobe with his horse Silver. The guy just gave it to me. So I called Eddie, "Man, have I got something for you. An autographed photo of Buck Jones." "Really?! Bring it over." I said, "I will, tomorrow. But I have to go to work now." Just within two minutes, Kathy called me and said, "Do you really have an autographed photo of Buck Jones?" "Yes, I really have. And it's for Eddie." "How much?" "Gratis. Free. I know how much he loves Buck. I'm just going to give it to him." So I go out there the next day, "Here you go, Eddie." He says, "Oh my god. Oh my dear god. Ohhhhh." He goes next door and I hear Eddie out on the porch, and he says, "Look at this! Look here what I've got. Nobody on earth has got an autographed picture of Buck Jones!" And the woman goes, "Who's Buck Jones?"

FORREST J. ACKERMAN For a while he called me up a great deal on the telephone, but he was always smashed out of his skull ... and there was nothing much I had to say to him, or could do for him or anything, I don't remember what in the world he wanted when he would call me up, it was sort of, "Well we got to get together, buddy," kind of thing.

ANTHONY CARDOZA Ed saved my life once. So, I'm swimming in the pool, the Lanaii apartments across from Warner Brothers. Anyway, I was drowning. And he dove off the second floor balcony and saved my life. Nine feet of water!

SCOTT ZIMMERMAN During the spring of 1975, *Bride of the Monster* was to be shown on an all-night movie show on Cincinnati tv. I and my best friend,another great Lugosi fan, waited with anticipation for 2 a.m. When the credits for *Bride* finally appeared, two sets of eyeballs and ears were at 100% attention for the next 90 minutes. I'd read about this film over the years, but there's a world of difference between reading about a film and seeing it. I clearly remember being thoroughly entertained by Lugosi's full-out performance and my initiation into a previously unknown realm of film.

I became increasingly intrigued as to who the director was. I dialed information in L.A. To my surprise the operator replied, "Ed D. Wood, Jr. — 469-4998." Immediately I dialed, armed with a list of questions. His wife answered, "No, Eddie's in the valley working on a skin flick. Give me your number, he always returns calls."

The next day while working at my father's restaurant, Dad mentioned he'd received a call at 3 a.m. from someone named Mr. Wood, returning a call to Mr. Zimmerman. Dad was confused by all this and pointed out that it was three in the morning, to which Ed replied, "It's midnight here!" I hightailed it home and called Mr. Wood. A hearty-voiced gentleman identified himself as Mr. Wood. Wow! I explained my father's ignorance of *Bride of the Monster's* significance and Ed appreciated this. He was more than generous in discussing his films with a teenage yokel from the midwest and my impression was that he was a cool guy.

I had never seen *Plan 9 From Outer Space,* so he gave me an invitation to see it anytime I was in L.A., he always ran films on Friday nights. You can imagine how that made me feel. He said, "I *hate* that title. It's *Graverobbers! Graverobbers From Outer Space!* There's a scene where Tor Johnson rises from the grave that'll blow your mind!"

He mentioned that he was looking for a photo of Buck Jones from *The Phantom Rider.* I'd seen half a dozen of Tod Slaughter's films on tv, they stuck in my memory, and I brought the name up. He said, "Oh, those things are so horrible! Oh, they're horrible! But I love 'em! I love 'em!"

He had a distinctive voice which sometimes reminded me of Lord Buckley. I asked him if he liked music. He said, "Yes, I do, very much. All the great operas." Was there anything he hadn't done that he wanted to do? "I've done everything in life I wanted to do." There was a pause, he exhaled on a cigarette, "except diving off those cliffs down in Mexico. Never got around to that. I'm too old now, of course."

ROBERT CREMER   It was the first time that the cast, what was left of the cast of *Plan 9* got together as a group to talk about Bela Lugosi. We went in the Small World on La Cienega and Ed Wood dragged me over to this woman sitting at the bar and said, "I want you to meet Christine Jorgensen." And he said, "She was supposed to be the subject of *Glen or Glenda,* but then she had to drop out because her parents had a fit. So that's when I had to talk Bela into coming in and doing the supernatural folderol and cut him into a movie that had basically already started shooting." Christine Jorgensen joked about it, said it was the best thing she ever did for her career, but Ed was in a good mood, it was one of those typical Hollywood jabs.

We left the bar and went over to Ed's place, we sat and drank for a while, then he put *Plan 9 from Outer Space* on. Ed would stop the film intermittently, and turn on the lights, and pour another drink, and then they would reminisce about the soliloquy that Dudley Manlove delivered, and I'm sitting there thinking, soliloquy? What are you talking about!? They had just blown *Plan 9 from Outer Space* into this incredible blockbuster major Hollywood epic, and I'm just sitting there thinking that I have crossed over, and Rod Serling was going to come in or something and tell me that it's time for a commercial break. It was just phenomenal!

My interview with Ed Wood was actually the last one I did [for the Bela Lugosi biography *The Man Behind the Cape,* Regnery, 1976], trying to fill out the unfinished pieces of the puzzle. It turned out that Ed really had more contact with Bela in the later years than anyone else. When we paid Wood for the interview, he was very straight and coherent and sober. Until after I delivered that first check. The first thing he did was send out for booze. After that, confusion really set in.

At the end of the last interview session, he started getting really angry at me, because he felt he was the person who should be writing it. He became despondent, then he became violent. He went out in the kitchen, grabbed a bottle of Wild Turkey to pour himself another drink, and there was nothing left in the bottle. He smashed the bottle on the kitchen counter and then came after me with it! He sort of lunged at me, but he was so drunk, I just pushed him back into the wall and he collapsed. And I just walked out the door, and said, "Okay Ed, I guess that's our last interview, I'll see you."

Idea Man

JOHN ANDREWS   Eddie was an idea man. He had a new idea every day. And he would work on it until it exhausted itself. And then he'd go on to the next idea. Anyway, he had an idea in about '51 for a Bela Lugosi comic book, which would be like *Dracula* and *White Zombie* and these things, but Eddie's original stories. He had a professional artist draw up some pagesand he sent letters to every comic book publisher. Not a nibble.

Eddie was in this pre-production office, early fifties, and who comes in off the street, George Zucco. He comes in after his medium success, but an outstanding success, because he had a quality about himself, the *Mummy* series, *The Mad Ghoul,* *The Mad Monster* with Glenn Strange at P. R. C. Now George was being driven by his wife. Poor George says to Eddie, "I'll take anything, I don't care what it is, I'll take any part, one line, I'll play it. But at that particular moment, Eddie didn't have anything. But Eddie would have loved to have done it. Eddie was a very sensitive man. He was pleased to see Zucco, but not in that condition, desperate for money, trying to support his family.

VALDA HANSEN   It was the late fifties, I was doing a play called *Accidently Yours,* and Ed and John Carradine came backstage. Ed was always up and down Hollywood Boulevard, and he met John Carradine, who was always very dramatic, going down Hollywood Boulevard, with his black cape, spouting Shakespeare.

EWING "LUCKY" BROWN   It was 1957, we were shooting down at Kenmore stage on Santa Monica — it was owned by Larry and Harry Smith. Ed was directing this wolfman thing with Lon Chaney, Jr. We had this great set — the outside of a building, the corner, where the stones are notched together. And Chaney climbed this goddamn thing! We were shooting — he got a finger and a toe hold with this mask and furry hands, and we were breaking up — we were shooting silent. Chaney says, "If you think this goddamn thing's easy — *you* try it! Goddamn it! We were cracking up as he was trying to climb this wall. Ed was trying to promote money on this. We did scenes for promo material. I worked on the camera with Bill "the Moose" Thompson.

TED ALLAN   Ed was to have written the *Dr. Acula* tv show for Bela Lugosi. But it never came about because Bela was getting very difficult and very hopped up, and it seemed that he was kind of out of it, so we didn't want to take the chance. I was having difficulties, too. Somebody was stealing my studio at the time, so, we couldn't have made it anyway.

GEORGE WEISS   He came in to New York in about '57, '58. He thought he could get a deal for making a couple of pictures back to back. That's the way they were doing it in those days. You sold a package of two that went on the same bill, so it didn't require double billing or whatever.

JOHNNY CARPENTER   Ed turned his cap around, with the bill going out the back, like a baseball player or a swat team man when he got busy. We were writing *The Lawless Rider* in his house on Riverside Drive and Victory Boulevard. Ed did everything, he was writer, production assistant, helped get people for me, we worked for each other for nothing. He would write a line of dialogue, and I would tear it up and throw it away. His dialogue was a little bit too perfect. The choice of words was not correct for the frontier.

HENRY BEDERSKI   Ed wrote the Johnny Carpenter western, *The Lawless Rider*. But on the screen it says, "Screenplay by Johnny Carpenter." Ed wrote it. But you see, anything to boost Johnny Carpenter. Johnny Carpenter couldn't write a story to save his life.

JOHN ANDREWS   Eddie ran an episode of his *Crossroad Avenger* tv western one Halloween night, on Bonner. This guy, a would be writer, shows up with a projector, and we ran it. Eddie had Harvey B. Dunne as an old prospector wear his .45 where his jock strap should be. That was supposed to be funny.

DAVID WARD   There was a scene where Tom Keene's horse was supposed to drink water, but the horse wouldn't oblige, so Eddie got below, out of camera range, and pulled the horse's head down to the water. Then there was another scene in it where he wanted to do a cameo, and ride through town on a horse. But he lost control. And though it ruined the scene, he kept it in. The horse goes tearing down the town street, with Eddie half in, half out of saddle — God it was funny.

RON ASHCROFT   I was cutting a sequence on my first picture, *The Astounding She Monster.* I got to a point where the invader comes upon a huge black bear. As the girl from outer spaces reaches out in a friendly gesture to touch the bear, it drops dead. I was having trouble with what we shot; I was very unhappy about it. Eddie came walking in the cutting room, and I told him my problem. He looked at the scene and said, "Listen, Ron, you go down to the costume company or maybe one of the prop houses and get one of those goddamn bear skins, not one of the silly things you wear to a party, but one that really looks real. And we'll get somebody into that bear skin and we'll go back to the same location"

So, I got the bear skin. Eddie promoted Kenne Duncan to volunteer to get in the bear skin, and a whole gang of us went up to Frazier Park. Lorraine [Ashcroft's wife, not the actress in the picture] got into the invader suit and put on the weird wig. Kenne crawled into the bear skin. Eddie grabbed the reflectors, Gene Grop was on camera. We made a couple of takes and all of a sudden we hear a voice coming from the bear. Kenne was yelling, "Goddamn it, stop, let me out of this thing!" Kenne had been smoking a cigarette in there, and the damn smoke was choking him! Anyway, Eddie's idea worked out. He had a lot of savvy about the business, how to get out of tight spots. We ran the footage at the lab the next day. It was great and we were able to put it into the sequence.

When it comes to friendships in Hollywood, they're rare. I'll say this thing about good old Eddie: whenever I was really in trouble and needed help, Eddie Wood was there.

KATHY WOOD He had most of his television commercials on reels when I first met him, then like everything else they disappeared. There was a commercial for Wesson oil which showed Eddie's goofy sense of humor. Here's these two explorers going through deepest Africa, and they get captured by these natives, who have this big pot of oil, and the cannibals, they're stirring the oil. One of the explorers says, "I'm too old to be cooked in oil and eaten," and the other one says, "I'm too tough to be cooked in oil," and the chief say, "Uh-uh. Nothing too tough to be cooked in Wesson oil!"

Eddie did industrial films for Autonetics. Some he wrote, some he directed. I think all those films for Autonetics were classified. Eddie was investigated by the F.B.I. He had clearance, secret clearance.

Wood directs and acts in a tv commercial for Wesson Oil, 1954.
Participants include Don Nagel, Phyllis Coates, and Conrad Brooks

[photo courtesy Don Nagel]

VALDA HANSEN Ed had a script, *Operation Salami,* a crazy script, a lot of comedy. Joe E. Brown came — this was after he made *Some Like It Hot* — and he said, "I love her, I want her for my leading lady." It was just perfect, Ed would just keep looking at me, he had a kind of a father love thing for me, protege love thing, and he'd wink at me, and he could see that I had stars in my eyes. Everything was going great, but then Joe E. Brown expired!

DON FELLMAN Wood was going to do the last teaming of Karloff and Lugosi. He was also going to get Joe E. Brown, who may have been swiped from him, because

Brown later turned up in *Comedy of Terrors* with all those other horror actors — they had everybody except Lugosi there. Wood said the picture was going to be called *Invasion of the Gigantic Salami*. That's right. *Invasion of the Gigantic Salami*. He was so tickled by the humor of it.

JOHN ANDREWS Ed had a bunch of stock footage, wild shots on Bela. But he shot it on nitrate. One morning he opened up the can — all this priceless footage, and it had gone to dust. All the poison, the vapors, hit him, and he threw up immediately. So that's what happened to his *Ghouls of the Moon* project.

DON FELLMAN He had written a script for *The Beverly Hillbillies*. And he said it was "rejected at the last minute."

TIMOTHY FARRELL The last time I talked to Ed was in 1974. He was drunk as a skunk but happy as hell. He had just gotten the money to make a picture. He had his attorney with him and kept putting people on the phone. I figured, Jesus Christ, he's going to drink up all the money before he makes the picture.

ROBERT CREMER Often Wood would say, "If I could have just put the right package together, things would have been different." And I think that's where the frustration came in, that he felt that he just never got some of the breaks that a lot of other guys, with no more talent than he had, were given.

I think the booze had a really serious impact on his ability to just reason and do business. The guy really went kind of crazy when he got around liquor. And then all of his frustrations came out, and his feelings that he was done over by Hollywood, and that Alex Gordon might have been in a position to help him...

DENNIS RODRIGUEZ Ed would call at night, just plastered, at two in the morning. It would always be about some very hush-hush big time deal. The Saudis were in town and they had five million dollars to make a movie, and he was meeting them tomorrow at the Bel Air — just complete hallucination.

JOHN ANDREWS *Island of Lost Souls* was playing on tv. Eddie calls: "Are you watching the picture?" I say, "Of course I'm watching it." He calls back when the picture's over and says, "I'd like to remake that picture, but this time, I would have them digging into the bodies, and I would have them pulling out gizzards and livers," and he went into this sick-ass shit, and I go, "That's fine, Eddie." What are you going to say to something like that?

DON FELLMAN Ed mentioned his script *Heads No Tails*, which was based on Tod Slaughter's *Demon Barber of Fleet Street*.

BARRY ELLIOTT I gave him some money for the script *(Heads No Tails)*, and I tried to rewrite it later. I think he charged something like 200 dollars for a script ... the poor guy was starving.

DON FELLMAN Wood was going to do a movie on Lugosi's last days, to be called

Post Mortem. He had the book going as I spoked to him, he was typing it as I talked to him. Peter Coe was going to play Bela, and it was going to be filmed by a multi-media company called Blue Dolphin. They wanted me to write a press release for their film. At first, it just struck me as ludicrous. Later on, I thought it would be something. Blue Dolphin was a manufacturer of rock and roll records, and Wood was trying to put himself in the right frame of mind, to respect the company, so as not to go against their image, which is funny, because Wood was a very uncompromising kind of man. He was commenting on rock and roll: "You know what it is?" I said, "Rhythm and blues?" He said, "I wish it was. I'll *tell* you what it is *It's blacks-and-reds-and-greens-and-purples- jumpin'-up-and-down-and-yellin'!"*

MONA McKINNON   There was a book that came out *[The Count: The Life and Films of Bela "Dracula" Lugosi,* by Arthur Lennig], and it said, "Edw. D. Wood, Jr., producer, director, promoter, made the worst movies in Hollywood." And it went on and on, panning him. It took his pictures apart. Eddie just laughed. He thought that was so funny.

DON FELLMAN   I don't know what brought it up, but he gave me a whole spiel on Lennig. He said, "He was just a little boy ... a *little boy.* I *lived* with the man!" At one point Wood quoted something negative Lennig had written about him from the book and bellowed out, "That pig Lennig! Wait'll my book comes out!" He said that with total disdain.

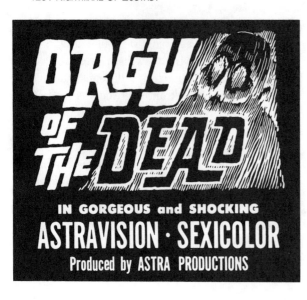

Left: Logo from pressbook

Bottom:
Still of crew on *Orgy of the Dead*.
Bottom Row:
Ed Wood (screenplay), Bob
Derteno (Art Director), Steve
Apostolof (Director-Producer),
Mark Desmond (Choreographer).
Top Row:
Bill Davis, T. V. Mikels (Gaffer),
unidentified camera assistant,
Bob Maxwell (Assistant
Cameraman). Behind the camera:
Robert Caramico,
(Cinematographer).

[photo courtesy Steve Apostolof]

Skin

> It is said on clear nights beneath the cold light of the moon, howl the dog and the wolf; and creeping things crawl out of the slime.
>
> — *Orgy of the Dead* by Ed Wood

SAM KOPETZKY It wouldn't surprise me that Ed got into skin. A lot of people got into skin, because you couldn't lose money.

STEPHEN APOSTOLOF *Orgy of the Dead* was the first film that Eddie and I made together. In addition to the screenplay, he was the production manager and helped on the casting. We had problems with Criswell, Eddie tried to help because he felt personally responsible. Criswell didn't know his lines and the son of a gun gets an entourage around him. It's like, "Bravo!" You can see in the picture that he's reading, looking below the camera where poor Eddie's sitting with the cue cards. During the lunch break, we were looking for Cris. And he was sleeping peacefully — in his goddamn coffin!

The greatest satisfaction I received was when we screened *Orgy of the Dead,* and Criswell started to cry. He said, "You made me look so regal." And I did, the son-of-a-bitch!

We're at a small commissary at KTTV, and Eddie nonchalantly walks in wearing the gold wig [that Pat Barringer wears in *Orgy of the Dead*]. Billy Barty the midget was there, and he starts joking. We're all laughing — the whole cafeteria was in tears. The next day he would come in with the Wolfman mask on. Another time he went in as the mummy, chasing everybody, scaring everybody. I said, "Eddie, shut up, we're not shooting at the studio here, they'll kick us out!"

JOHN ANDREWS Poor Pat Barringer. She had the Lou Ojena syndrome, she thought that she was going to be a big fucking star. And she couldn't even scream and make it convincing. She couldn't do shit. And those tits are plastic, by the way.

STEVE APOSTOLOF: Eddie did not know how bad his drinking habit was. In the middle of the picture, he hit me for some money, and the moment Eddie got some money, he got drunk. He was drinking bourbon. Old Crow. And sweet vermouth — an old fashioned. He got drunk as a skunk. You can see his eyes, they go like he's shooting dope. I sent him home. He sobered up, and the next day, everything was fine and dandy.

JOHN ANDREWS Eddie would go home and tell Kathy everything that happened during the day. She started calling Steve, "That Bulgarian bastard! That no good piece of shit!" And just on and on. If it wasn't for Steve employing Eddie, I don't know what the hell they would have done.

The girl in the gold pullover dress. At wrap, we're all getting loaded, and Ed says, "I want that dress." I said, "Well, I want one of those ceramic skulls." So I came back in and said, "It's in my car." Ed said, "Cool." And we had some Ballantine scotch out of styrofoam cups, which Ed hated, we couldn't find any Imperial. I went over to talk to Bob Caramico, the cameraman. Caramico said, "I know he was a leatherneck, just like me, but he's living from day to day. And if I were you, John, I wouldn't have anything to do with him." A few minutes later, I go back to the cup, and the scotch had eaten through it.

ED WOOD   Letter to Valda Hansen, 10/2/65:

> Love —
>
> I just made another film "Orgy of the Dead", Tried desperately to call you at GR 84639 (NO GO) — No time then to write — It was on time table Thing..
>
> New one coming — My new address is 6136 BONNER ST NORTH HOLLYWOOD —PO 96446 I bought a house with a swimming pool and a guest house —will write and talk more when I hear from you.
>
> Hope you're protecting my Blue angora
>
> Love
>
> Ed
>
> "Your usual — excellent — card received & appreciated"

Valda Hansen wearing her blue angora.

[photo courtesy Valda Hansen]

Ed Wood as "Alecia" in *Take It Out In Trade*

KATHY WOOD   *Take It Out In Trade* was made just before we lost our house on Bonner St. in 1970. I wasn't quite in my own mind ... they were in the process of taking our house.

It was a cute little film which he cut and edited in his den on a movieola. It kept me up all night, practically. He used some of our neighbors, Kenne Duncan's old girlfriend, Nona Carver, she played an old whore [Sleazy Maisie Rumpledink]. He wasn't really making any money out of it, and he never did ...

HARRY THOMAS   Nona Carver — big bazooms but very thin little legs. Chewing gum all the time. She was one of the top headliners at the Gaiety on Main St.

NONA CARVER   I met Ed Wood quite a few times over at Kenne's house.

There were two versions of *Take It Out In Trade;* I think one had quite a bit of pornographic business in it, and there was one that didn't. We made it in Lakewood, in some private home, in about two days. It was all non-union, but had a few SAG people. He had a couple of faggots in it. I played the part of a madam. I was supposed to be on the needle, running around in a little baby doll outfit. In the film this guy comes in, starts beating me up, and I scream and plead and cry. Evidently, it sounded so real the police came! That was kind of a big joke.

The way I understand it, Ed went out to some clubs and he met some guy who wanted to get hold of pornographic pictures. Ed says, well, instead of going out spending money on these things, I can make you a picture. If you got a couple thousand dollars, you can make some money, and I'll make two versions. One you can sell to the distributors, perfectly legit. And we'll get some scenes in there that we can cut out for your private collection.

RONNIE ASHCROFT   It was in the early 70's, Eddie had made a picture and had gotten out of sync. So he called me up one night. I go over there, ring the bell, the door opens, and there's Ed's dog Monster and these two feet with pink slippers on. I start to say, "Hello Kathy." But it's Eddie. He looked funny in this pink nightgown and big beard. But I just played it straight.

I glanced into the synchronizer ... it was a scene of two guys in a kitchen, kissing, or something. He got into a fight with the cutter; the cutter quit and went home. Eddie cut in an insert of a telephone bell, and then he was out of synch and he couldn't figure out why. And I had to tell him, "Eddie, when you cut a track in, you must remove the same amount of track that was in, otherwise it will be delayed."

MICHAEL DONOVAN O'DONNELL   We had worked on a picture Apostolof directed, *Hot Ice*. I believe Ed played a janitor in that. When this *Take It Out In Trade* thing came up, he cast me as Mac McGregor, private eye. He said, "You're the perfect guy." Mac McGregor — that's me. I made Mac McGregor Marlow. I always loved Marlow because he had a set of balls bigger than himself. Attack and try anything.

Ed gave you free reign, he let you do your thing. You showed him what you could do and then you went ahead and did it. Eddie let you improvise a lot. A lot. Because he was not stuck to any one particular concept or idea.

From *Take It Out in Trade:*
Monica Gayle & Linda Colpin frolic;
Michael Donovan O'Donnell is given
special treatment at Madame Puntacita's.

CHARLES ANDERSON   *Necromania* came about because Pendulum wanted a feature movie. Right away, Ed said, "I can do it — you want *Gone With The Wind?* Anything you want, I'll give it to you." So he had free reign to do anything he wanted, provided it was sexy and it fit in with their market. So at that point he came up with the *Necromania* idea, which was really just a spin-off of his involvement with Vampira and things like that from his early days. The film was going to be marketed for something like the Pussycat Theatres.

The last movies he ever made was something that we were doing for Pendulum. They were part of this home-study guide they were putting out. You'd get these 8 millimeter movies with the books, see? We were doing some sort of romantic, idyllic kind of situation with a husband and wife at home, and then it would progress into what was basically nothing more than a hardcore. But it had the pretense of being ... self help. We were co-directors. Our names never appeared on the screen at all.

A week before production on *Necromania,* Ed went on one of his binges. The days are coming closer and closer to the start of production ... and still no Ed. We'd call home, and Ed was indisposed, or whatever it was. Everyone was taking bets. A malicious person kept saying that Ed had been out of it so long that he was afraid to work on a film again. But Ed had the last laugh on everybody. The afternoon before shooting was to start, Ed showed up in his embroidered western outfit with copies of the shooting script. And they began.

He acted in *Necromania* as a sort of Orson Welles type, a wizard. He had some sort of weirdness going on with his scene, an evil doctor kind of thing.

JOHN ANDREWS   When Ed called me about *Necromania,* he said, "You are going to see a director in action." And he was good. *Necromania* was shot at Hal Guthu's studio, on a weekend. He had some flats set up that it looked like a motel, hotel, whatever it was supposed to be. The first thing that I remember is that the camera broke down! The Arriflex would jam up constantly! Couldn't get one shot. The cameraman said, "Let's go for an Eclair camera." Eddie didn't know what an Eclair was! I said, "Yeah Eddie, get the Eclair. And get a 12 to 120 zoom, you don't have to change the round, you can just push it." Eddie didn't have the first idea what I was talking about, and the producer said, "I don't think you're calling the shots here," and Eddie said, "I agree, I agree." So we went with the Eclairs. I was Eddie's assistant, got paid 75 dollars for two days. Hal Guthu's would allow nudity, but no hardcore. On the third day they shot on another stage to do the hardcore. It was a haunted hotel sort of thing, couples, lovers would go there to cure their sexual problems. It wasn't a bad idea.

TED GORLEY   Of Ed's two X-rated movies, *Necromania* was the better of them. It was about a woman who gave out love potions in a typical Ed Wood mystery house, the cobwebs, very Bela Lugosi type of thing. He was running around in this pink baby doll outfit, and Criswell came on the set. And we got the coffins mixed up. We picked up the wrong coffin from Criswell. One was from Lincoln's time, and one was

Top:
Ed Wood
directs
René Bond
and Ric Lutze in
Necromania,
1971

Left:
In Criswell's
coffin for a
hardcore
segment
of
Necromania

[photo courtesy
Kathy Wood]

modern. Of course the audience wouldn't be looking at the coffin, but it was part of the, uh, statement.

We sold it before we released it. It didn't take long to edit. We didn't want to bother with it. We weren't in the feature business at that time.

It was about 110 degrees in the studio. René Bond passed out. We had to put water on her to revive her ... but we all kept going, it was a struggle.

The cast loved Ed. He was very gentle, very patient. I hate to say this, but for him to direct in the pink baby doll outfit, it just seemed normal! Natural. Because he always wore pink satin shoes, velvet pants, and a pink angora sweater. With a bra. That was Ed Wood. When he would work, he was fantastic. But Ed Wood was his own worst enemy ... the bottle.

We made *Necromania* for 7000 dollars. And the other film was about the same price. The most expensive thing was the film stock. For the sets, the biggest thing we got was the coffin, and a stuffed wolf. Everything else was more or less improvised. And we picked the hottest day of the year to shoot the damn thing.

BUDDY HYDE   Criswell called me, "Eddie wants us to spend the afternoon at the shooting." It was hot as the devil. Eddie sat there in his director's chair, tight black pants, no shirt. There was a bedroom set, and off to the side, a set which had a casket and a stuffed wolf.

TED GORLEY   There were two guys. One could get it up, the other couldn't. The problem was, the guy that could get it up wasn't supposed to, and so on. We couldn't switch roles, so we just played it, and whatever came, came.

JOHN ANDREWS   In this hallway sequence, Eddie's trying to coach this would-be actor how to play his scene. Eddie assumes the personality and says, "No my dear, I must come first! I have to come first!"

MAILA NURMI   I was in General Hospital, not the tv show, the hospital, because I had some kind of attack of paralysis, and I was learning to walk again, and a guy came out of the back room of hematology and said, "There's someone on the phone for you." It was Ed Wood. And I talked to him at length, the last time I ever spoke with him. It had to be '71. Ed said, "I'm making a movie, I want you in it." I said, "Hey Ed, I'm in this wheelchair, I don't walk." He said, "That doesn't matter, that doesn't matter, honey. It's okay, I want you." He didn't tell me the name of the film, or what it was. About two months later I got a phone call, I don't know how they found me, but they did. This beer-guzzling type guy said Ed wants you, and then he proceeded to tell me what the thing was. "You're layin' in this coffin, you got nothin' on ... " I was stunned, and all I could say was, "You know, I can't walk." He said, "That don't matter, you can sit up, can't ya?" He said, "You ain't got nothin' on, you're in this coffin, and you sit up." I think my jaw was hanging open. He said, "Yeah, and this guy jumps on you, he says, 'Aaarooow!'" Then he said, "For a hunnert apples baby he's using your name." So anyway I told him wasn't interested. "Miss Garbo isn't working, I think she can probably sit up better than I can."

JOHN ANDREWS   Maila Nurmi was to be the ghoul-in-residence of this madhouse that these married couples and shack-ups would frequent. The one that comes out of the coffin was going to be Maila's part. She told me, "I've done professional suicide before, but I just don't think I should do this picture." So I took the message back to Eddie and he said, "Oh shit, I'll have to get somebody else." And he did. I made her up, in a way, the eyes, to give a Vampira look.

Then there was the weird moaning from inside the coffin. Danny nervously snapped to it. Shirley was held from any kind of fright by the comforting hand of Barb. Then Tanya slowly turned to face the bronze box.

"We await your appearance, oh, Madame Heles."

The moaning seemed to become more strong ... then it faded, then returned.

"We are all in attendance, Madam Heles," said the prayerlike voice of Barb as she mirrored some of the words Tanya had first spoken.

"I come ... " told the moaning words.

Then the coffin lid slowly creaked open. One might not expect such creaking from such a polished box, nor would one expect the sound of thunder racing across a mountain path, but the thunder was there and the sounds of a heavy wind ... and the figure which rose up from the depths of the purple, velvet-lined box might have been beautiful, but it was impossible to really tell through all the heavy make-up. But the lips were shiny and blood red, and the teeth, white, sharp, and long."

— *The Only House,* by Ed Wood

RIC LUTZE   Me and René Bond and Marie Arnold were in *Necromania,* and some other chick. Ed Wood was real dominant so I'm sure he gave himself a bit part a la Hitchcock because he looked at himself in that way. We thought he was making a comedy, to tell you the bloody truth. We were just a bunch of young kids, and we thought this was sort of a comedy thing ...

It was shot in one or two days, most of the movies in those days were shot — two days was like big. It was the only time I've ever made love in a coffin, that's not something you forget about. Ed would give us the lines and say, do it this way or do it that way, walk in here or walk in there. He thought it was going to be a real big thing, but you hear this from all the directors. The script would say, "go into sex" and then you had to make it all up yourself. The script itself was probably only 20 pages long.

ED WOOD   (From *Censorship, Sex and the Movies, Book I:)*

Recently one producer of former "B" pictures was asked to do a nudie flick for a young and very new producer. The former, the old-timer, produced pictures at a budget of between forty and sixty thousand dollars each. Thus when he asked what his budget would be, the new, young producer said five thousand dollars and the older man dropped dead on the spot.

The laboratory cost is nearly the entire budget ... the laboratory and the film. What little remains goes to the cameraman and the actors.

In *Necromania,* most of the emphasis is placed on the basic story. This film is in full, brilliant color filmed by two of Hollywood's best cameramen, has a hard line story, and is well acted by the principals.

It has a director who has more than twenty years in the business and an editor who has done more features than he cares to count. But it is a sure fire winner at the box office, and will set a new trend in sexploitation type of films.

Although the sex sequences are what the public wants and demands, they are also being treated to a well-balanced storyline which is sure to get rave notices in the publications which outline such films. And there is nothing offensive to the viewer. His intelligence is not insulted by bad performances from any of the behind-the-scene operations. And it is truly a sound film. The actors know their lines and deliver them with the competent, professional style mandatory in high calibre independent productions.

Necromania is selected here as an example because it is the trend toward better entertainment in the XX rated films. Thus when the patron lays down his 3, 5, or whatever bills at the box office he is not going to leave the theater feeling that he has in any way been cheated.

HAL GUTHU Ed did a lot of small parts in films I photographed. Maybe 10 to 15 of them. Small parts, walk-ons, bit parts, in regular straight films, and some of these mild girlie films. He played all different types of roles — he was an excellent actor.

JOE ROBERTSON In *The Photographer,* which I produced and directed, Ed wrote the screenplay and played the lead. This was totally softcore, 16mm, '68 or '67. He was half dragged out in that, switching back and forth from straight to drag. He'd be checking out the girl's clothes. In *Misty,* he was in a jacuzzi, and all dragged out.

PAUL MARCO I think he did some porno films in a little studio in North Hollywood. They were 10 minute long type of things. "Little short subjects" he called them. At one point I kept telling him, "When are you going to get back into legitimate?" He said that's what kept him alive, doing the loops and writing his books.

There are movie machines in every arcade in every town. For a quarter or fifty cents one might view what is called a "LOOP". This is a 16mm film either color or black and white which has a running time of approximately twelve minutes. However, the patron doesn't get that full twelve minutes for his first coin. The film is divided into parts, anywhere from 4 to 8 parts, all according to the vendor and his machine.

And these films are just about as HOT as any film can be made.

— from *Censorship, Sex and the Movies, Book I,* by Ed Wood

TED GORLEY He made a lot of loops. He did a loop where he played a Mexican jailer. Had a dildo and a big sombrero. And he took the girl away, but only for a second. Everybody was laughing so hard we could hardly keep the camera straight. It was an old Swedish Erotica movie, in the old days when we did nothing but silent ones.

Solly had led them through a dingy hall which was rutted from years of heavy shoes and high heels and boots walking its length. The stairs they went down were no better. The heavy stage door was opened and the stage itself equaled the rest of the building, although there was a fairly adequate kitchen, bedroom and living room set. The lights were ancient, but they worked, as Chris was to find out. And in a far corner there was a blue backdrop representing the sky and a bunch of plastic trees which could be switched around in any way which might be desired.

There were only three men on the set. A man named Hank, who held a still camera hung around his neck. Ernie, the man who ran the movie camera, and a young fellow named LeRoy, who was catch-all, but mainly he tended the lights. Solly introduced Chris around quickly and told both of the cameramen what he wanted.

The aging 16mm camera began to whir and the equally dated still camera began to click.

— from *TV Lust,* by Ed Wood

PHIL CAMBRIDGE When Caballero first started, they just did 8mm movies. They'd put one-liners, captions, on the bottom of the screen, just like silent films. They gave Ed a hundred bucks to write ten movies. There had to be fifty lines in each movie, minimum.

DAVID WARD Steve Apostolof [A.C. Stephen] was having a big party before they shot *Cocktail Hostesses* and *Dropout Wife*. And Apostolof rented a room at Michaels, which is a pretty ritzy place up on Los Feliz and Hillhurst. René Bond, the porno queen, everybody connected with these pictures was there. And Eddie, who wrote the screenplays, wanted me to go along, because he knew I didn't drink, and he was planning to get drunk, stinking drunk, and he wanted me to drive him home.

PETER COE I read one of his porno novels, and I was amazed that he would write something like that. He said, "I have to do it, that's what keeps my room and board, and the rent."

BUDDY HYDE Eddie did a lot of hardcore before *Deep Throat* came out. When *Deep Throat* was a big hit all of a sudden, Eddie said, "What the hell was that? I've been writing these for the last six years!"

BERNIE BLOOM To me, Ed Wood was a crazy genius. Way ahead of his time. Everybody was afraid to do the things that he would do. He was the most prolific writer I've ever known. And the fastest. He could write better drunk than most writers could write sober.

PAUL MARCO He was always like a Liberace, banging away, bouncing up and down on the sofa, banging on the typewriter. I can just visualize, closing my eyes, his butt going up and down while he's banging on the damn typewriter. Just like Liberace did when he played the piano.

KATHY WOOD He had written all his life. Even when he was in the Marine Corps he wrote and wrote and wrote.

He didn't sit down eight hours a day, seven days a week: he did it erratically, whenever the mood struck him. He was always with a pen and paper — it was part of him. He could be eating dinner and an idea would come to him.

I think he transposed some of his dreams into his stories. When Eddie was thinking, writing, composing, he walked round and round, back and forth, clenching and unclenching his right hand. He had remarkable concentration, and he could write oblivious to the gang who always seemed to be around, and he did love a crowd of his friends and buddies at all times.

Eddie was never too much on the research bit — he was too impatient. But he was so fast on that IBM Executive — Oh God he was fast!

BARRY ELLIOTT He showed up at nine one morning, his hands were shaking as usual, and he's got a pile of yellow paged notes, and he wanted to borrow a typewriter. He probably hocked his. And so I put him in a room with a typewriter. I brought him a cup of coffee about lunch time. By the time he got up at night he wrote a complete feature film. I couldn't believe it.

BUDDY HYDE It all came out of his head just like a machine gun. Real fast. He would sit down and do a whole book in something like four hours. He wouldn't rewrite or proofread or anything.

When he'd tell me an idea for a role in a film he'd want to write, he would ask me, "Who do you think would do that real well?" I might have run into John Carradine in a bar the night before, and he would be on my mind. So I'd tell him, "Ed, you know who would do that part real well? John Carradine." And he'd say, "Yeah. You know, I can just see him do that. Yeah." That's what he'd do, he would look for somebody in real life who he could visualize, then he could put it in words.

KATHY WOOD When he wrote, drinking seemed to help. We used to sit and talk, and it was such a nice progression of drinking and talking, and talking and drinking, and he'd wake up in the middle of the night and he'd think of something, and thank God he wrote most of it on paper. The drinking helped. He was always close to a pencil.

HARRY THOMAS He gave me a couple of his paperback books and autographed them. He'd call me up in the middle of the night and say, "How do you think this ending is?" He'd ask me how I would end this and what did I think of it, or he'd read a passage and say, "Is this authentic?"

PAUL MARCO There would be piles of scripts on the floor. Ed would have three-quarters of a script written, and he'd remember something about another script, reach down and grab it, start a chapter, and then put it down, get another piece of paper, and he'd be writing another thing. He had three or four of them going at one time. He'd have a shadow, being up all night long, and he'd have a funny little hat on, and an angora sweater, or leotards, and he'd look like an old man/woman.

David De Mering would come over with a bag of chicken, a bottle, and Ed would just fry it up and feed platter after platter. He'd have a chicken leg in one hand, a cigarette in his mouth, a bottle of vodka, the television in front of him. He'd watch television, look at me, get nagged by his wife, drink, and then, still talking, with the cigarette in his mouth, walk into the other room, take a bite of the chicken leg, put it on the coffee table, wash it down with the vodka, pick up the lit cigarette, pick up a manuscript page, bang away on the typewriter, hold a conversation and repeat everything I said to him. And he'd tell me what happened on television. You'd sit there with your mouth open — my God — how does he do it?

DON NAGEL Ed was ghosting for a lot of people. He'd ghost for 250 dollars cash, sometimes a thousand, depending what you could get out of them.

But ... he'd throw six balls in the air and couldn't find two of them ...

KATHY WOOD When Bernie Bloom left Golden State, Eddie went with him, then all of a sudden one day Bernie called Eddie and said, "I'm going to start my own company, Pendulum Publishing, come and help me." Duke Moore and I were at this high class Mexican bar one afternoon drinking tequilas, and Eddie and Bernie sat together trying to get the first two books done, *Raped in the Grass,* and *Bye Bye Broadie.*

BERNIE BLOOM The people I worked for were buying what we call "packages," magazines already packaged together, and I decided to start publishing my own magazines. And Ed was one of the first writers I hired. I hired five writers in all. I think Ed's work alone equalled the other four writers. he had a fantastic imagination, he knew how to write, smoke would come out of the typewriter when he wrote. He could take the same story, and re-write, change it around the characters, and change around the sets, and the scenes, and you wouldn't know the difference. He was one of the few writers in this business who used his real name. Ed would do about two or three magazines a month. We had writers sharing offices but Ed had to work alone because all the other guys used to resent him because he was too fast for them. He never rewrote ... you never saw any wasted paper in the basket — what came out of the machine was what you got. I've gone through dozens and dozens of writers, but I never knew anybody who could write as fast as him.

PHIL CAMBRIDGE   I got to know Ed around '74. Bernie Bloom had moved down to Santa Monica then, and Ed would sit at his table and write, and I would sit at my art table and draw. And I would always look over, and you know how Ed was dressed — his favorite wear was horrendous pedal pushers, which I guess were Kathy's, because they were too short. And he wore those women's cuffs, and always an angora top, an angora sweater. One of his many aliases when he was writing fiction was Ann Gora. But there was nothing sissy about him. I would look around and think, Jesus, his top is so tiny, I wish he wouldn't wear his bras so tight — they cut into his back! He was always on the sauce ... always. Blanche Bloom, who never found anything unusual about the fact that he wore women's clothes, would come in every day and discuss the latest fashions with Ed. And he loved to talk the fashions. I once said to him, "Ed, if you could have anything in life, what would you be?" He said, "I would come back as a blonde, a woman blonde." He denied having any homosexual relationships of any kind.

CHARLES ANDERSON   Ed wrote a transvestite study. Dick Trent was his most common name. He and I did a book together, a documentary study of fetishes and fantasies. He did the fetish part, and I did the fantasies part. When that book came out we had a big party. He took the writing very seriously.

DENNIS RODRIGUEZ   In 1968, if you wrote a paperback in the adult market, you could figure on a thousand dollars. That was 1968. But what they're offering you today for an adult novel is between three and five hundred dollars. It's a saturated market. Ed was stuck in it, in a sense. He was a transvestite, he wasn't going to put on a straight costume to land a job ...

JOHN ANDREWS   His drag name was Shirley. They all have a name. You'll notice in *Orgy of the Dead,* in the books, there's always a Shirley. It's him. Projection.

KARL JOHNSON   My dad used to call him Shirley. He liked that.

JOE ROBERTSON   Ed used to come into my bar, The Surf Girl. He always got drunk and someone had to take him home. He used to call himself Shirley. Shirley was like a 45 year old bar hooker. And he would say, "Shirley wants this," or "Shirley wants that." He'd be in total drag ... a gross silver dress — the grossest thing in the world. And with heels that were crooked, he couldn't walk in the goddamn things, it was comical. He wore a yellow blonde wig — he always had it on crooked.

So one night in the club, he got drunk, and I drove him home. He's sitting on the edge of my Jeep. One leg up in the air, one leg on the seat. In this gross silver dress. We're driving along, and the wind blows his wig off. So he runs out in the middle of the street, and all the people are jamming on their brakes, I get him back in the Jeep, and I'm trying to find his house, and there are a couple of young 14 year old girls walking down the street. So I ask the girls, "Can you tell me where Bonner Street is?" They take one look at Ed, and they run screaming down the street.

DENNIS RODRIGUEZ According to Ed, he knew every famous drag queen in Hollywood — Milton Berle, Jack Benny, Dan Dailey, Cary Grant. Ed would use that if anyone made a remark — that they always had women's underwear on.

JOHN ANDREWS When he had the second house on Bonner, he was in full drag, 24 hours. Ed said, "Vincent Price, Jack Benny, they'll all be here! Yeah, we'll have parties!" He loved to have drag parties. you see, that Jack Benny was a drag was a deep dark secret — like Errol Flynn mainlining — nobody knew that. He called me one day and says, "I'm stranded on Ventura." I said, "I'm stranded myself. I can't get out of the house." And he says, "I just had a terrible experience." He was quite drunk. I thought somebody beat him up or something. And he says, "Well, I went into the service station in drag, and there's these two mechanics, sitting there. And I say, 'Hey, can you help me with my car? It's stuck down the street.' 'Get out of here, you queer! Get out of here! Get your fucking ass out of here!'"

SCOTT RAYE He wore this watch — it was just like a little girl's watch, red, with a little rubber band on it, a play watch. But that was his feminine symbol. He wore earrings, but he would always take them off and put them in his briefcase. He said, "If I ever got caught going home, it would be hell. I got caught once and the police beat me up."

PHIL CAMBRIDGE I was driving a Mercury at the time, and one day the little mother conked out at work. So Ed Wood and I rode the buses from Santa Monica all the way back to Hollywood. And here I am with this guy who doesn't even look vaguely straight. Angora sweater and a cigarette. He smoked constantly. And he had this rolling gait, back and forth motion. He looked like nthing more than somebody in a bad gorilla costume — top heavy and really ridiculous.

The ride was sheer hell. We went to the back. I tried to pretend I wasn't with him — but he's talking to me, and he's drunk, too, right? So he doesn't give a shit what happens! I saw two seats, I have to cop out, I did not want to sit next to him! I said, "Sit there, Ed." So he sort of falls into the seat, next to the typical old lady, pince-nez glasses, shopping bags. I sat across the aisle, exactly opposite him. He'd roll out to me, say something, "Ha ha ha ha ha!" then roll back, bump into her, say excuse me, say the same line to her, see if she'd laugh. Abut the fourth time he did that, she moved up a few rows. Then she turned, and instead of looking at Ed, shot me the dirtiest look I have ever seen in my life!

SCOTT RAYE We used to go out on Pico near where we worked at Pendulum. There was a parking lot, an alley, and a porch across the alley. It was wide enough that we could sit down and have our lunch and lay back. We called it our "beach," made a big joke about going to the "beach." We sat down, had lunch, lay back. I was asleep, and I hear this click. There's only one click that sounds like that. I look up and there's a cop standing, spreadeagled, holding his gun with both arms. "Don't move. Neither one of you." I said, "Jesus Christ." I sat up, Ed sits up, scared to death, shaking — he shook all the time, but he's really shaking now. So his partner went around the side of us, his gun out, pointed at our heads. "One more move and you're dead meat." I said, "You guys got the wrong people." I thought, we're writing porno, but by god man, what is this shit? Ed couldn't even talk — he was just a nervous wreck. The cop says, "We got a message there was a break-in at this address." I said, "Do we look like we're fucking breaking in? We're sound asleep here at the beach." {This is no fucking beach, what are you talking about?" So we talked them out of it. Ed could hardly walk. He was a mess. We get back inside, he was white. Ed had been in his women's slacks, angora sweater with a bra, long hair, his little girl play watch with a red band. He started to laugh, he got hysterical, he's crying, he's laughing so fucking hard. "Jesus Christ, Scott, do you realize they didn't say anything about my titties — and I'm wearing a women's sweater."

"ITS KIND OF A GLOW"

She snapped out of her chair, slopped more whiskey into her glass and slugged it down; slopped in another glass full. "You like to drink, dearie?" She slugged that one down too and again refilled the glass."I do. Its kind of a glow you don't get from nothin' else and I ain't one of them bastard creeps that takes dope."

— from *Killer In Drag* by Ed Wood

MONA McKINNON   By 1975, you couldn't reach Ed after six p.m., because he and Kathy would go to sleep by then. In earlier years, he'd drink and call me all hours of the night. He got so he didn't want to take a bath. It got really bad there the last few years before he died. He said, "I'm not even going to have you to my apartment. I'm so ashamed of it. I'll meet you somewhere else." They didn't have any money, but he said, "I'll never go on welfare." He wouldn't do it, he was too proud.

STEVE APOSTOLOF   The poor bastard went to welfare, they wouldn't give him a dime. Because as a writer, that was part of the profession, to be unemployed.

ROY REID   Ed was his own worst enemy. He had vision ... he had ideas. Somewhere along the line he got lost. I told him, "As long as you're drinking, Ed, we can't do business." But he couldn't stop.

ALDO RAY   He always felt that he had to be the host. To have something at the house to drink. That kind of thing. His real big problem was, he would not eat. Maybe he'd go around the corner and get a hamburger and some french fries, that kind of shit. He would not eat properly.

We thought quite a bit alike about life and living, so that almost anything that he might say, I might say. We agreed a lot on ... well, what the hell. well, we're here now, take advantage of now! Because tomorrow may never come. But I'm afraid that that philosophy is also what led him to being a heavy drinker. Fuck it, I'm enjoying my drink, and let me drink!

HARRY THOMAS   Eddie was never tight on the job. He was alert. It was when he got together with some of his booze friends. It was when he was home, and had no phone calls, or somebody saying something derogatory, then he'd sip it ... and hit it. He was the type that let it get the best of him. He was very disappointed in people. You see, he believed in people. And they didn't measure up to what he wanted them to be.

He had a little bit of pity for himself ... remorse. He always lamented the fact that he should have done something that he didn't do. People who were supposed to be his friends — they had no respect for him. They said, "Well, he's a drunk." Eddie said, "They're supposed to be my friends ... who the hell do they think they are? I don't need 'em."

PAUL MARCO   He'd always say, "My God, I've given everything away, I should have a million bucks."

CHARLES ANDERSON   He never drank vodka — it was Brown Royal. He didn't do what you would think someone in this business would do, and buy the cheapest- I think that stuff was 12 or 14 dollars a bottle.

If he was working on a job like at Pendulum, he would start as soon as he got home. That would continue until about the time he would pass out at about 9:30 or 10, and then he would go to sleep wherever it was he passed out, wake up about 4 in the morning, and head immediately for the refrigerator for a big pitcher of Kool-Aid.

JOHN ANDREWS   My pancreas is shot to hell — I had major surgery for it — and Ed Wood was a contributor! Ha ha ha! I really started drinking when I got with Eddie. Jesus Christ! Everything was Imperial whiskey. Big ones. Two a day. Jim Beam? Never. It had to be Imperial straight whiskey, room temperature, with a water chaser. Ice water chaser. He switched to vodka because Ralph's on Highland and Fountain, which was his source of Imperial, went out of business! Ha ha ha ha! So he switched to vodka!

BERNIE BLOOM   A couple of times I had to let him go, 'cause the drinking got too much. And he'd call me up and say, "Pappy, pappy, I need you, I need you." And I said, "Are you straightened out now?" "I've straightened out now, I swear." I said, "Okay, come on back to work."

KATHY WOOD   Eddie wasn't nice when he was drunk.

JOHN ANDREWS   Eddie was a violent drunk. He called me one morning, we talked to each other, three, four times a day. He says, "I nearly killed O'Hara last night. I ... " "Oh no. What happened now?" He says, "She was mouthing off in the kitchen, and she wouldn't shut up, I told her to shut up, and I told her to shut up, and finally I went in there and I let her have it." And — he knocked her cold.

CONRAD BROOKS   Ed would go to the extremes. It depressed me because I didn't want to see a friend of mine wasted away on that stuff. He would be talking to me and just black out. I was his drinking buddy, I'm what you call a good drinker but Eddie couldn't handle his booze. If you're going to drink, you're supposed to sip on the booze. But Ed would take a straight shot, or a double shot, and straight. With a water chaser.

BLANCHE BLOOM   Every time he tried to stop drinking, he told me "I'd go on the wagon and I'd go home and she'd have a bottle, she'd offer me a drink, and then I'd be back on the booze again." Then they'd go into hiding and would be drinking for weeks at a time.

JOHN ANDREWS   One day Ed called me, "John-John." I was either John-John or Old Father. "Hey Old Father, you fuckhead, what are you doing! — you shitbird —

get over here! Kenne's coming over, can you bring a bottle of Imperial? I am without funds." Kenne was there when I walked in, he was saying, "Ed, you've destroyed yourself. You've wrecked your career. Look at Kathy. Look at you. Look at this dump." And it wasn't that bad a place. I didn't like that. I said, "What do you think caused all this, Kenne?" He said, "That stuff you brought." But I noticed he took his share of it without being forced.

STEVE APOSTOLOF   He was a proud man. He knew what he was becoming. He knew what was happening. I spoke with him and he agreed to stop. And then he'd say, "O'Hara is as drunk as a skunk." And when she gets drunk, she starts screaming at him, and then Eddie starts ...

KATHY WOOD   Tor gave Eddie a life mask of himself as Lobo from *Bride of the Monster*. Eddie gave it away. Eddie gave everything away.

JOHN ANDREWS   When they would move to a new house, they would go to the liquor store, one of them, to establish credit. Kathy would say, "I wonder if you have any of my husband's books." She would con her way into credit. I mean it was just this constant, constant put on. It was just this constant rip-off. Not paying rent. Not paying tabs.

BUDDY HYDE   Eddie was the kind of a guy, if you needed a hundred bucks, he'd go, "Here." And he might have needed it more than the person who was asking for it. Kathy would go, "Eddie, why did you do a damn fool thing like that?" "Because I wanted to!"

KATHY WOOD   Eddie was so gullible that I was in constant turmoil. Because he was always getting screwed up by some cheap bastard. Eddie was a big dumb nut when it came to handling money.

CHARLES ANDERSON   I would get listings of movies for sale, and sometimes I would show it to him, and he would say, "Oh, this is mine! I made this." And he wished he had the money to buy the prints.

KATHY WOOD   With Steve Apostolof Eddie thought he was writing for a little bit of money — he didn't know he was writing for nothing! He never knew what he would be getting, and he had to beg for the pittance that he got. And sometimes the pittance was a check that would bounce! My God almighty you can't imagine what a horror that was, what a horror. And the whole thing went around and around and around ...

STEVE APOSTOLOF   He had no conception of money. Money, no conception. He was always broke. Always. No matter what, I was always good for a hundred bucks. Eddie didn't want a bank account — he pays this week's rent, he has the booze for the weekend, well, drop the bomb tomorrow, who cares! The two houses they bought was because I gave a phony letter to Eddie, how much he made. They were evicted because they didn't pay the rent. They had so little money, and they were boozing it up like the dickens.

With me and Kathy, it used to be a love/hate relationship. I'll come one day, "Oh, Steve, excuse the dirty house." Shit, the house was always dirty. The last time I talked with her — "You goddamn son of a bitch, you're taking advantage of Eddie, you don't pay him enough, you ... " She said this many times. Eddie said, "Ah, Kathy, shut up!"

DAVID WARD   Things really got bad for him when he moved to Hollywood, to this place on Yucca. That was a dive.

KATHY WOOD   Betty Woods was the manager when we first moved into that god forsaken apartment building on Yucca. She wanted Eddie to write her a screenplay, in return for which we would get free rent. So he did.

PAUL MARCO   There was a run of people, in and out, I would always run into John Agar, Aldo Ray, Duke Moore. It was a nice little building, then all of a sudden a 7-11 came in, and it became quite a hustler place. It got so bad out there they had to close the bar out in the Lido Hotel. And Ed got stuck there, really. Or couldn't afford to move out.

KATHY WOOD   At first, on Yucca Street, there were a bunch of racetrack people, a couple of hookers — nice and interesting people, it was exciting. The scene was sort of like Damon Runyon.

NONA CARVER   On a couple of hot nights, I wanted to get out of the apartment, so I went up to the dump on Yucca. The place was just horrible. Somebody would bring a bottle in, and, before you know it, everybody in the building, like a bunch of chickens running for the corn, would be knocking on the door for a drink. I said, "how do they know?" Ed said, "I don't know, they just smell it." Before you know it, you had all these strangers on the mooch to drink. Ed and Kathy must have been hurting pretty bad at the time. I went there one time, and they had nothing to eat all day. They thought David Ward was bringing something to eat. He didn't show up, so I went up to the corner and bought 10 or 12 dollars of bacon and eggs, groceries and stuff.

CHARLES ANDERSON   It was the kind of place, when you walked in, you just had the feeling, this creeping feeling all over, that you might not even survive this walk down this hallway.

JOHN ANDREWS   You know what we used to call it? Yucca Flats! "Where ya gonna be tonight?" "Well meet me over at Yucca Flats." Okay. I rented a room there for myself once, from a black guy, black as the ace of spades. His name? John Andrews.

KATHY WOOD   Florence [Dolder] was a good friend in those days, they lived right across the hall, she and her daughter. She tried to help us move out of Yucca. But

Eddie was, by that time, kind of going down the drain. But Aldo Ray, John Agar, Ed and myself, the four of us ... we used to go on some real hoots ...

ALDO RAY   I used to go over to that real raunchy place at Yucca and Cahuenga, and sometimes, Jesus, the doors would be bolted because the cops had raided the next door neighbors, and half the time he'd answer the door in his underwear, and well, we'd sit down, start talking, and who was going to finance this, and finance that, you know, filmwise, who's gonna pay for the script and all this bullshit, but we just happened not to have ever got anything off the ground.

When I went over to Ed's, I must say, it was always pleasant, always positive. He was a perennial, perpetual optimist. Yeah. I guess that's why I didn't mind dropping in in that zone, that den of iniquity. The thing is, like I say, the goddamn doors were bolted and everything else, oh Jesus. Robberies on one side or the other, they'd even try to break into his place with the goddamn chain on the door. Whenever I walked in, it seemed to be like a feeling of relief because, as long as I'm there, nothing happens. There's an aura about a so-called person of my position, an aura that, automatically — ptoom! Deflates tension, or whatever the hell it is. It's one of those things. I used to be a cop, years ago, a constable. And people, when they see me, they figure, he's a Marine, he's a killer.

PHIL CAMBRIDGE   Bernie would pay him on Friday, and Ed would shuffle home in his terrible little slippers. He would go down to Pla-Boy liquor, they would cash his check because he would buy the weekend's liquor. Five or six bottles. Ed would buy his liquor, step outside, and always, a couple of black guys would grab him and say, "Alright, what do ya got?" And rather than get beaten up, he would give them all his money. Every weekend. I'd say, "Well, why do you do it, Ed?" He'd say, "Well, what can I do?" I said, "Leave some of the money with the store keeper until the next time you go." He said, "Yeah, that's an idea." So then he would start leaving 20 or 40 bucks in his pocket and the rest, a hundred bucks, he'd leave with the liquor store owner. And the guys wouldn't get all his money.

BUDDY HYDE   John Agar and Eddie had been drinking. Ed called me. "Bud, we're over here, we're a little low on funds, we need a bottle. Can you lend me twenty bucks?" I said, "Sure, but can you come over, I have some people here." So they came by, a guest took a picture of us in my front yard. I gave Eddie the twenty and off he took!

JOHN AGAR   I met Ed through a fellow by the name of Baron Von Brenner. John Von Brenner was a hypnotist. Ed and I weren't buddy-buddy, but I would stop over occasionally and say hi. I was at that Yucca Street place just once. He and his wife, and they were having such a rough time, and I went over there one afternoon. It was too depressing for me ... very depressing.

DAVID WARD   There would be dog shit, right in the halls, loud music, yelling. I met John Agar there. I shook his hand, and the guy marvelled at my handshake. For

Right: John Agar, Ed Wood,
Buddy Hyde, 1977

Below: The apartment building
at Yucca and Cahuenga

five minutes that's all he talked about. The handshake. Eddie told me this story; He and John Agar were drinking together, watching the news on tv, and they had John Agar's obituary.

JOHN AGAR   It was ABC. That's a true story. Ed said, "You're not dead, and I'm gonna tell 'em!" I told him, "Forget it, I don't care what they say." Well, Ed called up the television station and said that I hadn't died, that I was sitting right there with him, and I went in the next day, and they put me on the air.

JOHN ANDREWS   When he was at "Yucca Flats," he called me, and he said, "John-John! You gotta come over here! You gotta help me! These niggers are trying to steal my typewriter!" I said, "They don't want your typewriter. What are they going to do with it? And how are they going to walk down the street with it? What are they going to get, 20 dollars?" He kept it on the table in front of him and it was usually busy. He was a prolific writer. He said, "You gotta come down and spend the night here—they're gonna kill me!" So I went up there, and he says, "John-John, sleep on the floor tonight, when they get here, I'll wake you up." So I said, "Yeah, okay." It was early a.m., way before sunrise, and he's waking me up ... and he's in drag. He's got this fucking negligee on, and he's got a baseball bat in his hands. He's kicking me by this time, "Get up, get up." He's looking out the kitchen window, and there's two spooks out there: and he says, "That's them! That's them! There they are! John, lure them in here — I'll beat 'em up with this bat!" And he's in a pink negligee! "No, man, no, I'm going to call the cops." I call the L.A.P.D. — "Listen, there's a couple of guys trying to break in ... " And there's a helicopter over us, and the light's shining down, and all this shit. And Kathy's yelling, "Oh these fucking niggers!" He turns the bat on her, "Shut up! Shut up!" I said, "Please, Kathy, my god, I mean our lives are at stake."

So two cops come to Eddie's door. Eddie's door had a bullet hole in it the size of a quarter. One of the cops said they robbed a store down on Cahuenga, and the chopper reported to us where they were, they've been taken away." And he said to Eddie, "So your typewriter isn't in any danger, sir." And he's standing there in this pink nightgown, it was a Pegnoir set, it was like a slip — he looked like Audrey Hepburn, *Breakfast At Tiffany's.*

SHANNON DOLDER   If there was noise in the hallway, Kathy would yell out, "Shut up, you motherfuckin' niggers!" I thought, man, they're going to kill her. And she was always doing that when they would walk by the windows — "I don't want no nigger trash walking by my window!"

FLORENCE DOLDER   One night, there was terrible screams in the hall. When those screams started, Eddie pounded on my door and said, "Don't come out, lock your door, don't call the police, don't do anything." There was a drag queen and some men, I don't know who they were, how many or what, but they beat him to death in the hall. As drunk as he was, Ed thought enough of us to warn us, because as witnesses, we could have been killed, that's what Eddie said later.

This girl upstairs was renting out her one child, a girl, to porno movies. She was about four or five. The mind went — you could see it. And then she said she had to put her away because she wasn't right in the head. Eddie called up and reported it. He was furious.

SHANNON DOLDER   It was a pretty exciting building. The building next door was even worse. And the cops used to have shoot-outs. And our apartment, was right next to it. So the cops would yell, "Get on the floor."

So you'd sit on the floor and watch T.V. while they had the shoot-outs. The first time we got scared, but we got used to it. This happened all the time ...

Two prostitutes were murdered in the Hollywood 8 Motel, right around the corner on Cahuenga, on the other side of the 7-11. Eddie and Kathy did tell us they heard screaming, but they thought it was the typical thing of a pimp beating up one of his girls.

KATHY WOOD   Most of the time we would have bottles delivered. Once in a while Eddie would get brave and go down to the store. I would sit there with baited breath waiting for him to get back.

DAVID WARD   I drove him down to Pla-Boy Liquor one time ... he had the shakes. Toward the end, when he hadn't had his booze, he would get the shakes ...

OTTO DOBROWSKI   Yeah, he would come in here just about every day. He'd get the pint bottle of Popov vodka, the lower priced vodka. Or Gallo Port, the small $1.85 half pint bottle. Usually when they hit that it's about the end of the line. Before that, we delivered to his house. He would order the bigger bottles then. That's when he had money in his pocket. Sometimes he would come in here with people who didn't have any money, pretty much under the influence.

I remember his saying to me, "I used to direct movies, and I still can go out and do it." I told him, "Oh sure you can. Why don't you just take it easy and you'll be fine."

KATHY WOOD   One time, somebody broke down our door ... and I happened to be standing in the way. The door was off its hinges for a day or so. It was all confusion ... violence and confusion ...

SHANNON DOLDER   Ed decided he was going to make me a big movie star. He thought I had talent to do something. And he was going to do this movie about the Venus de Milo's lost arms, what happened to her arms. We were supposed to film it over in Greece and he told me to get the passport. I think I was supposed to have been the model for Venus de Milo.

He took me down to this agent on Melrose, he got all dressed up in a suit and everything, and the agent liked me. My brother would not give me the money to get the passport, because he said, "There's not going to be any movie." I truly believed that there would. It didn't work out. He got sick. I don't think it was like a pipe dream, but maybe his health, maybe a backer dropped out. I was very flattered he wanted to have me in it.

JOHN ANDREWS   When Kathy was angry at him, which was most of the time, she would call him Wood. "Look, Wood, don't you give me any shit," He would go into the kitchen and pour this big glass of ice water and he would stand in front of her and say, "You'd better shut up, O'Hara. You're gonna get it. You'd better shut up!" "Oh, fuck you!" And he'd throw the ice water in her face! And it was just something every day. Criswell told me one time, "You know ... I've always had the feeling ... one would kill the other. And if you were there ... the killer would say you did it!" I told that to Mike Angel, good actor, good writer. He said, "Do you know I've always had that feeling? One has to kill the other. It's just a question of who gets who first."

SHANNON DOLDER   They'd fight over who lost the bottle of liquor, who left the refrigerator door open. I never heard any fights about anything that made any sense. And Kathy had a vile mouth on her ... really filthy mouth, every vulgar word you could think of she'd say to him, and he'd turn it right back on her, then they'd realize what they were doing and they'd make up. There was something they did I used to think was cute. They only had one pack of cigarettes, and they'd share the pack. She'd ask him for a cigarette, even if they were fighting, "Give me a cigarette, you old bastard." He'd light it for her, and then he'd continue yelling.

DAVID WARD   When they'd start fighting, oh boy, you should have heard the *names* they'd call each other. And then Eddie would take Kathy's head and bang it against the wall! Then she'd be quiet for a while.

KATHY WOOD   We were fighting one time. He dragged me over the floor for a couple of minutes, and my left hand, it's pretty well gone now, it doesn't go straight out. It's not Eddie's fault, but it's half his fault ...

FLORENCE DOLDER   When he'd leave Kathy, he'd leave with his typewriter and scripts under his arm. Well, supposedly he'd leave. He'd go out in the back and scream at the window at her. I think what was killing him was writing porno. He was too good for porno. And I think it was eating away at him. Eddie was a gentleman, he was brilliant, very brilliant. And very very witty. And then, the porno bit. Like sometimes I'd go over and he'd be sitting in his chair, and just looking out the window, and say, "I've got to get out of this. I've got to get out of this." You could hear him and Kathy fight about it. "I'm not going out there to write this ... this crap. I'm not going to write it." And then — "Well how the hell are ya gonna pay the rent and eat?" We'd just turn up the television. One time, he came out of the 7-11 with this bottle. He said, "You know, this helps me write, when I have to write, to pay for the groceries. I feel like taking them and throwing them on the sidewalk and just keep walking." "Where would you walk to, Eddie?" "I don't know, I'd just keep walking."

PHIL CAMBRIDGE   By the time that five o'clock rolled around [at the office at Pendulum], Ed'd be swishing down the halls, carrying on a mile a minute. Bernie

Bloom put his foot down and told me, "Phil, when you pick Ed up tomorrow morning, if he's drunk, you leave him home and say, 'No, Ed, not today.'" When I'd go pick Ed up in the morning, he'd be waiting for me, shivering all over like he was going to fall apart. I wanted to get him a drink or something, but he said, "No, no, I'll be alright." It finally dawned on me; he'd be drinking before he got in the car, and I just couldn't smell it on him. By the time we'd get to Santa Monica, he'd be drunk.

JOHN ANDREWS   At the end, Ed totally lost his mind. Completely. Just flat-ass lost his mind.

Delusions. Illusions. Paranoia. I'm alcoholic, all alkies are paranoid. All alcoholics. But at the end, he was not the Ed Wood I fell in love with, so to speak. I'm not talking homosexual: Eddie and I just dearly loved each other. Dearly, dearly. And we were on the phone three or four times a day.

Towards the end, he became someone else. The dark side came out. If he saw a shadow he'd hide under the bed.

Eddie wrote a horror script that would have been fine for 1934 but not 1974. So he sends it to the story department of Universal Pictures. Three days later, they send him the script back with the standard "It's not bad but we're not in that market now." A polite kiss-off. So I go to Yucca Flats to see him, he opens the door and says, "Come in here! Benedict Arnold! You fucked me up! You've ruined me!" I said, "Who ... did ... what?" He says, "You called Universal. You killed my deal." There was never a deal. Eddie really got out of it, man. I mean, out of it. Between the booze, the hallucinations, the self-grandiosity, the disappointments, the heartbreak. He was heartbroken but he wouldn't admit it.

BERNIE BLOOM   I tried to keep him as busy as possible, because the harder he worked, the less he had time to drink, and get himself in trouble. Sometimes I'd catch him — he'd have it in a Coca-Cola bottle, he'd have it in a coffee container. Vodka. He drank vodka because it didn't smell ... you can't tell on the breath. But I knew Ed well enough that I could tell when he was drinking and when he wasn't drinking.

KATHY WOOD   Over the years Eddie bounced back and forth between Bernie Bloom and Steve Apostolof like a ping pong ball. I hated when Steve would try to get Eddie away from Bernie — "We're gonna make another picture Pappy, come on Eddie, come on Pappy." How many times did I plead with Ed to stay with Bernie and a regular guaranteed paycheck. You know, Bernie did love Eddie in a way, and I know Eddie loved Bernie. He tested Bernie too many times. Eddie was such a kid in a way. When Bernie fired him, it broke his heart.

DON FELLMAN   In the course of a phone conversation he said, in a lamenting voice, "I was ... good looking ... I had a beautiful wife ... *look what I got now!*" Then, in the background, I could hear Kathy: "Oh, shut up!" When I asked what he was doing, he said he was "cleaning the pool and washing the limousine."

KATHY WOOD   Dudley Manlove was the last one who really tried to help Eddie.

He showed up at our place, before we got kicked out, with his beautiful big white Cadillac. He stood in the doorway of that hovel — "Come on, Woody, let's go to the Veteran's hospital." But he wouldn't do it.

> They would be remembered for a moment then would be forgotten as if they had never walked the earth.
>
> — from *Parisian Passions,* by Edw. D. Wood, Jr

VALDA HANSEN   He was actually preoccupied with death ... He used to phone me at midnight, 1 o'clock in the morning. He says, "I want to talk about death. Death." So he used to tell me the most way-out things! When a person dies, and how, maybe their heart stops, but the organs in them are still living. And he'd say, "You know, just because you think you're dead, you're not dead!" And oh my God, he'd go on and on.

MAILA NURMI   He was too heartfelt a man, you know what happens to people who are too heartfelt, most of them kick the bucket that way.

KATHY WOOD   Ed loved that damned song, "Amazing Grace." It kind of hit him, somehow. And he wrote that book, *Saving Grace.* It was written when he was getting more and more depressed.

They say that people, when they feel they're going to die, that they get kind of religious, and Eddie, something kind of happened to him, I don't know what it was, but he wrote this crazy book. And I felt kind of strange about it, like a chill up my spine.

PHIL CAMBRIDGE   Someone back East was having an "Ed Wood Day" and were going to show his films, and when he got that letter, he was just ... thrilled. I mean, he brought it into work, and he read it to me twice, and said, "You read it!" I read it. He said, "Isn't that nice that somebody remembers me, that someone thinks of me." And Ed Wood, to me, had always been this old drunk who wrote porn.

ED WOOD   (From a letter to Richard Bojarski, dated March 18, 1978)

> My plans other than here with my publishing firm is to make a film this summer called "The Day the Mummies Danced." This I hope to shoot in Mexico where the actual mummies are in a cave as a big tourist attraction. But of course I will make a horror film out of it. I started the book some years ago, but got side tracked. Now with the horror pictures being on the uprise again, I feel this might be the vehicle to put me back in the field. The stars I have in mind, who are great drinking buddies with me will be, John Agar, Aldo Ray and the fellow who played Eros in "Plan 9 from Outer Space", Dudley Manlove, who, by the way, is putting up much of the cash for the venture.
>
> My script, "I Awoke Early The Day I Died", looks like also a summer production, but to be shot in Norway. I doubt very much if I will go there

as there is too much on the fire here ... This is the entirely silent movie about the last three days in the life of a madman. Aldo Ray wants to do it so bad he could bite his tongue. The commitments are piling up steadily, one of the reasons I want to get moved, there's too many screaming kids in the place since the new owners took over ... all Mexicans, none who speak English ... even pidgeon-English ...

RICHARD BOJARSKI   I entered the apartment, introduced myself, and he was very friendly. It was hot and stifling in that apartment and he was lying flat on his back. He offered me a drink, and we both started drinking. I was asking him about Bela, which was the reason I went out there, and he gave me a few standard answers to a few standard questions. Eventually, a stranger came in and exchanged some friendly insults with Ed Wood, threw down a few dollars on the coffee table. After he left, Ed resumed drinking and brought out a 16mm print of *Plan 9 from Outer Space*. I think he was going to offer it to me for sale, but I didn't push the conversation in that direction. His wife opened a can of spaghetti and warmed it up on the stove. He did say, "It's tough for a guy to make a living in L.A., I should have gone to Oregon. Or Colorado." He said he could make a better living out there, I didn't know what he was talking about.

I kept on drinking, and I was really getting drunk. I soon found myself very sick, crawling on my hands and knees to the bathroom, that's how sick I was. I heard his wife say, "Dick, why did you drink all that booze, you didn't leave any for me and Ed."

KATHY WOOD   He hocked his typewriter to get money for booze ... so many times, we had to do it. Most of the times we got it back. He loved his IBM Executive. It was a big son-of-a-bitch, and it was so beautiful. And we both were so fast on it. It was a great big heavy thing, an office typewriter, it took about half the desk. We carted it around with us for years. When we had money, we'd have it in our house. When we needed money, we'd hock it. I can't tell you the last time, but it was ... a bad day. It was a very sad day when we lost that typewriter.

DUDLEY MANLOVE   He called and said, "I'm writing dirty books and I don't have a typewriter. I pawned my typewriter to buy some liquor, and I can't get it out of hock. Do you have an extra typewriter?" I said, "Well hell yes," I had an upright Underwood, a Smith-Corona portable. I took three typewriters down there, and I thought, well, for God's sake get to work now, if you're gonna make a buck, you've got three typewriters to work on. I think he took the Underwood to the liquor store and traded it for a bottle of booze. This was toward the very end ... of his demise. It was a horrible, horrible ending, and something which is heart-wrenching when I even think about it.

KATHY WOOD   About two or three months, maybe a month before he died, he'd sleep upstairs at Bernie's, and he got ticks. Ticks — on his neck.

FLORENCE DOLDER   Bernie Bloom said Eddie had to go out to Santa Monica for his paycheck. Eddie said to me, "I'll give you 10 dollars if you drive me out." He was getting awfully, awfully white. The color was like maybe somebody had been in prison for years and years in solitary. A terrible color. I asked him to go to the doctor and he wouldn't. When he came out of Bernie Bloom's his head was bent. He said Bernie got rid of him.

DUDLEY MANLOVE   Ed called me one night and said, "Look old buddy, I want to borrow five dollars." And I said, "Why, Ed?" He said, "Well, Kathy and I don't have any food in the apartment, and we're hungry." I said, "Don't you worry your bloody head about it, I'll bring you more damn food than you can eat in the next 30 days." He says, "No, don't do that. I'm asking for the money, not the food." So I knew what he wanted the money for. I said, "Look, if you're hungry, I will store your house with more food than you can eat in a month. But I'm not going to give you money to go out and buy alcohol, Ed. Do you understand? Am I coming across? Is this loud and clear? You're not getting money to go out and buy booze." He said, "I thought you were a friend." And he hung up.

HARRY THOMAS   He called me about a week before he died. He said he was moving. We reminisced a little bit about the house that he had in the Valley, and the parties we had over there. And I said, "Gee, Eddie, I hope you get something like that again." He said, "I've got some books, I'm typing some stories."

I think he would call whoever was home ... whoever would listen to him and talk to him late at night.

Ed Wood's last manuscript, 1978.

[courtesy Kathy Wood]

He Stared Into a Starless Space

FLORENCE DOLDER   Eddie had a mind that wouldn't move once he made up his mind. No, they weren't going to take his things and put him out because his wife was sick. The landlord said he wanted them out of there, the fights were horrible. Eddie went down with the cash, the landlord wouldn't take it. I told him, "Eddie, what you do, you write a check, and on the back of it 'payment towards rent.' And if they refuse it, you don't have any problem." When he left here, he said he would go to the bank and get a certified check. He was not drunk. He was scared. So, instead, he spent the money, he and Kathy had a real good ball.

A couple of days later, he and Kathy had a fight, andhe called me up, said he wanted "to throw the bitch out into the street." We got to talking, "Did you get a receipt from the landlord?" He said, "I wasn't going to give that fucking Mexican, this spic." "Oh, Jesus, Eddie, they're going to throw you—" "Oh, no they're not. No they're not. We're sick people. I'm well known in Hollywood, I've got all kinds of friends." He could never believe that it would happen again. Not out of that place.

DAVID WARD   About a week before he was evicted, he gave me a box of his paperback novels for safekeeping. He knew it was coming ...

KATHY WOOD   Eddie must have known, had some sort of premonition, about dying. A week or so before it all happened, he took the dogs, Casey and McGinty, out to the kennel.

PHIL CAMBRIDGE   Things got worse in the building. Ed was, in those last few weeks, deathly afraid that someone was going to break in and kill them both. There was somebody who didn't like somebody next door, there had been gunshots, some guy came down the hall and kicked in two or three doors, and then came and pounded on Ed's door. Ed and Kathy lay on the other side, dresser up against the door and said, "Go away — we have nothing, leave us alone, we have nothing!" They were trying to get the tenants out; it had become a dope-drug hangout on that floor.

Then one day he called me up, "Phil, there's something wrong with my legs, I can't walk." I said, "Get to a hospital, Ed." I was on my way to work, and in my mind it was more important to go see Bernie. He said, "Yeah, yeah, that's what I'll do. I'll go to the hospital."

KATHY WOOD   Eddie had been sick on and off ever since he lost his job. He had pains in his legs, his chest, he was getting sicker and sicker. There were a lot of clandestine things going on, the landlord was pulling a dope deal, and we knew it. If I had control of my faculties, I would have put my foot down, I would have called City Hall, I wouldn't have allowed them to move Eddie. But I was so worried about him, I was so broken apart, it was terrible, I had no fight left in me. That's why they gave us the bum's rush.

It was about nine in the morning, Eddie had been up about an hour, he was sick, lying on the couch. But the horror of it all, opening the door and these two marshals standing there in their uniforms. We weren't expecting them. Eddie showed the marshals the check, and he said he had the cash. He told them that they wouldn't accept our money, they wanted us out. I tried to tell the sheriff that Eddie was sick, that he shouldn't be moved. But they were so nasty, they made us go and weren't going to let us take anything out. Then we protested, and they let us go back in and grab some things. But we weren't thinking straight, it happened so quickly, it was like a nightmare. At nine in the morning you're not ready for anything. I don't think Eddie even had his socks on. It was cold that morning. He had his things all scattered around. They allowed us one suitcase. Ed had this handwritten manuscript on Bela Lugosi that was almost finished. It was called *Lugosi: Post Mortem*. It was funny, oh God it was funny. It may have kept him alive just to have that one book. It broke Eddie's heart to leave that behind. Eddie's files, papers, scrapbooks, it was all lost.

FLORENCE DOLDER   Eddie used to say that if there was a fire that was what he was going to grab — the Lugosi book and his typewriter. And we used to kid him, what are you going to do with Kathy? "She can follow me."

KATHY WOOD   One thing he did take was one of the last scripts he wrote, one he really loved, *I Woke Up Early the Day I Died*. And this one angora sweater that he loved so much.

FLORENCE DOLDER   There was a kid that lived upstairs, he saw me on Selma one day. He said, "Hey, you know that loud couple at the end of the hall? They got rid of them. Yeah, he put up an awful fight, I thought they were going to arrest him."

The witnesses said that Eddie couldn't believe it. First he yelled, he was screaming he had all kinds of contacts in Hollywood, then he got real nice, begging for a couple more hours to call up people. The sheriff said he was sorry, it had to be. Kathy was out there, screaming, calling the sheriff every name in the book, they told her they were going to arrest her if she didn't shut up.

One of the women told me that he finally slumped down when he realized he was really going. That he slumped down in the hallway, against the wall, and just sat there and cried.

He called everybody he knew and they all turned him down. He had nobody. Now, when they went over to Peter's, the drinking was heavy. Very, very heavy....

PETER COE   He called me just about Christmas time, and he said, "I'm in trouble. They took all my possessions, we are hungry, I have no place to go." And I told him, "Don't worry about it, I'll put you up for as long as you need it."

The first thing he put his arms around me, and he said, "Oh God love you, you're a real, dear, dear friend, and I won't forget what you have done for me and Kathy." And we bullshitted, and he made some telephone calls, calling friends. It was the holiday season, and we were all happy, I guess. And then we began to drink. He kept asking me if I would be interested in doing that movie about Bela Lugosi.

FLORENCE DOLDER   Even though Peter drank, with those two, the empty bucket never filled. Eddie lay in the bed, in his little outfit, refusing to get up. Kathy was on Peter's couch, throwing up ... Peter called me and said, "What am I going to do with these people?" I told him to take Eddie down to the welfare office. Peter said, "Well, would you come with us, because Eddie will listen to you." I made the arrangements but Eddie wouldn't get out of bed that day. He would not get out of bed. He would not go on welfare — he was a director, a veteran, etcetera, and refused to go. Peter screamed, "Well, what are you going to do? You have no money!" But Eddie wouldn't budge.

ALDO RAY   I was really shocked when I found out how he got killed. What I heard was, he was with this guy, who was a wild, wild character, a stuntman or whatever that lived over near Hughes Market. They were both drinking pretty heavy. Now this is what I heard, this is my version of Ed Wood's death: They were gassed going down La Brea, and the cops were chasing them because the guy was weaving and everything, and the guy was trying to outrun them and made a left turn on Exposition Boulevard, way out where La Brea, toward the airport. And they made a left turn and the guy was going so fast, trying to escape the cops, that they slammed into a telephone pole and it killed them both.

LILLIAN WOOD   I wished I knew just what he died with besides a heart attack. I have an idea of something else but I don't dare to say it out ... I don't want to say, but, I don't know, it's one of those things that's had me upset, not knowing what happened.

PETER COE   Kathy came and said, "You know, I don't think Eddie's feeling too good." I asked Ed, "Are you feeling good? You're drinking too goddamn much." He was drinking vodka straight, triple, quadruple shots like crazy. I said, "Ed, it's going to kill you. On Monday, I am going to take you to the hospital. I am going to take you if I have to beat the shit out of you and drag you! I want you to be examined." And then on Sunday, we woke up to get some breakfast, and the first thing he wanted was a double shot of vodka. And I said, "Ed, don't! Don't! We are going to see the doctors tomorrow at the Veteran's hospital." So he said, "Well, can I go into your bedroom and watch the football game with you?" I said, "Of course. Why not?" I started to cook spaghetti and watch the game. He had that one double shot of vodka. When that was gone, he said, "Peter, please give me another one." I said, "Eddie, this is the last one, because I want you to be sober, otherwise they won't even admit you." And he said, "Okay, okay, I promise." He had another shot of vodka around 10:30, 11 o'clock, and he said, "I feel sick." I told him to lay down. I think the four shots of vodka put him back to sleep again; I didn't pay any attention. Some friends of ours came over. And this old lady, Beulah Ames, who was a nurse said, "Where's Eddie?" I told her, "Ed's in the bedroom, resting."

KATHY WOOD   Eddie didn't like football. When he went into Peter's bedroom he had just cussed me out, he said, "Kathy, get me another drink." At the very last I heard him screaming, "Kathy, I can't breathe." I just ignored him. I ignored it.

Because he was always ... telling me what to do. And that's when I said to Beulah, "Why don't you go and see how he's doing."

PETER COE   Beulah comes out of the bedroom: "Ooooooooooh! My God! Eddie's dead!" I said, "What?" I just couldn't believe it. It just struck me like something absolutely impossible, incredible.

KATHY WOOD   I still remember when I went into that room that afternoon and he was dead, his eyes were wide open. As long as I live, I'll never forget the look in his eyes. He had this awful expression. It was an awful, awful look in his eyes. He clutched at the sheets. It looked like he'd seen hell. What do you suppose he saw in those last few moments? What do you suppose he saw?

PETER COE   I remember them taking his body out in a garbage bag. It made me sick.

STEVE APOSTOLOF   In his book, *Death of a Transvestite,* I think Ed described his own funeral. I had a sneaky feeling that maybe he didn't want anybody to be at his funeral. Because, even if he was cremated, they dress you, and he wanted to be dressed as a bride.

KATHY WOOD   He may have wanted to be buried in drag, or he may not have wanted to, but he never said it to me. I just know one thing: he didn't want to be buried ... he had a horror of the thought of being under the ground.

(Criswell, Paul Marco and Steve, Buddy Hyde, David Ward were present at the memorial service. David De Mering officiated. Edward D. Wood, Jr. was cremated at the Utter-McKinley mortuary; his ashes were scattered at sea.)

FLORENCE DOLDER   It wasn't the liquor that gave him the heart attack — it was his pride.

VALDA HANSEN   Inside, he suffered. But he never showed it. I've seen him suffer to the point of just.... Even Kathy said, "I feel so sorry for him, Valda." She said, "There's nights when he just can't sleep. Nights upon nights. He's like a lost being on this earth. He doesn't belong here ... it's like he's visiting. But he doesn't belong here."

Ed Wood, age 53, taken three months before death.

7B-158190	CERTIFICATE OF DEATH STATE OF CALIFORNIA	0190-055284

Edward Davis Wood Jr. — December 10, 1978 — 1403

Male — White — 9 — October 10, 1924 — 54 YEARS

New York — Edward Wood Sr., New York — Unknown, Unknown

United States — 090-16-1719 — Married — Kathleen Everett

Writer-Producer — 30 — Self Employed — Movie Industry

5636 Laurel Canyon Blvd — Apt 4 — North Hollywood

Los Angeles — California — Kathleen Wood — Wife

Home — Los Angeles — 5636 Laurel Canyon Blvd apt 4

5636 Laurel Canyon Blvd — North Hollywood — North Hollywood, California

(A) ARTERIOSCLEROTIC CARDIO VASCULAR DISEASE — 78-15360

NO

NO

NO

THOMAS T. NOGUCHI, M.D., CORONER — 104 N. MISSION RD., LOS ANGELES, CALIF. 90033 — 12-11-78

Cremation — 12-18-78 — Memory Gardens Crematory, 455 W. Central Ave., Brea, California — 3140

Utter McKinley Van Nuys — DEC 15 1978

7 — X — 4124

Biographical Notes

(The following notes are about the people who speak in the book. Those individuals who wished to retain anonymity and whose names in the text were pseudonymous, will not be listed in this section.)

FORREST J. ACKERMAN   World's foremost collector of fantastic fiction and film memorabilia. Edited *Famous Monsters of Filmland* magazine from 1958 to 1984.

JOHN AGAR   Actor. Films include: *Fort Apache, Sands of Iwo Jima, The Brain from Planet Arous, The Mole People, Curse of the Swamp Creature.*

TED ALLAN   Cinematogapher and reknowned Hollywood still photographer. He was the original cameraman on *Bride of the Monster* and was to have produced an Ed Wood created television series for Bela Lugosi, *Dr. Acula.*

CHARLES ANDERSON   Writer and editor who worked with Ed Wood at Pendulum Publications in the 1970's.

JOHN ANDREWS   "I'm currently at liberty — still on my feet — and I raise hell every day." Friend of Ed Wood's whose acting credits include: *Orgy of the Dead, Suburbia Confidential, Movie Star, American Style, or, LSD, I Hate You!*

CARL ANTHONY (CARL WUCO)   Played Patrolman Larry in *Plan 9 from Outer Space* and the smut film director Johnny Ryde in *The Sinister Urge.*

STEVE APOSTOLOF (A. C. STEPHEN)   Producer-director. Films include: *Journey to Freedom, Orgy of the Dead, The Divorcee, Class Reunion, Hot Ice, Suburbia Confidential, College Girls, Lady Godiva Rides, Fugitive Girls.*

SAMUEL Z. ARKOFF   Co-founder, with James H. Nicholson, of American International Pictures. Currently heads Arkoff-International Pictures.

RONNIE ASHCROFT   Director, producer and sound-effects editor. Credits include *The Astounding She Monster, Girl With an Itch, Mr. Peek-A-Boo's Playmates (Like Wow!).* Assistant director on *Night of the Ghouls.* Died after a long illness in December, 1988.

HENRY BEDERSKI   Bit player in Ed Wood movies "whenever he could get away from the bakery." Also appeared in the John Waters films *Female Trouble* and *Polyester.* Wrote "Stars Over Hollywood" column for the *Los Angeles Herald Dispatch.*

BERNIE BLOOM   Publisher, Pendulum/Gallery Publications. Died April, 1986.

BLANCHE BLOOM   Widow of Bernie Bloom.

RICHARD BOJARSKI   Writer/cartoonist. Books: *The Films of Boris Karloff; The Films of Bela Lugosi.*

JOHN "BUNNY" BRECKINRIDGE   Played "The Ruler" in *Plan 9 From Outer Space*. "I am writing my memoirs. It's called *My Shadow As I Pass.*"

CONRAD BROOKS   Played small roles in several Wood pictures. Recent credits: *A Polish Vampire in Burbank, Vampire at Midnight, Death Row Game Show.*

EWING "LUCKY" BROWN   is a motion picture editor based in Hollywood.

BOB BURNS   Special effects and make-up artist; assistant to Paul Blaisdell on *Invasion of the Saucermen* and *It Conquered the World.*

PHIL CAMBRIDGE   Artist who worked with Wood at Pendulum Publications.

ANTHONY CARDOZA   Writer/producer/director of motion pictures and television movies for the last 30 years. Credits include: *Playground, The Beast of Yucca Flats, The Hellcats, Bigfoot, Outlaw Riders, Raw Force.*

JOHNNY CARPENTER   Actor/stuntman. Star of *The Lawless Rider,* also appeared in *Night of the Ghouls.*

NONA CARVER   Worked in burlesque, played "Sleazy Maisie Rumpledink" in Wood's *Take It Out In Trade.*

Nona Carver, aka "Sleazy Maisie Rumpledink" today. [photo by Rudolph Grey]

PHIL CHAMBERLIN   Now married to Dolores Fuller; organized the film department at the L.A. County Museum of Art and Filmex.

PETER COE   Actor with extensive movie and television credits, including *The Ten Commandments, The Secret Invasion, The Mummy's Curse, House of Frankenstein.*

GEORGE COOPER   Actor, stage director, musician who knew Wood in the early Hollywood years.

ROBERT CREMER   Author, *Lugosi, The Man Behind the Cape*.

ROBERT DERTENO   Director/editor. Art director on *Orgy of the Dead*. Films include *Pin Down Girl, Pin-Up Girl, Gun Girls, Girl Gang*.

ED DE PRIEST   Producer/director/editor/photographer. Movies include *The Kill, Hedonistic Pleasures, The Affairs of Aphrodite, The Hard Road, Skin Tight*.

FLORENCE DOLDER   Friend and neighbor of Ed Wood. Mother of Shannon.

SHANNON DOLDER   Ed Wood's neighbor on Yucca Street. "I was on the punk rock scene for a while, a lot of my friends wouldn't miss Ed Wood's films."

BARRY ELLIOTT   was one of the pioneers of early television.

MICHAEL "DINO" FANTINI   Played sex-maniac Dirk Williams in *The Sinister Urge*.

Dino Fantini today. [photo by Rudolph Grey]

TIMOTHY FARRELL   Actor who worked in numerous '50's exploitation movies. Played Dr. Alton in *Glen or Glenda*. Films include: *Dance Hall Racket, Test Tube Babies, Gun Girls, Pin Down Girl*. Played gangster Vic Brady in *Jailbait*. Died May, 1989.

DON FELLMAN   Renegade artist-writer, inspired by anonymous junk-snapshots, street scenes in 1950's films and space age industrial design. Proposed films: *Yesterdonia* and *A Number Like N*.

DAVID FRIEDMAN   Exploitation movie producer, responsible for such films as *B-O-I-N-N-N-G!, Bell, Bare and Beautiful, Scum of the Earth, A Swallow of Brine, Mondo Depravados, She Freak, Brand of Shame, The Lustful Turk, Thar She Blows!*

DOLORES FULLER   Actress/songwriter. Film credits: *Glen or Glenda, Jailbait, Bride of the Monster, Outlaw Women, Mesa of Lost Women, Body Beautiful, The Moonlighter, Play Girl, Night Music, Opposite Sex.* Co-wrote songs with Nelson Riddle, Billy Sherrill, Don Costa, Sammy Faye for Elvis Presley, Nat King Cole, Peggy Lee, Duane Eddy and Tanya Tucker. Songs include: Rock-a-Hula Baby, I Got Lucky, Do the Clam, Spinout, Beyond the Bend.

BEN FROMMER   Charactor actor. Played the derelict in the police station in *Bride of the Monster.*

ALEX GORDON   Producer. Films include: *The She Creature, Voodoo Woman, the Day the World Ended, Apache Woman, Requiem for a Gunfighter, Motorcycle Gang.*

HAL GUTHU   Cinematographer. Cameraman on *Necromania* (softcore scenes), *Mrs. Stone's Thing, Take It Out in Trade.*

FRANCINE HANSEN   Valda Hansen's mother. Died June, 1987.

VALDA HANSEN   Actress. Played Sheila, the White Ghost, in *Night of the Ghouls.* Also appeared in *The Great Northfield Minnesota Raid, Slaughter's Big Rip-Off, Bikini Bandits, Outer Space, Norma, Outlaw Riders,* others. "I've been psychic all my life. I'm Scorpio with Capricorn rising — like Elvis Presley, very earthy."

BUDDY HYDE   Produced Criswell's television show in the late 1960's. Friend of Ed Wood's. Died June, 1988.

KARL JOHNSON   Son of Tor Johnson. Formerly a Lt. for the San Fernando police.

LORETTA KING   Female lead in *Bride of the Monster.*

SAM KOPETZKY   Sound man on *Night of the Ghouls, Wild Guitar, Targets, Space Thing, Hells Angels of Wheels, Love Me Like I Do, Girl In Gold Boots.*

CHUCK LA BERGE   Actor. Appeared with Ed Wood in *Streets of Laredo,* and on stage with *Peg O' My Heart* and *Casual Company.*

REV. LYN LEMON   Reverend Lemon now lives in Texas and enjoys showing *Plan 9 from Outer Space* to friends and family.

RICK LUTZE   Porn actor. Appeared in Wood's *Necromania,* among many others.

DUDLEY MANLOVE   Played Eros in *Plan 9 From Outer Space.* Grew up in vaudeville, became a singer, concert pianist, and staff announcer on NBC radio. Partial credits: *Final Curtain, Creation of the Humanoids, Alfred Hitchcock Presents, Highway Patrol, Restless Gun, Official Detective, Schlitz Playhouse.*

MONA McKINNON   Played Paula Trent in *Plan 9 From Outer Space*. Also in *Jailbait, Mesa of Lost Women, Teenage Thunder, Unwed Mother*.

PAUL MARCO   Kelton the cop in *Plan 9 from Outer Space, Bride of the Monster, Night of the Ghouls*. Films include *Hiawatha, the Young Savages, My Soul Runs Naked*. Also seen on *77 Sunset Strip, G. E. Theatre, Voice of the Heavens*.

MARGARET MASON   Widow of Tom Mason, Bela Lugosi's double in *Plan 9 From Outer Space*. "Bela Lugosi thought Tom looked very much like him. They had the big ears together."

DON NAGEL   Film and television actor who appeared in the Wood films *Crossroad Avenger, Jailbait, Bride of the Monster* and *Night of the Ghouls*.

MAILA NURMI (VAMPIRA)   Horror film hostess on KABC and KHJ tv in the early 50's. Seen in many beauty pageants and on Broadway with Mae West in *Catherine Was Great*. Movies include *If Winter Comes, Plan 9 From Outer Space, Too Much, Too Soon, The Beat Generation, Sleeping Beauty, The Big Operator, I Passed for White, Sex Kittens Go to College, The Magic Sword, James Dean, the First American Teenager, Bungalow Invader*. "I'm busy doing the illustration for my new book *The Googie-ites*, which is half-finished. It'll be a small cocktail table book and suitable for a tv series about an out out-of-work actors' hangout in the 50's. Populated with those "truth is tranger than fiction" people, many of whom later became famous. I'm also making tombstone rubbings from graves of celebs in Hollywood, for sale by mail order."

Maila Nurmi in her Hollywood apartment, 1987. [photo by Rudolph Grey]

MICHAEL DONOVAN O'DONNELL   Played detective Mac McGregor in *Take it Out in Trade*. Other films: *Satan's Cheerleaders, The Snake Gang, Beyond the Valley of the Dolls, Death Trap, Vixen, Hi Riders, Inside Straight, Speedbirds, Paint Your Wagon.*

ALDO RAY   Actor, Ed Wood's drinking buddy. Films include *We're Not Angels, Men in War, The Naked and the Dead, God's Little Acre, Nightmare in the Sun, Sylvia, Dead Heat on A Merry-Go-Round, The Power,* many others. Died March, 1991.

FRED OLEN RAY   Director/producer. Films include: *Death Corps, Bio Hazard, Prison Ship, Armed Response, The Tomb, Commando Squad, Beverly Hills Vampire.* Ray had contacted Wood to write a screenplay titled *Beach Blanket Bloodbath*.

STEEVE REEVES   Mr. America, 1947, Mr. Universe, 1950. Films: *Jailbait, Athena, Hercules, The Last Days of Pompeii, The Giant of Marathon, The Avenger, The Trojan Horse, Duel of the Titans, The White Warrior.* Today he raises Morgan horses on his ranch outside of San Diego.

ROY REID   Veteran exploitation film producer and promoter. Roy helped promote such movies as: *Reefer Madness, Narcotic, Mad Youth, Wang-Wang, High School Girls, Jungle Virgin, Unashamed Women, Sins of Bali, She-Devil Island, Youth Aflame, Teen Age, Her Wedding Night, Bedroom Fantasy, Hoodlum Girls.* Produced *The Sinister Urge* and *The Violent Years* for his Headliner Productions. Died August, 1987 at the age of 95.

JOE ROBERTSON   Producer/director. Credits include: *The Slime People, The Crawling Hand, Mrs. Stone's Thing, The Chambermaids, The Photographer, Dr. Caligari.*

DENNIS RODRIGUEZ   Writer, editor at Pendulum publishing. Credits include *The Terminator* series for Pinnacle Books, teleplays for *Knight Rider, Hunter, Adam 12, 1990.*

LYLE TALBOT   Veteran actor seen in movies since the early 1930's, including *Glen or Glenda, Jailbait, Plan 9 From Outer Space, City of Fear, Atom Man Vs. Superman, Return of the Terror, Three on a Match, Chinatown Squad, Torture Ship.*

HARRY THOMAS   Make-up artist. Credits include: *Glen or Glenda, Bride of the Monster, Jailbait, Night of the Ghouls, Plan 9 From Outer Space, Kiss me Baby, Little Shop of Horrors. She Demons, Frankestein's Daughter, She Freak, From Hell It Came, The Naked Kiss.*

THEODORA THURMAN   Fashion model for European *Vogue*. Played gangster Timothy Farrell's moll in *Jailbait*. Worked extensively for radio and television, including a long tenure on *The Jack Paar Show.*

JOHN CRAWFORD THOMAS   Worked with Ed Wood on stage as an actor in *The*

Blackguard Returns and financed and acted in Wood's 1948 western *Crossroads of Laredo.*

MARGE USHER   Hollywood theatrical agent; clients included Tony McCoy and Valda Hansen. Died in 1989.

GREGORY WALCOTT   Played airline pilot Jeff Trent in *Plan 9 From Outer Space.* Former contract player for Universal and Warner Brothers.

DAVID WARD   Stage, televison and movie actor. "My great grandfather was Lou Doxstedder, the minstrel, he gave Al Jolson a job." A movie based on his life, *Edward Ford,* is in preparation.

GEORGE WEISS   Independent exploitation film producer who financed *Glen or Glenda.* Under his Screen Classics production banner he produced such films as *Test Tube Babies, Dance Hall Racket, Girl Gang, Blonde Pick-Up, Hollywood After Midnight, Chained Girls.*

EVELYN WOOD   No relation to Ed Wood. She played Sheila, whose transvestite brother stretched her sweater all out of shape in *Glen or Glenda.*

KATHY WOOD   Born in Vancouver, Canada, Kathy Wood lived with Ed Wood from 1956 until his death in December, 1978.

LILLIAN WOOD   Mother of Ed Wood. Born July 5, 1903, in Red Hook, New Jersey. Died May 16, 1989 in Poughkeepsie, New York.

MILDRED WORTH   Wife of composer Frank Worth, who wrote the original score for *Bride of the Monster.*

Lillian Wood
and
Rudolph Grey,
1984

Kathy Wood
and McGinty,
1988

Edward D. Wood, Jr.
A Chronology

1924	Oct. 10: Edward Davis Wood, Jr. born in Poughkeepsie, NY to Edw. Davis Wood, Sr., and Lillian Phillips Wood.
1931	Ed Wood, age seven, sees his first horror movie: Bela Lugosi in *Dracula*.
1935	Ed Wood gets his first movie camera on his 11th birthday.
1941	June: Wood graduates from Poughkeepsie high school, gets work as an usher at the Bardavon Theatre.
1942	Wood enlists in the U.S. Marine Corps. Stationed in the Southwest and Central Pacific, sees action at Tarawa and Nanumea.
1944	Private Wood in Naval hospital in South Pacific.
1945	Japan surrenders.
1946	Corporal Wood discharged from the Marines. Studies at Kings School of Dramatic Arts, Frank Lloyd Wright Institute, Washington, D.C. Joins a travelling carnival where he plays the half-man, half-woman and the geek.
1947	Wood arrives in Hollywood. Acts in stage productions.
1948	Meets veteran Hollywood cameraman, Ray Flin at Monogram Pictures. August 28: with Ray Flin on camera, Ed Wood directs and writes his first Hollywood movie, *Crossroads of Laredo*. Oct. 25: Wood directs and acts in his play about the Marine Corps, *The Casual Company,* at Village Playhouse, Hollywood.
1949	Wood does a long run as the Sheriff in *The Blackguard Returns* at the Gateway Theare. Ed Wood forms Story-Ad Films with the photographer of the Nazi war trials, Robert Ganon.
1950	Works as stunt double (in drag) in Samuel Fuller's *The Baron of Arizona*.
1951	Wood joins the Screen Actors Guild to do bits and parts. Dec. 17: Directs half hour tv drama, *The Sun Was Setting* at KTTV studios.

1952   Introduced to producer George Weiss by cinematographer William Thompson. Writes screenplay for *The Lawless Rider*.

1953   Ed Wood meets Bela Lugosi; films *Glen or Glenda* under the working title, *Transvestite*. Lugosi announces projected Wood-Lugosi television series, *Dr. Acula*. Wood writes and directs the color tv pilot *Crossroad Avenger*. Produces, writes and directs *The Bela Lugosi Review*, a take-off on *Dracula*, featuring Lili St. Cyr, at the Silver Slipper, Las Vegas.

1954   Wood films *The Hidden Face*, later released as *Jailbait*. June: dialogue coach for Lugosi on *The Red Skelton Show*, which also features Vampira and Lon Chaney, Jr. On Oct. 29, *Bride of the Atom* begins filming at Ted Allan Studios.

1955   April: Shoots Lugosi footage later used in *Plan 9 From Outer Space*. A couple weeks later, Lugosi is hospitalized for drug addiction. May: *Bride of the Atom* previews. Ed Wood meets Kathy O'Hara Everett.

1956   June: additional footage shot of Lugosi, later incorporated into Plan 9 From Outer Space. July: *Bride of the Atom* is released in the U.S. and the U.K. as *Bride of the Monster*. July: Begins filming *Rock and Roll Hell*; project abandoned. *The Violent Years* is released, from Wood's screenplay *Teenage Girl Gang*. August 16: Bela Lugosi dies. November: Shoots *Grave Robbers From Outer Space*.

1957   Wood films *Final Curtain* for projected tv series, *Portraits in Terror*. March 15: *Grave Robbers From Outer Space* previews at Carlton Theatre, Hollywood.

1958   Wood forms Atomic Productions with Major J.C. Foxworthy, U.S.M.C., with plans to film 18 low-budget pictures over the next three years. Writes and directs *Night of the Ghouls* for Atomic Productions. *The Bride and the Beast* released, from Wood's screenplay *Queen of the Gorillas*.

1959   *Night of the Ghouls* previewed as *Revenge of the Dead*. July: Hal Roach's Distributiors Corporation of America releases *Grave Robbers From Outer Space* with the new title *Plan 9 From Outer Space*. Wood plans *Ghouls of the Moon* to utilize unused footage of Lugosi.

1960   July: Wood directs *The Sinister Urge*. December: *The Sinister Urge* is released; a sequel, *The Peeper*, is abandoned. Wood begins 27 weeks at Autonetics writing and directing short government films.

1961   August: Films new sequence for *The Sinister Urge*. Unfilmed screenplays: *The Silent Night*, *Last Town North*.

1963   Wood's first novel is published: *Black Lace Drag*. *Shotgun Wedding*, written by Wood, is released. Wood confers with Boris Karloff and Joe E. Brown for the unrealized project, *Invasion of the Gigantic Salami*.

1964   Works for Sam Yorty at KTTV.

1965   September: Wood works as an assistant director on *Ghouls and Dolls* (from his script). *Black Lace Drag* is reissued as *Killer in Drag*. *Ghouls and Dolls* is released as *Orgy of the Dead*.

1966   March: Wood's novelization of *Orgy of the Dead* is published. April: *69 Rue Pigalle* (from Wood's novel) set to roll; production cancelled when front money falls through. *Parisian Passions (69 Rue Pigalle)* published.

1967   Novels published include: *Devil Girls, Death of a Transvestite, It Takes One to Know One, Drag Trade, Security Risk, Watts ... After*.

1968   Novels published include: *Purple Thighs, Sex Shrouds and Caskets, Hell Chicks, Bye Bye Broadie, Sexecutives, Night Time Lez, Sex Museum, Raped in the Grass*.

1969   Wood writes and stars in Joe Robertson's *The Photographer, Misty* (uncompleted) and Jacques Descent's *Operation Redlight* (from Wood's novel *Mama's Diary*). Novels published: *Carnival Piece, Toni: Black Tigress, Mama's Diary*.

1970   Wood writes, directs and acts in *Take It Out in Trade*. Produces a .45 record: *The Day the Mummy Returned* (read by Tor Johnson) / *Final Curtain* (read by Criswell). Release uncertain.

1971   May 17: Tor Johnson dies, age 68. June: Ed Wood writes, directs and acts in *Necromania*. Sept: Wood writes and directs *The Only House*. Directs numerous uncredited loops for *Swedish Erotica*. Dec. 29: *Necromania* premieres at Hudson Theatre, NY.

1972   Feb 5: Kenne Duncan dies, age 69. Novels published: *Mary-Go-Round, The Producer, The Only House.*

1973   *A Study in the Motivation of Censorship, Sex & the Movies,* two volumes, published.

1974   Wood writes and plays two roles in *Fugitive Girls.* Novels published: *Forced Entry, Diary of a Transvestite Hooker.*

1975   Wood writes/directs 12 short films for the Sex Education Correspondence School.

1976   August: negotiates a movie/book deal for *Lugosi: Post Mortem.* Nov. 16: James "Duke" Moore dies of a heart attack, age 63.

1977   Wood's unrealized project, *Venus De Milo,* in preparation. *TV Lust* published.

1978   Unrealized projects: *The Day the Mummies Danced* (to star Dudley Manlove); *I Awoke Early the Day I Died* (to star Aldo Ray, John Carradine). *Swedish House* published. December 10: Ed Wood dies of a heart attack, age 54, at 5635 Laurel Canyon Boulevard. Cremated at Utter-McKinley mortuary, his ashes are scattered at sea.

Bibliography

All of Ed Wood's novels were issued as paperbacks, usually of the mass market sized format. The earliest title dates to 1963; Wood continued to produce these books until his death in 1978. Wood was proud of his books, giving them out as Christmas presents. (Unlike most pornographers, Wood used his own name whenever possible.) While nearly all of his possessions were lost or sold through the years, Wood carefully saved his novels, inscribing the date of issue and "from the personal collection of Edw. D. Wood, Jr." in each book.

There is no way of knowing precisely how many novels Ed Wood published. He did use a pseudonym on occasion, and title changes were common in the "adult" field. In 1967 and 1968 Wood had 22 known titled published, nine issued in September and October of 1968. It is conceivable that Wood wrote as many as 75 books.

BLACK LACE DRAG
(Raven Books RB 713, 1963, 160 pp.)

Glen Marker, alias Glenda Satin, is a killer for "the Syndicate." When an old queen is murdered, Glen suspects a frame-up, and leaves for Colorado where he hides out in a carnival.

Wood's earliest known published novel is more dense and detailed than his later books. There are seemingly autobiographical touches; in particular, the protagonist Glen Marker's job as a female impersonator in clubs across the country, including Washington. Wood's own resumé lists a credit as "headline performer" at the Kavockas Club, Washington D.C. Art Pepper, in his autobiography, *Straight Life*, described it as "a jazz club filled with the black pimp type cats and the hustling broads and the dope fiends." The character of the wealthy homosexual Dalten Van Carter seems to be a roman à clef riff from the life of silent film director William Desmond Taylor who, like Van Carter, had a black transvestite as his butler. Taylor was murdered in 1922 in a famous case which involved actresses Mabel Normand and Mary Miles Minter. The novel was reissued in 1965 as *Killer in Drag* (Imperial 793), and in 1967 as *Black Lace Drag* (Columbia CN 433), and *The Twilight Land* (1967, attributed to "Sheri Blue," Pad Library PL-549). The sequel, *Death of a Transvestite*, appeared in 1967.

From *Black Lace Drag:*

> Dalten Van Carter was an old man, a very old man, who drank too much and he thought too much of feverent [Wood's neologism], perverted sex. He flounced around his apartment like a fluttering old auntie, like a nymph in a flower bed; a fairy in the scented woodlands. He wore a faded pink satin wrapper which was trimmed in ancient, almost decaying, white

fox — reminiscent of his much younger days. He didn't try to cover up the fact that he was of the male sex, nor the fact that at one time he had been as beautiful a "drag" as Glenda was now...

The aged "drag's" eyes all but popped out of their socket when they lighted on Glenda as she glided into the room. He stepped back in amazement — awed at the beauty of the "girl" he beheld. He had seen a lot of them in his day but this was by far the loveliest thing he had ever laid eyes on. He shut the door without removing his eyes from her and when the door was closed he took three studied tours around her, looking her up and down then muttering, "Exquisite. Beautiful. Sensational. Ohhh — This will be grand." He was thinking of later...

Dinner was served by Wilma, a negro boy flawlessly dressed in a short skirted maid's outfit of black satin, then Dalten prepared several more drinks which Glenda and he consumed slowly. Dalten had to show the costumes he had in his wardrobe — "From my better years," he had explained. He opened his pink wrapper to show black lace panties with pink bows.

ORGY OF THE DEAD
(Greenleaf classic GC 205, 1966, 160 pp., photo illustrated)

A GREENLEAF CLASSIC

Special introduction by Forrest J Ackerman

The novel *Orgy of the Dead* was issued after the movie's release. According to director Steve Apostolof, Wood was paid $600 for the book. It incorporates much of Wood's short film *Final Curtain* and his story *The Day the Mummy Returned,* marginally rewritten. The Banshee episode appears to be based on his short film *The Night the Banshee Cried,* and the undertaker tale is similar to episodes in two other Wood books, *Suburbia Confidential* and *For the Love of the Dead.* Unlike the movie *Orgy of the Dead,* there is no werewolf character in the novel. Cover painting by Robert Bonfils.

From *Orgy of the Dead:*

Shirley struggled in vain against her bonds as the mummy walked back toward the dark edge of the circle, heading toward the spot where he had left the unconscious Bob. She was in near hysteria. "Let me loose, you fiend!"

"All in good time. I do not see why you struggle. Are you not one of us? Are you not here to be judged with the other sinful dead?"

"Fiend! You're mad!"

"Mad is it! Why is it I am mad?" The black creature's words were dangerously calm. "One is always considered mad when one says or does something which others cannot comprehend." He laughed, and the sound was the rattling of skeletons and the thunder of the tomb.

PARISIAN PASSIONS
(Sundown Reader 611, Corinth Publications, 1966, 191 pp)

In Paris, a succession of strippers are found strangled in the Rue Morgue. Unable to solve the murders, Inspector Goulet brings in Sheriff Buck Rhodes from Texas, who in turn brings in Lorraine Peters, female impersonator.

Originally titled *69 Rue Pigalle,* a script based on the novel was set to be produced by A. C. Stephen (Steve Apostolof).

Alternately absurd, comic and poetic, the book has its share of terse philosophic observations:

"Sights sure look different in hand cuffs, from the back seat of a police car..."

"Habit, Monsieur, is extremely easy to acquire, yet so difficult to eliminate."

"It has been shown — proved over the centuries, if one does not conform, one is considered mad."

"It is such a wicked world ... many times I wonder why we fight so had to remain with it..."

(In a printing error, the author "J. X. Williams" appears on the cover, though Wood's name is used on the title page.)

WATTS — THE DIFFERENCE
(Pad Library PL 564, 1966, 192 pp.)

Flashbacks alternate between the early memories of two lovers, Rocky, a black television cowboy actor, and Angie. Wood keeps the story line interesting by continuing to return to the present, as the couple drink, argue and make love. The character Rance Holliday, an independent movie director, has a fetish for angora sweaters. Reissued in 1969 as *Burn Baby Burn* under the pseudonym "Ray Jones" (Selected Adult Library SAL 559).

From *Watts — The Difference:*

He sighed, then, as he got up from the arm of Angie's chair. "Ahh, girls have so much more going for them — so much more fun than boys," he expounded while he lazily stretched out on his studio couch. "They're pretty to look at — Oh, so soft bodies.... The clothes....: he whispered and Angie thought he had climaxed just thinking about them. "My God, the clothes," he breathed and his eyes closed momentarily in his ecstasy, then when he opened them once more, they fastened on the girl. He was feeling her up with every force his eyes could generate. "Hurry dear child... Do hurry ... I must get those things on.

Angie got slowly to her feet. "Everything?" She spoke in a sexy whisper and she knew what the answer would be.

"Everything! I must feel everything as they are on you now... with the dainty fragrance of your body still impregnated in them — the warmth of your body, only your body could leave there ... Everything ... Do a striptease for me straight to the skin."

Angie went to her purse where it rested beside the desk. She took out her lipstick and returned to him. Thus when he had finished reddening his lips he took her in his arms and kissed her long and hotly ... His tongue racing in and out between her lips. "Oh, Angie ... Angie ... You are going to be the best one ever — the very best of them all — I can tell —I've had them all — all kinds and all shapes ... this sweater of yours," and he went into the ecstasy of sight and feel of the garment again..." You can't imagine the beauty of the feel ... or perhaps you can."

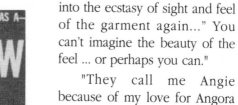

"They call me Angie because of my love for Angora sweaters. I have, man ... I can grab your feeling for it alright ... You must be in seventh heaven right now...."

SIDE-SHOW SIREN (Sundown Reader SR 618, 1966, 190 pp.)

When Karl the Abominable Snowman escapes from a carnival, a series of gruesome murders ensues.

Changed from the original title *Naked Bones* as more marketable for the paperback trade, *Side-Show Siren* is possibly the first of Wood's carnival novels. It resembles films like *The Ape* (with Boris Karloff, Monogram, 1940) and *Circus of Horrors* (AIP, 1960). The character of Jinx Dixon, a cowboy sharpshooter, is modeled after Wood's close friend, Kenne Duncan.

From *Side-Show Siren:*

> The car shot forward in one long, grinding, uncontrollable motion. The dark shadow of the driver could be seen trying desperately to regain control of the vehicle. It was immediately apparent that control was impossible as the car slammed wildly through the ride area. Yet the driver kept a heavy foot on the accelerator — skidding and screeching across the mud and grime until it finally cut across Kari's crushed body, and smashed to a stop against the stationary rigging of the Ferris wheel.

> Donna, still wearing the brown skirt and pink mohair sweater, forced open the partly sprung door on the driver's side, and got out. She held a pistol in each hand. The barrels pointed at Tomms, Miles, Jinx and Duke, who were the first to reach the stalled car.

> Hard, determined eyes accompanied the muzzles of the guns, and even harder words "I didn't get outta prison so you lousy bastards can put me back again." It was Clay Warner's voice that dominated the rouged lips, that spat the words at the startled group.

> Far in the distance, the ambulance siren wailed faintly. It grew steadily louder with each gust of the wind. A wail of the forlorn — the lost —not the forgotten — but the lost.

DRAG TRADE
(Triumph News TNC 106, 1967, 159 pp.)

Ed Wood is pictured in drag on the cover. The stories concern Raymond Gomez, who is dressed as a child in pink dresses, and grows up to enter a life of crime as "Sheila Gomez," liquor store hold-up drag artist. Other characters include: Martin Harmony, known professionally as Mary Harmony, the Jello girl, a female impersonator whose career selling stolen cars is interrupted by the FBI; Big Nellie, who runs a drag bar for whites only, gives in to a "swish-in" demonstration to allow black drag queens entrance into his club; and Yahio Mura, Japanese student and drag prostitute ("sister boy") who assasinates a politician with a samurai sword.

From *Drag Trade:*

Life had been one long procession of dresses ... seldom he wore the same panties more than once or twice ... once the dainty garments entered water they lost their newness and feel ... this is of the utmost in importance to the transvestite ... clothes are his very existence.

BLOODIEST SEX CRIMES OF HISTORY
(Pad Library NTG 814, 1967, 160 pp.)

Under the pseudonyms of "Spenser and West," Wood's study covers Elizabeth Bathory, necrophiles, Sgt. Bertrand, vampirism, cannibalism, Albert Fish, and Fritz Haarman.

SECURITY RISK
(Pad Library PL 580, 1967, 192 pp.)

Espionage, Wood style, involving communists, sabotage at a movie set, and hard-loving, hard smoking and hard drinking Col. Harvey Tate.

From *Security Risk:*

> Joe Lazar came to just as the headlights flashed straight across into nothingness.... In that brief instant he didn't know what was happening to him ... but in the next he knew, as the car dipped forward and he was thrown against the windshield.... Then he found himself slammed from door to door ... roof to floor ... the steering wheel slammed against his guts ... His head hit the windshield ... then his arms went lifeless as the motor crushed back against it ... His leg became entangled in the steering wheel ... His other leg tore loose from its socket and lodged between the two front seats ... His mouth screamed ... then his mouth hit the gear shift and his false teeth broke and tore through both his upper and lower lip ... The broken leg tore loose from the seat and flopped crazily toward the right door which flew open, then slammed shut, locking itself over the already lifeless leg. Joe tried to scream again, but only blood spurted through his open, gaping mouth. Then he was on the ceiling again, and slammed again into the burning motor which had come between him and the front seat. The rear end of the car burst in a sound of tearing metal. The unbreakable glass splintered and broke, shooting slivers of glass like rifle shots, and one large one stabbed through Joe's adam's apple....

WATTS ... AFTER
(Pad Library PL 578, 1967, 191 pp.)

Rocky Alley, black television star of *The Tucson Kid,* tangles again with fanatical black nationalists.

A follow up to *Watts ... The Difference,* which includes the return of transvestite movie director Rance Holliday, who tells how he "went out and solicited money for my own films, and I made them. I was lucky to find the proper old character actor who was on the skids and I — only I took enough interest in him and brought him back to do one more film. The one more film went into five."

DEVIL GIRLS
(Pad Library PL 566, 1967, 189 pp.)

In the small town of Almanac, Texas, Sheriff Buck Rhodes tangles with drug smugglers and teenage gangs, including the wild girl gang, The Chicks. A series of sexual liaisons and violence culminate in their tragic end.

A Tor Johnson like character appears: Chief, the 350 pound Indian with a "deep, scratchy voice," who works as a cook at Jockey's Hamburger Joint.

From *Devil Girls:*

> She snapped to him with the glazed eyes which demanded immediate action. "Now, Lark, now. God damn it now. You got my girls, you got me. We'll get your stuff. Now, damn it, get me the stuff now ... I'll do whatever those whore bitches want. I'll kiss 'em. They can kiss me. They can screw me, they can jazz me. They can whip me. I'll take the high heels in my back, my stomach. I'll take the whip, the paddle. They can kiss my ass for all I care. Just get me a fix. Get me a fix before I die right here on the sidewalk.

IT TAKES ONE TO KNOW ONE
(Pad Library IMP 786, 1967, 191 pp.)

A femme boy, Don, is raped on campus. Hitching a freight, he meets a young lesbian who encourages him to become Donna. In Colorado, Don / Donna is initiated into the secret world of gay-drag parties.

The only known Wood novel with chapter titles. They are: "A Matter of Rape"; "Jimmy Felt Kindly"; "Incident on a Freight"; "Heading West"; "A Way of Life"; "More Than a Lesson"; "The Light of the Day"; "Patricia"; "Time is the Healer"; "Substitute Sister"; "The First Day"; "Friday"; "She Passed This Way"; "A Very Gay Party"; "Crook-A-Day Cruise"; "The Changing Times." In the last chapter Wood has his say on transvestite rights via a long discourse from the central character Don / Donna.

From the final chapter, "The Changing Times":

> Hollywood Boulevard is SWISH. The Sunset Strip is SWISHIER. And there are other places which are the most.

On the Boulevard there are no men's shops per se.

Oh, of course one can buy a straight suit ... the men can that is. But featured in the same men's shops are the frilly purple, pink, yellow and black lace shirts — and full FEMALE wardrobes, and private booths so one can make sure of the proper fit. And velour is the most prominent in all the shops in all the GAY colors. I shall call it velvet, because velvet by any other name is still velvet. My thoughts also apply to the shirts. A shirt, no matter how frilly it becomes, is still a shirt. I of course prefer blouses — and the trend toward blouses is there — the change is there.

The beret, which I have advocated for years and the lovely June high in the mountains over Denver collected so lovingly, is more evident than ever before. In order to give them the mannish appeal they are called car hats, as the fur coats are called car coats. Even the furs and the angoras I have had in my wardrobe for years is all the style. It would seem that anyone riding a convertible car will sooner or later be wearing a beret, or a car coat. The fuzzier the better, it would seem.

I've owned a white fox jacket with a hood of the same luscious fur, for many years. At a time, when not completely in DRAG, I was laughed at many times. Now the fur jacket is the "IN" thing — the "SHAGGY LOOK" as the men's magazines call it.

In front of KTTV studios in Hollywood the other day, I'd have sworn the GIRL I saw was strictly of the female specie ... SHE wore a bright orange velour V necked blouse, green capris and black medium heeled boots ... HER blonde hair, tied back in a pony tail reached in soft waves to HER waist line.... Two things to prove HER manhood which I was quick to notice, was the lack of breasts, rubber or otherwise, under the velour blouse — and there was the growth of a pencil thin mustache under HER nose.

But at that, maybe SHE was smart. SHE was wearing the female garments she so undoubtedly desires out in public — yet who could bust her, should such a thing be possible in this day and age. What could be the charge. She certainly wasn't masquerading. The mustache, no matter how thin and how covered with make up, proved she wasn't masquerading.

One last point about this long haired DRAG. The green capris were so tight around HER firm butt, that the double leg bands of her panties made definite lines there — no male shorts ever made interesting lines such as that.

The fuzzier the sweater, the better I've always liked them, as I have stated from the time I left the east. Throughout my meeting with Pat and the lovely June. My desires had always been there. It just took the proper person, at the right time to make me realize it. Pat on the train those many days. And the realization when June and I dressed as twins. There was a

GIRL leading the life she desired. My uncle, crook as he might be, gave me an insight which has calmed any nerves I might have had because of my beliefs that I was in reality born two persons. One outwardly and one inwardly.

Conquest!

The time is now to speak out ... and as I have done, write every line we feel. Some one will publish it.

The toughs have invaded our territory. The days of the Roman empire and their long hair and their dress-like toga is returning.

Back then we had the right of our attire — it slipped away from us. WE must not permit this to happen again. Any more than WE should permit the SLUGS and the TOUGHS to invade our territory of attire without us taking full advantage of them. There is a time to live and a time to die. We are alive, so obviously NOW is the time to live — our lives the way we were designated and destined to live it.

I read an article in a Glendale paper the other day of a character dressed in a green dress, red sweater and blonde wig who held up a liquor store. The TOUGHS — the INVADERS. The police picked him up in a telephone booth still dressed as such — and a mighty poor combination of clothes I might add. There was another only recently who escaped from a

work camp as a girl. He got a ride by hitch hiking, then proceeded to knock his benefactor over the head. Another held up a gas station in North Hollywood, wearing a beige dress and white sweater....

These people give all of the true transvestites a bad name.

DEATH OF A TRANSVESTITE
(Pad Library NT 821, 1967, 192 pp.)

Glen Marker, a transvestite hit man on death row, agrees to a taped confession in return for his last request: to die in drag.

Alternately titled *Hollywood Drag*, this is a sequel to Wood's *Black Lace Drag*. The two books comprise what

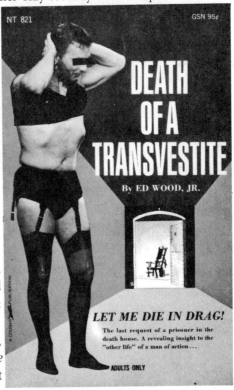

NT 821   GSN 95¢

DEATH OF A TRANSVESTITE

By ED WOOD, JR.

LET ME DIE IN DRAG!

The last request of a prisoner in the death house. A revealing insight to the "other life" of a man of action...

ADULTS ONLY

must be considered Wood's strongest novelistic ventures. *Death of a Transvestite* has different incidents in the protagonist's story reconstructed through L.A. police reports, taxi drivers, syndicate members, court files, bellboys, diaries, the warden's commentary and Glen's own tape confession.

Death of a Transvestite was reissued in 1969 by Selected Adult Library (SAL 557) as *Let Me Die in Drag* by "Woodrow Edwards."

The transvestite pictured on the cover is Hugh Hooker (who at one time was Richard Basehart's stand-in) in a scene from A. C. Stephen's *Suburbia Confidential*.

From *Death of a Transvestite:*

> Another spasm sent the blood rushing from my wounds and up through my mouth. I couldn't move any longer; not even my arms or my hands. Such simple little movements I had done all my life. There was none, and I knew that I'd had it. I felt the end was close, but I fought for every precious second of it.
>
> Everything suddenly seemed so silly to me. The whole scheme of things. I wanted to laugh, but I couldn't focus my senses to even that privilege. I was not to be permitted even that last movement towards fate. But I did realize I was still in DRAG. I would die in the clothes I had always hoped for. I only wished I could reach the angora sweater and the wig. But I had outwitted the Killer. The Killer was not to see me die with or without the clothes of my choice. It was the one glowing thought.

SUBURBIA CONFIDENTIAL
(Triumph News Co. TNC 305, 1967, 159 pp.)

Case histories told to a psychiatrist by a succession of patients with various sexual problems and deviations. The doctor interjects his notes throughout the taped confessions.

Excerpt for the basic theme, this book is unrelated to the 1966 movie *Suburbia Confidential* directed by A. C. Stephen, who says Wood did not have anything to do with the movie. Written under the pseudonym "Emil Moreau."

NIGHT TIME LEZ
(Columbia PE 446, 1968, 168 pp.)

The initiation of the beautiful Paula Thomas into the twilight world of lesbianism — the "fluffs" and the Butch dykes."

There is an endless succession of martinis and bourbons in this colorful novel of "the outer spheres of sexuality." The sex passages are euphoric and imaginative.

BYE BYE BROADIE
(Pendulum Pictorial 001, 1968, 157 pp.)

A peeping tom rapist spies on a group of young women making love in a boarding school. He approaches them and joins in on the action. The man-hating schoolmistress, Mrs. Grundy, discovers the orgy and beats the man to death with her cane. The headmistress then coerces the girls to assist her in burying the body in a nearby pet cemetery. After the burial, a hand appears out of the ground and grabs one of the young girls. The bloodied "corpse" smashes Mrs. Grundy with a shovel, sending her off into eternity. After another young girl falls victim to his revenge, the now blind young man staggers off toward the swamp water.

Accompanying photos are only marginally related to the story. Claims are made that they are from a "motion picture production," but the stills are obviously posed.

RAPED IN THE GRASS
(Pendulum Pictorial 002, 1968, 157 pp.)

From Wood's introduction:

> The story centers around two American girls on vacation in a mythical Central American country who get captured by a small band of Guerrillas hiding out in the woods. The hatreds and frustrations of these people are released in their treatment of the two girls. The girls are forced to endure all sorts of torture and degradation to satisfy the barbaric and brutal needs of the Guerrillas. They are beaten, raped and tortured by the men and when at last, they think they have satisfied their animalistic needs, they are then "taken over" by the one female in the band ... who is a sadistic lesbian.

> The girls struggle, fight and rebel throughout their nightmarish experience in the hope that they will be allowed to live through it all and return to their own country.

> In the end, they are caught up in the whirlpool of this animalistic existence and find that they really do not desire to leave. Instead, they remain and join the band to help them in their struggle and to satisfy some of their frustrations and cravings.

This "pictorial novelization by Ed Wood, Jr." has 80 black and white photos. The book jacket states: "Photos and novel adaption from the film *Raped in the Grass*, produced by D-M Productions, Los Angeles, Cal." Research has unearthed no trace of such a film, and the photos all have a posed look to them. It is likely this delirious, sleazy porn with a fair amount of dark humor was written around the posed shots.

THE PERVERTS
(Viceroy Books VP 294, 1968, 160 pp.)

By "Jason Nichols," *The Perverts* was ghostwritten by Ed Wood. "A SHOCKINGLY bold uncovering of the deviations taking place in our GREAT society!" Includes chapters on necrophilia, troilism, prostitution, fetishes, sadism, masochism, bestiality, homosexuality, transvestism, incest, lesbianism.

From *The Perverts:*

> The weird lot may very well have a wife at home, or a girl friend but she is not enough. When this comes into value we find that the man or the woman is so predominantly controlled by the thing between their legs that no other thought is worth considering. New experiences no longer satisfy. There has to be something else. Perhaps for a time this type of person may attempt rape in the park or even one or more forms of homosexuality. There are many cases on record where the male has shoved his stiffly erected shaft into a gas tank of his car after it had been lined with slabs of pork liver ... and of girls who have attempted screwing the gearshift of similar vehicles.

THE GAY UNDERWORLD
(Viceroy Books VP 292, 1968, 192 pp.)

Similar to Wood's *Drag Trade* of 1967, with several episodes slightly rewritten.

SEX, SHROUDS AND CASKETS
(Viceroy Books VP 291, 1968, 187 pp.)

An episodic sex exposé of religious charlatans and their manipulation of the poor. From the back cover copy:

> After reading *Sex, Shrouds and Caskets, Fanny Hill* is like reading a dictionary. Once more Ed Wood, Jr. has rocked American readers to their inner souls...

> From the author of *The Gay Underworld, Sex Shrouds and Caskets* will stimulate the intellectual mind, and for certain, SHOCK all!

From *Sex, Shrouds and Caskets:*

> Send me — send me — send me — Please dear God, send me — send me to hell if you must," she screamed ... "But send me!"

> Her legs locked around him suddenly in one sweeping motion, and the preacher's hot lips clamped tightly over hers. The greatest of all her screams centered itself into his throat. The sky blew up and the ceiling crashed in around them. The bed flew up to meet the ceiling and the floor drifted away into some past existence..."

THE SEXECUTIVES
(Private Edition PE 457, 1968, 156 pp.)

Much humorous expounding on love, money, sex and death in this narrative about a gang of female sex spies ("Instant Secretaries, Inc."). Wood's old associate Don Davis filmed the novel in 1968 as *For Love or Money*. Davis produced and directed many sexploitation films in the '60's and '70's and died in 1983.

The photo illustrated paperback of *For Love or Money* appeared in 1968 (Olympic Foto Reader F107). This novel "corrects" Wood's idiosyncratic syntax of *The Sexecutives,* rendering it ordinary and unappealing.

From *The Sexecutives:*

> He got up and paced the floor with a trail of smoke drifting out after him as he lit the tobacco on the move. Waiting was the most unpleasant part of life. Waiting and the insecurity of just what one is waiting for. Time always told the story in full. But time always took so damned long in running its measured space in the Universe. When time held heavy on a man's hands, that's when he didn't think entirely straight....

THE **SEXECUTIVES**
by DAVID L. WESTERMIER   PE 457 $1.50
The price was high for a few hours of stolen pleasures !

The incredible SEXploits of a gang of sex spies who used grotesque measures to blackmail their victims.

SEX MUSEUM
(Viceroy Books VP 299, 1968, 156 pp.)

Sexual rites and rituals in antiquity, including sex in the Old Testament, Aztec sacrifice of the virgin ("Only the girl really isn't a virgin at all. She has been taken by one or more of the High Priests on several occasions before the ritual. No God wants some broad who is inexperienced."), orgies in the Roman Empire, voodoo, LSD, Ilsa Koch, Japanese "sister boys" and "brother girls" et al. Ghosted for "Jason Nichols."

THE LOVE OF THE DEAD
(Viceroy Books VP 310, 1968, 156 pp.)

From the back cover:

> NECROPHILIA! Many dark pages of history are devoted to the sex crimes of sadists, masochists, flagellants, sodomites, pederasts, bestialists, fetishists and their ilk. But by far the most heinous of all is ... the necrophiliac, the violator of dead bodies!

Through the ages, mankind has witnessed many sexual horrors. Deviates and perverts have been a blight on civilization since its very beginning.

THE LOVE OF THE DEAD reveals the limitless depths to which man can sink in his sexual cravings. A REAL SHOCKER!

From *The Love of the Dead:*

More so we might, for a moment take up the ancient Pharoahs of Egypt ... the great temples built in their honor, their memorials ... their tombs ... Their demand of the female mate or mates and Eunuchs to accompany them through the land of the dead. It is not above thought that the brides of the corpse (the Pharoah) have taken him on sexually even in death. Most men actually die with a hard-on and the instrument must be broken before he can be folded into his everlasting box.

The ancients didn't bother to break the thing of the Pharoah. After a time the girls took care of that for the undertakers. Dead or alive no man can keep a hard-on forever.

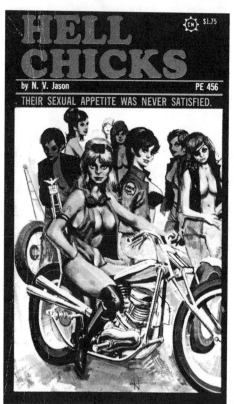

ONE, TWO, THREE
(Viceroy VP 311, 1968, 156 pp.)

A study of orgasm ghosted again for "Jason Nichols." Chapters include: "The Mecca for Twisted Sex," "Clothing and Auto-Erotic Sexuality," "The Secret Sex Sorority."

YOUNG, BLACK AND GAY
(French Line FL-38, 1968, 156 pp.)

A homosexual transvestite adapts to prison life, taking the female sex role while absorbing convict philosophy. He winds up the victim of a brutal beating in a filthy alley.

HELL CHICKS
(Private Edition Books PE 456, 1968, 188 pp.)

Ghosted under "N. V. Jason," *Hell Chicks* is one of Wood's most crazed, anarchistic novels. The complete disregard for normal rules of grammar suggest that it was written in one sitting. Unleashed in distorted, alcoholic twists of consciousness, the novel takes the girl gangs from his screenplays for *The Violent Years* and *Fugitive Girls* to the ne plus ultra of sex and violence. The Hell Chicks are twelve rough tough broads in black leather jackets. Their credo: "Rules are LAWS and LAWS were meant to be broken." Hopped up on grass and beer they roar across the countryside on their hogs, raping any man they can get their hands on. Pussy, Pisser, Prancer, Sissy, Syph, Boobie, Cherry and Flame meet their inevitable end in a climactic bloody showdown with the law.

PURPLE THIGHS
(Private Edition PE 461, 1968, 156 pp.)

Originally titled *Lost Souls Delivered,* this is Wood's fantastic take on hippies and drugs, as an outsider.

CARNIVAL PIECE
(Private Edition PE 473, 1969, 160 pp.)

Imbroglios concerning carnivals, a murdered dancing girl and her stunning young blonde replacement who attracts the attentions of the local sheriff, the owner of the carnival and Mama Tate, a fat lesbian. Characters include Wheezy the Skeleton, who prefers wine to food; the Geek, another wino who bites the heads off snakes and chickens; Bertha the 450 pound fat woman; the tattoo man; the magician ("a ham bone lush"); the wolf man who "glues hair on his body everyday while he sniffs the glue and pops heroin into his veins"; and Matty, the female impersonator who does the half-man, half-woman act.

The author's pseudonym, "Kathleen Everett," is Kathy Wood's maiden name.

TONI: BLACK TIGRESS
(Private Edition PE 474, 1969, 188 pp.)

Toni, a pretty 18-year-old black girl, is trained by a militant black organization. In Madame Rose's whorehouse, she learns about the weaknesses of men. As in his Watts novels, Wood portrays militant black groups as essentially corrupt organizations manipulating "the rabble." Wood's inscription in a copy of the book to an associate: "Don't let 'em have my address or phone number ... a bombed out house I don't need."

MAMA'S DIARY
(Tiger Books / Powell Publications 129, 1969, 224 pp.)

A popular sex novelist is "drafted" to run a chain of whorehouses in Vietnam. The characters are caricatures evoking the sex cartoons of Bill Ward. According to Kathy Wood, "Eddie treasured that book. It was something that he did that he really liked and I liked it too ..." Apparently, Wood wrote a screenplay of the book which was made into a movie called *Operation Red Light* by Jacques Descent Productions. Wood was reportedly not entirely pleased with the results.

TO MAKE A HOMO
(Little Library Press 3003, "Classic Adult Series," 1971, 191 pp.)

A high school student is blackmailed into homosexual relations with an older boy, who hooks him on drugs so he will remain a sex slave. Drugged, homosexual rape is the centerpiece of this sexual "tragedy." Probably the most sexually explicit of Wood's novels, it is particularly interesting for the descriptions of a transvestite:

> As if by instinct his free left hand began to lightly travel up and down the side of his body. When it connected with the soft angora his hips trembled. then the hand went up the sweater front and took the breasts, one at a time. They felt as soft and real as any girl's tits he'd ever felt. He made himself believe they were real and they were actually connected to his own body. He closed his eyes to retain the mental thoughts he had conjured up ... it was he, naked again, and dressing in the clothes he had on ... but then it was not the body of a male which he saw. It was the body of a lovely teenage girl with his face. The thing he held in his hand was not his own tool, but looked very much like the one Tommy had between his legs ... the one he had sucked on such a long time ago ... and Paul used that instrument to force open the lips of the vagina he believed had suddenly appeared there. He dug the meat deep inside and the deeper it went the more his body trembled for release. No longer did he feel he was masturbating the male penis ... it was inside him and he was screwing the girl within ... for indeed he did feel all girl at that point ... if there was any doubt, all he had to do was open his eyes and look into the mirror and the girl, Pauline, the name he suddenly adopted, would be looking back at him.

MARY-GO-ROUND
(Little Library Press 3010, 1972, 191 pp.)

Mary, a 19-year-old virgin, finds a job with Glamour Bros. carnival, where she is initiated into the "queer jungle of human wrecks" and the world of sex. Similar to *Carnival Piece,* but more raw, especially in sexual descriptions and the carny vernacular. His inscription to Steve Apostolof: "Let's get a million budget and make this one into a film."

From *Carnival Piece:*

> Shirlee then looked up directly into Mary's eyes. "You ain't never seen a prick before ... a cock ... a penis ... a dork ... the banana ... the jimmy-john ... the dink ... the jack-in-the-box ... the private prong ... the wang ... the wheenie ... the meat whistle ... the golden rivet ... the syph pounder ...

the gulping meat ... the black jack ... the cheese cutter ... the pussy prober ... the peter ... the meat and two vegetables ... the tool ... the hot dog ... the jerking iron ... the hot rod ... the joy stick ... the snake ... the stalk ... the tellywhacker ... the organ .... the red hot poker ... the red cap .. the poon-tanger .... the phallus .... the ying yang ... the dick ... the throat spoon ... the jock? You ain't never seen this thing before?" And again the man / girl pulled up the skirt and slipped aside the frilly panty crotch and exposed the dick again. Only this time it was hard as a rock and stood out more than eight inches and the head which had the foreskin over it before was in full view, throbbing and purple.

A STUDY OF THE SONS AND DAUGHTERS OF EROTICA
(Secs Press SP 122, 1971, 192 pp.)

This Wood book is attributed to the compilation of "Dick Trent with Dr. T. K. Peters." Covers swingers, scopophilia, lesbianism, homosexuality, transvestism (called "Eonism"), Sacher-Masoch and Marquis De Sade, the occult arts, erotopathy, prostitution. Wood quotes from Criswell and from Anton LaVey's *Satanic Bible*.

SEXUAL PRACTICES IN WITCHCRAFT AND BLACK MAGIC
(Secs Press SP 112, 1971, 191 pp.)

By "Frank Lennon with Dr. T. K. Peters," this one includes such chapters as: "Why White Women," "The Necromancer," "Hypnosis," "Witches," "The Fickle Finger," "Lycanthropy and Zoanthropy," "Vampires and Ghouls."

BLACK MYTH
(Secs Press SP 116, 1971, 192 pp.)

"A detailed analysis of the sexual and sociological misinformation surrounding black sexuality." By "Dick Trent with Dr. T. K. Peters."

THE SEXUAL WOMAN, BOOK TWO
(Secs Press SP 125, 1971, 191 pp.)

By "Mandy Merrill with Dr. T. K. Peters." "The sexual woman! What makes her different? An in-depth study of female sensuality ... for men or women."

THE SEXUAL MAN, BOOK TWO
(Secs Press, SP-127, 1971)

By "Frank Leonard with Dr. T. K. Peters."

THE ONLY HOUSE
(Little Library Press 2016, 1972, 159 pp.)

A married couple seek the help of a sorceress to solve their sexual problems. Through various surrogates, the wife's frigidity is cured though the husband's premature ejaculation is not so easily remedied until he climbs into a coffin with the sorceress and finally becomes a man who can please a woman.

The Only House appears to be the plot of Wood's 1971 film *Necromania*. At the same time, Wood also made the film *The Young Marrieds,* which may also be known as *The Only House.* The novel was published in short story form as "Come Inn" in *Young Beaver* magazine, 1971.

A STUDY OF FETISHES AND FANTASIES
(Edusex Press ED 113, 1973, 191 pp.)

Part of Gallery Press' "continuing Encyclopedia of Sex. The complete series covers every aspect of sexual information and knowledge." Digest-sized, presented in "educational style" format with graphic photographs in color and black and white. "By Edw. D. Wood, Jr. and Norman Bates."

A STUDY IN THE MOTIVATION OF CENSORSHIP, SEX & THE MOVIES, BOOK 1
(Edusex Press ED 111, Gallery Publications, 1973, 190 pp.)

Covers the history of censorship in movies, stag films, the motion picture code, themes of sex films, problems of low budget filmmakers, taboo-breaking mainstream movies, loops.

A STUDY IN THE MOTIVATION OF CENSORSHIP, SEX & THE MOVIES, BOOK 2
(Edusex Press ED 112, 1973, 192 pp.)

Covers the murder of William Desmond Taylor, the Fatty Arbuckle scandal, George Weiss and the "forty thieves," *Glen or Glenda,* early sexploitation movies, Bill Thompson, the future of sex movies. Photographs are from hardcore sex loops.

TALES FOR A SEXY NIGHT, VOL. 1
(Gallery Press GP 101 Vol. 1, 1973, 159 pp.)

This volume consists of one novelette and 14 short stories culled from Gallery Press magazines. "The Devil and the Deep Blue-Eyed Blonde" by "Dick Trent" is Wood's story, and concerns a blonde undercover agent and her mission in an unnamed country during a revolution.

TALES FOR A SEXY NIGHT, VOL. 2
(Gallery Press GP 102, 1973, 159 pp.)

In this companion volume, Wood has the following stories:

"Final Curtain" , based on Wood's short film. An actor, after the final performance of a horror play, wanders backstage, drawn by an unknown force.

"To Kill a Saturday Night." Two derelicts in a small town speculate on their activities for the night. Based on Wood's script of the same name.

"Craps." After his funeral, a legendary crap shooter's friends talk about his death.

"Calamity Jane Loves Hosenose Kate Loves Cattle Anne." When Calamity Jane's beloved, Wild Bill Hickok, is shot dead, she has words with Hosenose Kate, owner of the High Dyke saloon. She speaks of revenge against Cattle Anne, one of Wild Bill's lovers.

"In the Stony Lonesome." Hector, a sadistic bully who calls himself The Grim Reaper, forces young girls to succumb to his sexual demands in a graveyard atop the marble slab of old lady Kanthru, "the rich old witch."

OUTLAWS OF THE OLD WEST
(Mankind BM 012, 1973, 153 pp.)

This book, compiled and edited by Charles D. Anderson, has a nine page Wood story titled "Pearl Hart and the Last Stage," which concerns the last stage robber and her capture. Wood worked with editor Anderson at Pendulum Publications.

DEATH OF A TRANSVESTITE HOOKER
(Eros Goldstripe CLS 104, "Connoisseur Library Series," 1974, 182 pp., photos)

"By Randy, as told to Dick Trent." Brief and sordid episodes with a Hollywood Boulevard transvestite prostitute. "The pink fades fast under the lash."

FORCED ENTRY
(Eros Goldstripe BLS 105, Blackpool Library Series, 1974, 181 pp.)

Unsatisfied wife learns to love anal sex. "By John Quinn."

From *Forced Entry:*

> She went directly to the living room and sought out Ralph's scotch. She seldom ever drank. She actually couldn't even remember what the stuff tasted like. But she always heard that when men have certain problems they call for a drink. It always seemed to pick them up right away ... give them that new and extra needed lift to set them straight again ... at least that's what she had always heard ...
>
> One didn't do it. Two blurred her eyes. And the third made her giggle. Was that what they meant by setting everything straight again? It must have been because she felt good all over. Not the kind of good she got when

she got sexed, but the kind of good when she felt ... well ... good and giddy, like she wanted to laugh all the time.

TV LUST
(Eros Goldstripe TSL 102, 1977, 180 pp.)

Before going out on a hit, a transvestite killer for the underworld mixes martinis and flashes back on his formative experiences: a traumatic moment occurs when his father discovers him dressed in female undergarments, masturbating to climax in front of his bedroom mirror. His father never speaks to him again and dies soon afterward, slumping in front of the television. The transvestite attends his father's funeral dressed in black — as a woman.

From *TV Lust:*

> Chris pushed up the sleeve of the fur coat and the angora and looked at the watch. It was time. "Solly will be coming out of that door of the diner in one minute. That gives me just time." He reached for his gun case, opened it and took out the pistol.
>
> He got out of the car and put the pistol into the coat pocket, and the high boots moved through the deepening snow. The heavily falling flakes felt good on his face. He loved the feeling of snow.
>
> The end of the alley was one step away when Richard fired the automatic pistol, then was gone. Chris had seen who it was in that split second before he was on the ground dying, the snow falling on his dead face softly like small bits of the angora fur he had always loved.

OTHER ED WOOD BOOK TITLES INCLUDE:

Hollywood Rat Race; Hollywood Sext Book; Riot, Rape & Revelry; And He Rode All Night; The Producer; The Greek Connection; They; The Pleasure Dorm; Saving Grace: The Last Lash; The Trouble With ----?; Swedish House.

SHORT STORIES

Wood had literally hundreds of short stories and articles published in *Pendulum, Calga* and *Gallery Press* magazines from 1968 to 1978. He used pseudonyms as well as his own name. The following is a partial list:

"Castle of Dracula," "Voyage of Dracula," "Lust of the Vampire" appeared in

Monster Sex Tales, Vol. 1, No. 1, Gallery Press, Aug / Sept. 1972.

"Cease to Exist," Bums Rush Terror," "The Witches of Amau Ra," "The Rue Morgue Revisited," "Scream Your Bloody Head Off," "Hellfire," Gore in the Alley," appeared in *Horror Sex Tales,* Vol. 1, No. 1, Gallery Press, 1972.

"Wanted: Belle Starr" in *Woman's World,* Vol. 2, No. 2, Gallery Press, 1973.

"Dracula Revisited" in *Wild Couples,* Vol. 3, No. 3, Gallery, 1971.

"That Damned Faceless Fog" in *Beavers,* Vol. 6, No. 1, Pendulum, 1972.

"Try It You'll Like It" in *Woman's World,* Vol. 2, No. 1, Gallery, 1973.

"In the Stony Lonesome," in *Sex Stars,* Vol. 2, No. 1, Gallery 1974.

"Not So Freewheeling," in *Goldiggers,* Vol. 7, No. 1, Gallery, 1975.

"Ever Hear of a Dingbat?" in *Deuce,* Vol. 2, No. 1, Gallery, 1973.

"Flowers for Flame Lemarr" in *Bi-Sex,* Vol. 2, No. 1, Gallery, 1975.

"Whorehouse Horror" in Garter Magazine, Vol. 1, No. 1, Gallery 1974.

"The Fright Wigs," in *The Wild Cats,* Vol. 5, No. 2, Pendulum, 1971.

"Out of the Fog" in *Two Plus Two,* Vol. 3, No. 2, Pendulum, 1971.

"Come Inn" in *Young Beaver,* Vol. 5, No. 4, Pendulum, 1971.

"No Atheists in the Grave" in *Hot Fun* Magazine, Vol. 2, No. 2, Calga, 1971.

"To Kill a Saturday Night" in *Black and White,* Vol. 2, No. 1, Pendulum, 1972.

"Final Curtain" in *Belly Button,* Vol. 2, No. 2, 1971.

"The Wave Off," *Freaked Out* magazine

"Missionary Position Impossible," "Captain Fellatio Hornblower," "Phantom of What Opera?" no information available.

Ed directs *The Sinister Urge*

Filmography

1948

THE STREETS OF LAREDO (also: **CROSSROADS OF LAREDO**)

Unreleased — no soundtrack — 16mm — 30 min.

Produced by Tony Lawrence and John Crawford Thomas

Written and Directed by Edward D. Wood, Jr.

Camera by Ray Flin and Ed Wood, Jr.

Cast: Duke Moore (Lem); Ruth McCabe (Barbara); Don Nagel (Tex); Chuck LaBerge (Sheriff); John Crawford Thomas (Deputy); Ed Wood (Cowboy); Bill Ames (Bartender)

Notes: Wood's first real movie was never completed. Shot silent, a soundtrack (which was to consist of cowboy ballads and sparse dubbed dialogue) was never added.

1951

THE SUN WAS SETTING (also: **THE SUN ALSO SETS**)

Empire Productions / W.D.B.C. Prod. Inc. — 16mm — 20 min.

Written, Directed and Produced by Edward D. Wood, Jr.

Cameraman: Ray Flin

Cast: Angela Stevens, Tom Keene, Phyllis Coates

Synopsis: A woman is dying in her New York apartment. Two friends visit and she tells of her desire to go to Chinatown and the village. They attempt to dissuade her. After they leave, the woman, unable to bear her confinement, leaves the room and dies.

Notes: Shooting was at KTTV studios, Sunset and Van Ness, during the week of Dec. 17, 1951.

1952

THE LAWLESS RIDER

United Artists (Oct. 1954 release) — 62 min.

Directed by Yakima Canutt

Screenplay by Edward D. Wood, Jr. (Credited to Johnny Carpenter)

Camera: William C. Thompson

Cast: Johnny Carpenter (Rod Tatum); Frankie Darro (Jim Bascom); Douglas Dumbrille (Marshal Brady); Frank Carpenter (Big Red); Noel Neill (Nancy James); Kenne Duncan (Freno Frost); Bud Osborne (Tulso); Bill Coontz (Red Rooks)

1953

GLEN OR GLENDA (I LED TWO LIVES; I CHANGED MY SEX)

A Screen Classics Release, April, 1953 — 67 min.

Written and Directed by Edward D. Wood, Jr.

Produced by George Weiss

Photography: William C. Thompson; Camera Operator: Bert Shipham; Makeup: Harry Thomas; Sound Technician: Ben Winkler; Music Consultant: Sandford Dickinson; Medical Advisor: Dr. Nathan Bailey; Settings: Jack Miles; Unit Director: Scott McCloud

Cast: Bela Lugosi (The Spirit); Dolores Fuller (Barbara); Tim Farrell (Dr. Alton/Narrator); Lyle Talbot (Inspector Warren); Daniel Davis [Edward D. Wood, Jr.] (Glen/Glenda); Charles Crafts

(Johnny); "Tommy" Haynes (Alan /Anne); Captain DeZita (The Devil/Glen's Father); Evelyn Wood (Sheila, Glen's Sister); Shirley Speril (Miss Stevens); Conrad Brooks (Reporter/pickup artist/bearded drag); Henry Bederski (Man with hat and receding hairline); William C. Thompson (Judge); Mr. Walter (Patrick/Patricia); Harry Thomas (Man in nightmare); George Weiss (Man at transvestite's suicide)

Notes: *Glen or Glenda* was shot at Jack and Helen Miles' Larchmont Studios under the title *Behind Locked Doors; Transvestite;* then *I Changed My Sex.* It was first released as *Glen or Glenda* with the alternate titles *I Changed My Sex* and *I Led Two Lives* for different territories. It was reported also known as *He or She?* Additional footage of women in scant clothing and a mild bondage theme from a Weiss production directed by Merle Connell was later added to subsequent prints (*I Lied Two Lives* and *I Changed My Sex)* for commercial reasons. It was released world-wide and played in France and Belgium as *Louis ou Louise,* Argentina as *Yo Cambie Mi Sexo.* It also played throughout the orient. Wood's comments on this film in his own books is of interest. From *A Study in the Motivation of Censorship, Sex & the Movies,* 1973:

> I wrote and directed several films, including *Glen or Glenda* in the early 1950's when the sex change had been a national sensation.... The producer with the guts to attempt bringing such a deviant type of film to the screen was a delightful, gutsy little fellow named George Weiss. He produced films in a small, barn-like studio affair just off Santa Monica Boulevard in Hollywood. He didn't have a hell of a lot of money (he screamed at me for spending $26,000 on Glen or Glenda), but he couldn't see where anyone should tell him what he could or could not produce.

> The title later changed to *I Led Two Lives* in order to capture in on two very important shows of the period. The Christine Jorgenson sex-change case and the very popular *I Led Three Lives* television series.

> It was a film which was to have discussions with the censors many times ... Bela Lugosi carried the spirit like God who arranged all these things on Earth.

> There was the moralistic value. As long as there was a God or a Judge taking the curse off at the end, there was the moralistic value which was proven. As long as the wrongdoer, the deviant-doer, the evildoer is put down at the end, the films generally passed the censor.

And from *The Sons and Daughters of Erotica,* he wrote in June, 1971:

> [The transvestite] must wear female attire during the [sex] act —and frustrating as it can be — he has to search out a mate who will give in completely to his deviant pleasures....

> Such a frustration has caused many transvestites to dress and make up to perfection, then commit suicide after leaving a note of instructions to the undertaker, instructing him as to burial arrangements. He is to be buried in the female attire he was wearing at the time of death. A famous movie depicting this type of case was produced and distributed [...] some years ago. The title was *Glen or Glenda* (later retitled *I Changed My Sex)* which was shown in nearly every country of the world, including the US Air Force hospital in Japan and a recent series of performances on the Island of Formosa.

Dolores Fuller suffers under the weight of Ed Wood's transvestism in *Glen or Glenda*
[photo courtesy Michael Luca]

1953

CROSSROAD AVENGER: THE ADVENTURES OF THE TUCSON KID

Tucson Kid Productions — 25 min. — color
Written and Directed by Edward D. Wood, Jr.
Produced by Lew Dubin
Associate Producer: John E. Clarke
Camera: Ray Flin
Sound: Tribby
Film Editor: Lou Guinn
Art Director: Cowboy Slim
Cast: Tom Keene (Tucson Kid); Tom Tyler (The Deputy); Lyle Talbot (Bart); Don Nagel (Dance); Harvey Dunn (Zeke); Forbes Murray (Roger); Kenne Duncan (Lefty); Bud Osborne (Max); Ed Wood, Jr. (Pony Express Rider)

Notes: Wood filmed a sequel, *Crossroad Avenger Returns* (no credits available) and the two unsold tv pilots were combined in a 50-minute film called *The Adventures of the Tucson Kid* (1953). According to Wood, his *Crossroad Avenger* pilot was passed up in favor of *Wild Bill Hickock*, with Guy Madison.

1953
BOOTS
Tucson Kid Productions
Written and Directed by Edward D. Wood, Jr.
Approx. 25 min.

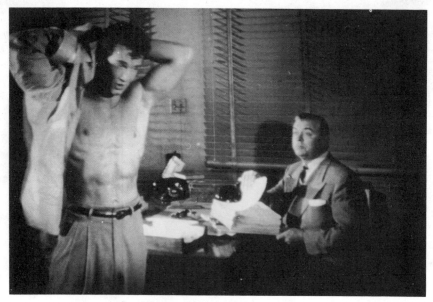

Steve Reeves and Lyle Talbot in *Jailbait*

1954
JAILBAIT (also: THE HIDDEN FACE)
Howco Productions. Release date: May 12, 1954 — 72 min.
Produced and Directed by Edward D. Wood, Jr.
Screenplay by Alex Gordon and Edward D. Wood, Jr.
Photography: William C. Thompson
Editors: Charles Clement and Igo Kantor
Music: Hoyt Curtin
Make-up: John Sylvester and Harry Thomas
Sound: Dale Knight
Lighting: Harry Folz
Dresses: Gene D. Evans
Lingerie: Chic & Pandora
Special Effects: Ray Mercer
Cast: Lyle Talbot (Inspector Johns); Dolores Fuller (Marilyn Gregor); Steeve Reeves (Lt. Bob Lawrence); Herbert Rawlinson (Dr. Boris Gregor); Theodora Thurman (Loretta); Clancy Malone [Scott McCloud] (Don Gregor); Timothy Farrell (Vic Brady); John Robert Martin (Det. McCall); Cotton Watts and Chick (Themselves); Bud Osborne (Night Watchman); Mona McKinnon (Miss Willis); Don Nagel (Det. Davis); La Vada Simmons (Miss Lytell); Regina Claire (Newspaper Woman); John Avery (Police Doctor); Edward D. Wood, Jr. (Radio News

Announcer); Conrad Brooks (Medical Attendant/Photographer); Henry Bederski (Suspect in Police Station).

Notes: Herbert Rawlinson, former silent film star, died of lung cancer the morning after his night's shooting was completed. According to Alex Gordon, Rawlinson's role as Dr. Boris Gregor was originally intended for Bela Lugosi, who couldn't do it. Gordon's idea for *The Hidden Face* came from producer Edward Small's 1935 *Let 'Em Have It* (British title: *False Faces)* which concerned a gangster who has his face altered by a plastic surgeon to elude the law.

According to *Variety, Jailbait* cost $22,000 and was previewed at the Monterey Theater in Monterey Park, CA., where several sequences were filmed. (Mona McKinnon enters a theater in an angora hat and witnesses a robbery-murder).

Howco producer-director Ron Ormond suggested the title change from *The Hidden Face* to *Jailbait.* The music in *Jailbait* by Hoyt Curtin (composer of the music for *The Jetsons* and numerous Japanese cartoons) was previously used in Ormond's *Mesa of Lost Women.*

The black vaudeville number was from Ron Ormond's *Yes Sir, Mr. Bones!*

1955
BRIDE OF THE MONSTER (BRIDE OF THE ATOM)

A Rolling M Production/Banner Productions Release — 68 min.
Produced, Written and Directed by Edward D. Wood, Jr.
Executive Producer: Donald E. McCoy
Associate Producer: Tony McCoy
Photography: William C. Thompson and Ted Allan
Special Effects: Pat Dinga
Music: Frank Worth
Editor: Warren Adams
Technical Supervisor: Igo Kantor
Sound: Dale Knight and Lyle Willey
Sound Effects: Ray Erlenborn and Mike Pollock
Cast: Bela Lugosi (Dr. Eric Vornoff); Tor Johnson (Lobo); Tony McCoy (Lt. Dick Craig); Loretta King (Janet Lawton); Harvey Dunne (Capt. Robbins); George Becwar (Prof. Strowski); Paul Marco (Kelton); Don Nagel (Martin); Bud Osborne (Mac); Jake Warren (Jake); Anne Wilner (Tillie); Dolores Fuller (Margie); William Benedict (Newsboy); Ben Frommer (Police Station suspect); Conrad Brooks (Policeman/Suspect).

Notes: *Bride of the Monster* was originally title *The Monster of the Marshes,* and began filming Oct. 26, 1954 at the Ted Allan Studios as *Bride of the Atom.* Ted Allan shot the scenes featuring the newspaper background, and Lugosi entering a trap door. Shooting was halted when actor George Becwar complained to the Screen Actors Guild. Shooting resumed in March, 1955, at Centaur Studios. Segments of the movie were shot on location at Palm Canyon in Griffith Park.

Assistant director William Nolte was a veteran producer/director of "B" westerns of the '30's and '40's *(Range Busters, Boot Hill Bandits,* etc). He directed the 1938 *Blonde Venus,* with Lena Horne.

Wood gave Alex Gordon co-screenplay credit for giving him an idea about a swamp and an octopus, although the screenplay is entirely Wood's. Wood's salary for directing *Bride of the Monster* was $350.00. The original Hollywood premiere was May 11, 1955, at the Paramount Theater. It went into general release in 1956.

A scene from *The Violent Years* [photo courtesy The Fred Mollin Collection]

1956

THE VIOLENT YEARS

A Headliner Production Picture. Produced by Del Productions. 58 min.
Produced by Roy Reid.
Director and Associate Producer: William M. Morgan
Screenplay by Edward D. Wood, Jr.
Photography: William C. Thompson
Editor: Gerard Wilson
Music Supervision: Manuel Francisco
Set Director: Jack Miles
Wardrobe: Victor Most of California
Cast: Jean Moorehead (Paul Parkins); Barbara Weeks (Jane Parkins); Arthur Millan (Carl Parkins); Theresa Hancock (Georgia); Joanne Cangi (Geraldine); Gloria Farr (Phyllis); Glen Corbett (Barney Stetson); Lee Constant (Sheila); Stanford Jolley (Judge Raymond Clara); Timothy Farrell (Lt. Homes/Narrator); Bruno Metsa (Manny); Harry Keaton (Doctor).

Notes: The picture was based on an original story by B. L. Hart (Roy Reid) titled *Teenage Killers. The Violent Years* was originally slated for release as *Girl Gang Terrorists* and *Teenage Girl Gang*. The director was recruited from television and died a few years after the film was made. It was re-released in 1966 as *Female. The Violent Years* was a box-office winner on the exploitation circuit on its original release.

1956

PLAN 9 FROM OUTER SPACE (GRAVE ROBBERS FROM OUTER SPACE)

A D.C.A. release, July, 1959. 79 minutes.
Produced, directed and written by Edward D. Wood, Jr.
Executive Producer: J. Edward Reynolds
Associate Producers: Hugh Thomas and Charles Burg
Music Supervisor: Gordon Zahler
Photography: William C. Thompson
Editor: Edward D. Wood, Jr.
Special Effects: Charles Duncan
Sound: Dale Knight
Set Construction: Tom Kemp
Make-up: Harry Thomas and Tom Bartholomew
Set Dresser: Harry Reif
Wardrobe: Dick Chaney

Cast: Tor Johnson (Inspector Clay); Vampira (Vampire Girl); Tom Keene (Col. Edwards); Gregory Walcott (Jeff Trent); Dudley Manlove (Eros); Mona McKinnon (Paula Trent); Duke Moore (Lt. Harper); Joanna Lee (Tanna); Bela Lugosi (Ghoul Man); John "Bunny" Breckinridge (The Ruler); Lyle Talbot (Gen. Roberts); Criswell (Himself); Carl Anthony (Patrolman Larry); Paul Marco (Kelton); Norma McCarty (Edith); David DeMering (Danny); Bill Ash (Captain); Conrad Brooks (Patrolman Jamie); Gloria Dea (Mourner); Ben Frommer (Mourner); J. Edward Reynolds (Gravedigger); Hugh Thomas (Gravedigger); Tom Mason (Lugosi's double); Rev. Lyn Lemon (Minister, Clay's funeral); Don Davis (Drunk); Karl Johnson (Farmer Calder); Dick Chaney (Man Carrying stretcher); Edward D. Wood, Jr. (Man holding newspaper).

Notes: *Plan 9 From Outer Space* began shooting at Merle Connell's Quality Studios towards the last part of Nov., 1956 as *Grave Robbers From Outer Space*. Actual shooting time was between 4 and 6 days.

According to Ed Wood, "Lugosi needed a thousand dollars, so I just shot some footage of him." Lugosi's scenes were probably shot in Spring, 1955, before Bela entered Norwalk hospital. Though it has been claimed that this footage was shot for *The Vampire's Tomb,* they bear no relation to the script.

The space station was built by Tommy Kemp; the space costumes were created by the uncredited fashion designer Robaire. Phil Tucker, director of *Robot Monster,* assisted Wood with the editing. Russian composer Mossolov's "Iron Foundry" is used for *Plan 9's* title credits, and is played throughout the movie.

Plan 9 was previewed as *Grave Robbers from Outer Space* at the Carlton Theater, Los Angeles, March 15, 1957. It went into general release in the US in July, 1959, as *Plan 9 from Outer Space,* on the bottom of a double bill with D.C.A.'s *Time Lock.*

1957

FINAL CURTAIN

Atomic Productions — 20 min.
Produced, Written and Directed by Edward D. Wood, Jr.
Executive Producers: Ernest S. Moore, Anthony Cardoza, Thomas Mason, Walter Brannon
Photography: William C. Thompson

Music Supervision: Gordon Zahler

Sound: Dale Knight

Cast: James "Duke" Moore (The Actor); Dudley Manlove (Narrator); Jenny Stevens (The Vampire)

Synopsis: After the last performance of a horror play, the vampire star wanders in the empty theater, compelled by an unknown force to seek an unknown object.

Notes: *Final Curtain* was the script Bela Lugosi was reading when he died. Duke Moore was later given his role. *Final Curtain* was a pilot episode for a projected anthology series called *Portraits in Terror*. Parts of *Final Curtain* later turned up in *Night of the Ghouls*. Executive Producer Ernest Moore was Duke Moore's brother. *Final Curtain* remained one of Wood's favorite films.

1957

THE NIGHT THE BANSHEE CRIED

Atomic Productions — 22 min.

Produced, Directed and Written by Edward D. Wood, Jr.

Charlotte Austin and Spanky the Gorilla (Ray "Crash" Corrigan) in *The Bride and the Beast* [photo courtesy David J. Hogan]

1958

THE BRIDE AND THE BEAST

Al Allied Artists release — 78 min.

Produced and Directed by Adrian Weiss

Screenplay by Edward D. Wood, Jr., from a story by Adrian Weiss
Script Consultant: Dr. Tom Mason
Photography: Roland Price
Music: Les Baxter
Editor: George Merrick
Assistant Director: Harry Fraser
Special Effects: Gerald Endler
Make-up: Harry Thomas
Cast: Charlotte Austin (Laura); Lance Fuller (Dan); Johnny Roth (Taro); Steve Calvert/Ray "Crash" Corrigan (Spanky the Gorilla); William Justine (Dr. Reiner); Jeanne Gerson (Marka); Gil Frye (Cameron); Slick Slavin (Soldier); Bhogwan Singh (Native); Jean Ann Lewis (Stewardess).

Synopsis: On their wedding night, Laura is curiously attracted to a pet gorilla in her husband's cellar. Through hypnosis, it is revealed that in a previous incarnation she was the Queen of the Gorillas.

Notes: The original title for *The Bride and the Beast* was *Queen of the Gorillas*. The assistant director, Harry Fraser, an associate of Wood's, directed many PRC westerns in the '40's, as well as *Chained for Life* (1951), an exploitation picture starring Violet and Daisy Hilton, the Siamese twins who also appeared in Tod Browning's *Freaks* (1932).

Stills showing a semi-nude Charlotte Austin and the gorilla are not represented in the version which played television.

1958
NIGHT OF THE GHOULS (REVENGE OF THE DEAD)
Atomic Productions — 69 min.
Written, Directed and Produced by Edward D. Wood, Jr.
Executive Producer: Major J.C. Foxworthy, USMC, (Ret.)
Associate Producers: Marge Usher, Tony Cardoza, Tom Mason, Paul Marco, Walt Brannon, Gordon Chesson
Director of Photography: William C. Thompson
Music Supervisor: Gordon Zahler
Make-up: Harry Thomas
Lighting: John Murray
Assistant Directors: Ronnie Ashcroft, Scott Lynch
Art Director: Kathleen O'Hara Everett
Sound: Harry Smith
Costumes: Mickey Meyers
Cast: Kenne Duncan (Dr. Acula); Duke Moore (Lt. Daniel Bradford); Valda Hansen (The White Ghost); Tor Johnson (Lobo); John Carpenter (Capt. Robbins); Paul Marco (Kelton); Don Nagel (Sgt. Crandall); Jeannie Stevens (The Black Ghost/Mannikin); Bud Osborne (Mr. Darmoor); Harvey B. Dunne (Henry); Thomas R. Mason (Wingate Foster's Ghost); Marcelle Hemphill (Mrs. Wingate Yates Foster); Clay Stone (Young Man); Margaret Mason (Martha); Henry Bederski (Drunk); James La Maida (Hall); Tony Cardoza (Tony); John Gautieri (Boy); Karen Hairston (Girl); Karl Johnson, Leonard Barnes, Frank Barbarick, Francis Misitano, David De Mering (The Dead Men); Criswell (Himself).

Notes: Filming on *Night of the Ghouls* (previewed as *Revenge of the Dead*) began in late April of 1958. Originally scheduled to appear in the film were Dudley Manlove, Mona McKinnon, Tom Keene, Lloyd Simons, Tom Duggan, and Roy Barcroft. Filming was reported to have been completed at the end of May, according to *Daily Variety.*

A snatch of film showing a fight between Wood and Conrad Brooks originally shot for Wood's 1956 *Rock and Roll Hell (Hellborn)* is included to illustrate the problem of juvenile delinquency. The scenes of Jeannie Stevens as the mannikin which comes to life were from *Final Curtain,* as were the scenes of Duke Moore ascending the staircase with the cold, clammy railing.

According to Valda Hansen, the film played as *Revenge of the Dead* in Hollywood at the Vista theater.

Jean Fontaine, Jeanne Willardson, Carl Anthony in *The Sinister Urge.*
Note lobby cards for Wood films on the wall.

1960
THE SINISTER URGE
Headliner Productions — 75 min.
Producer: Roy Reid
Story and Direction: Edward D. Wood, Jr.
Associate Producer: Edward D. Wood, Jr.
Director of Photography: William C. Thompson
Set Designer: Jerome Lapari
Film Editor: John Soh
Special Effects: Ray Mercer
Musical Arrangement: Manuel Francisco (Mischa Terr)
Set Dressings: J. B. Finch

Assistant Director: Jim Blake
Sound: Jim Fullerton
Miss Fontaine's Wardrobe: Eileen Younger
Cast: Kenne Duncan (Lt. Matt Carson); James "Duke" Moore (Sgt. Randy Stone); Jean Fontaine (Gloria Henderson); Carl Anthony (Johnny Ryde); Dino Fantini (Dirk Williams); Jeanne Willardson (Mary Smith); Harry Keatan (Jaffe); Harvey B. Dunne (Mr. Romaine); Kenneth Willardson (Theatrical Agent); Reed Howes (Police Inspector); Vic McGee (1st Syndicate Man); Nick Raymond (2nd Syndicate Man); Conrad Brooks (Connie); Ed Wood (Danny), with April Lynn, Toni Costello, Kathy Kendall, Fred Mason, Betty Boatner, Dick Lamson, Claudette Gifford, Jean Bare, Clayton Peca (Drag Cop), Henry Kekoanui, Sylvia Marenco, Vonnie Starr, Paul Main, Raphael Sporer, Rhea Walker, Henry Bederski, Lisa Page Ward, Honey Bee, Candy Paige, Vickie Baker, Carole Gallos, Carmen Lee, John Carpenter.

Notes: *The Sinister Urge* began as a script Ed Wood wrote in 1959 called *Racket Queen*. Wood revised the screenplay for Roy Reid in March of 1960 for the amount of $250.00. *Racket Queen* began shooting Friday, July 15, 1960 for four consecutive days in Jerome Lapari's Rocket Studios on Sunset Boulevard in Hollywood, and then a day for outdoor shots.

Kenne Duncan brought in Lisa Page Ward, Honey Bee and Candy Paige, as well as his girlfriend at the time, Betty Boatner, seen in the opening sequence. Other parts, besides Wood regulars, were cast though Harry Keatan, who ran an acting workshop.

The "Jake's Pizza Joint" sequences were filmed by Wood in 1956 for the partially completed *Rock and Roll Hell*. From a long list of titles, which included *Act of Compulsion, Hollywood After Dark, Immoral Intruder, Chains of Evil,* the final title *The Sinister Urge* was chosen for Headliner Production no. 112.

An additional scene was shot in late August, 1961, in which Dino Fantini (Dirk Williams) rips Rhea Walker's blouse off. This footage replaced a scene in the original release of two high school girls talking of going to Hollywood for fame and fortune.

Wood's salary for directing *The Sinister Urge* was $1000.00, plus a bonus.

1960 - 1961
During these years, Wood wrote, directed and produced the following industrial films for Autonetics: *Aviation Fuel Measurement Systems; Space Capsule in Flight; Radar; Chronometer; Sextant; Minute Man Missile Program*. Wood also directed Autonetics' closed television productions on subjects such as dust free areas for the gyroscopic systems.

1963
SHOTGUN WEDDING
Boris Petroff Productions. Released by Pat Patterson Productions, 12/9/63.
Color — 64 min.
Produced and Directed by Boris Petroff
Screenplay by Edward D. Wood, Jr.
Cast: J. Pat O'Malley (Boy's Father); William Schallert (The Minister); Jenny Maxwell (The Girl); Valerie

[Ad Mat courtesy Jimmy McDonough]

Allen (The Wife); Nan Patterson (The Daughter); Jack Searl (Girl's Father).

Notes: Director Boris Petroff worked under the pseudonym Brooke L. Peters. His films included *The Unearthly* (1957) and *Anatomy of a Psycho* (1961).

1965
ORGY OF THE DEAD

Astra Productions. Released by F.O.G./SCA Distributors
Filmed in Astra Vision and Sexicolor — 82 min.
Produced and Directed by A. C. Stephen (Stephen C. Apostolof)
Screenplay by Edward D. Wood, Jr., from his novel
Assistant Director: Edward D. Wood, Jr.
Music: Jaime Mendoza Nava (conducting the Chilean Symphony Orchestra)
Director of Photography: Robert Caramico
Choreographer: Mark Desmond
Cast: Criswell (The Emperor); Pat Barringer (Shirley / Gold Girl); Fawn Silver (Black Ghoul); William Bates (Bob); Louis Ojena (The Mummy); John Andrews (The Wolfman/Giant); Rod Lindeman (Giant); John Bealy (Detective); Arlene Spooner (Nurse); Colleen O'Brien, Barbara Norton, Mickey Jones, Nadejda Dobrev, Dene Starnes, Texas Starr, Bunny Glaser, Rene de Beau, Stephanie Jones (Dancers).

Synopsis (written by Ed Wood):

The night is dark, a deep darkness only produced by a threatening storm — a blackness cut at brief intervals by the crisscross of violent lightning flashes. The torrents of rain hit with resounding force.

Into this pressure of blackness and the foreboding mountain roads cuts another shaft of light — that of a set of automobile headlights.

A young writer and his fiance drive the perilous dirt road in search of an ancient cemetery, necessary in his research for a new novel ... They have been lost for some hours, unable to find their quest, or to find their way out of the mountains ... When the storm hit, it gave them little chance of turning back ... They could only continue on....

Then ... the accident ... a lightning-felled tree across the road — the squeal of brakes — the scream of injured tires — the crash!!!

A full moon flooded the ancient cemetery with light, even though a heavy fog lay over the entire area — the Master of the Dead and his equally infamous Princess of Darkness left their tomb to seat themselves on marble thrones, once again ready to judge those, the newly

Texas Starr & Lou Ojena in *Orgy of the Dead*
[photo courtesy Steve Apostolof]

dead, brought before them ... THE JUDGEMENT DAY....

The young writer and his fiance, gaining consciousness after the crash, stumble, accidentally, upon these fantastic happenings ... these horrifying rites ... and are soon captured by the "Things" of the Night who take them before the Master, which orders them tied to ceremonial posts so they may watch the proceedings before they too join the others.

The Emperor hears, through interpretive dancing, the pleas of the many newly dead ... The Main Street Prowler who lured men to her apartment and then fleeced and killed them ... The Slave Girl who once was a princess and is now beaten by those who had been the slaves she had beaten ... The Bride who murdered her husband and now must reside with his skeleton ... The Indian Girl who tossed her lovers into the fires ... But for an eternity now must toss herself into the fires continually ... The Island Girl who loved snakes — used them to dispose of her lovers, and who now forever will live with snakes ... The Girl who loved cats, and will remain a cat ... and the One who worshiped Gold above all else — thus she is turned into solid gold.

The Princess of Darkness is about to take the young girl as her own slave when the first rays of the morning sun glisten upon the shiny blade of the knife. The Princess of Darkness, as all the others, are turned back into the skeletons and dust that they really are....

The young writer and his fiance are then rescued from their wrecked car. Was it a dream?

Only the Night People know.

Notes: *Orgy of the Dead* began life as an eighteen page script called *Nudie Ghoulies*. It was to have been composed of ten dances (approx 42 min.), with twenty minutes reserved for the story. The original script was without the wolfman and the mummy characters, and Criswell's "Emperor of the Dead" was called "Skull," a caped figure with "a skull where the head should be," and taloned hands. The cape Criswell wore was Bela Lugosi's Dracula cape from *Abbott and Costello Meet Frankenstein*.

Filming began in Sept., 1965, and the movie was known for a time as *Ghouls and Dolls*, according to assistant Ted V. Mikels (director of *The Astro Zombies*, *Doll Squad*, etc.). Criswell suggested the title *Orgy of the Damned*, which director Steve Apostolof changed to *Orgy of the Dead*.

The uncredited score is by Jaime Mendoza-Nava, who has done numerous motion picture soundtracks. The cameraman, Robert Caramico, went on to direct his own movie, *Sex Rituals of the Occult*, as well as photographing the tv series *Falcon Crest*. Criswell was a frequent guest on Johnny Carson's *Tonight Show*, and would plug the film often.

1969
FOR LOVE OR MONEY
Don Davis Productions / Color 80 min.
Produced and Directed by Don Davis
Adapted from Ed Wood's novel, *Sexecutives*

1969
ONE MILLION AC/DC
Canyon Distributing Co. / Color / 80 min.
Produced and Directed by Ed De Priest
Screenplay by Akdov Telmig (Ed Wood)
Photography: Michael Weldon, Ed De Priest, Eric Torgesson
Historical Consultants: R. L. Frost, Bob Cresse
Cast: Harvey Edmundt, Lawrence Richey, Douglas Martin, Robin Glanz, Jacqueline Fox,

1969
OPERATION REDLIGHT
Jacques Descent Productions / Color
Screenplay by Ed Wood, from his novel *Mama's Diary*
Cast: Ed Wood

1969
GUN RUNNERS
Don Davis Productions / Color
Produced and Directed by Don A. Davis
Screenplay by Ed Wood

1969
THE PHOTOGRAPHER
Robertson - Kay Productions / Color / 63 min.
Produced and Directed by Joseph F. Robertson
Screenplay by Ed Wood
Photography: Hal Guthu
Historical Consultants: R. L. Frost, Bob Cresse
Cast: Ed Wood (Mr. Murphy), Linda Colpin (Linda)
Synopsis: Mr. Murphy, a nudie photographer, interviews an endless parade of women. A group of girls arrive who force Murphy into a dog collar on a chain to act as their slave. He is made to wear a baby doll nightie and women's shoes, and he submits to their fetishistic demands.

1970
TAKE IT OUT IN TRADE
Ashdown-Gonzalez Productions
Color — 80 min.
Written and Directed by Edward D. Wood, Jr.
Produced by Richard Gonzalez and Edward Ashdown
Director of Photography: Hal Guthu
Second Unit: Ben Incremona
Associate Producer: Roy Corrigan
Film Editors: Michael J. Sheridan and Edward D. Wood, Jr.
Assistant Director: Don Nagel
Cast: Donna Stanley (Shirley Riley); Michael Donovan O'Donnell (Mac McGregor); Duke Moore (Frank Riley); Ed Wood (Alecia); Nona Carver (Sleazy Maisie Rumpledinck), with

Casey Lorrain, Linda Colpin, Monica Gayle, Emilie Gray, Donna Young, Lynn Harris, Andrea Rabins, James Kitchens, Hugh Talbert, Judith Koch, Phyllis Stengel, Elaine Jarrett, Linda Spheres, Lou Ojena, Jack Harding, Herb Webber

Synopsis: A private eye's search for the missing daughter of wealthy socialites bears fruit when she turns up working in "Madame Penny's Thrill Establishment."

Notes: *Take it Out in Trade* loosely resembles Ed Wood's sex novels, but with an emphasis on sight gags. Donna Stanley and Monica Gayle starred in the 1969 3-D sexploitation hit, *The Stewardesses.*

The movie marked Wood's return to directing after a hiatus of ten years. Wood demonstrates a preference for the color red: red carpeting, red couches, red stairs, red drapes, red table covers, red bedcovers, red panties, red nighties, etc. Visual puns and slapstick are intermingled with conventional softcore sex scenes.

The detective's global forays are suggested in the most extreme terms: a character in a beret holding a wine bottle staggers past a travel poster of Rome (the same character later is seen whispering to a sexy woman at a cafe table with his bottle of vino, and receiving a stinging slap). A pair of red scanties flies onto a travel poster of Argentina, etc. There are other inventive bits: hooker Sleazy Maisie Rumpledinck has a "no credit" placard on her wall; Papa Riley gets a card from the private eye ("working on a hot tip" — "I wonder what he means by that?"), cut to the detective eagerly licking a woman's nipple.

There are odd touches of para-psychedelicism and surrealism: a woman wearing a black and yellow-striped raincoat carries a yellow umbrella inside Madame Penny's, to the sound of thunder, lightning and rain, nude women endlessly ascend and descend a bright red staircase. There is also the black marble skull on the whorehouse lamp table, as well as the large cobra figurine on the house coffee table. But the most curious, inexplicable touch is the flash of light accompanied by a distorted thunder-like crash which saturate a shot of a couch and curtains at various intervals.

The most remarkable sequence is a seven-minute segment featuring Ed Wood (billed under the name "Alecia") decked out in a lime-green dress, fluffy orange sweater, white plastic boots, and a blonde wig in an extraordinary performance.

Take It Out in Trade was originally to have been handled by MarJon Film Distributors *(Here Comes Dodie, Love Children, Orgy in the Ozarks, Pussy Posse, Dracula Sucks, Strange Hunger, My Butch Stud,* etc.) and was listed in their catalogue, but was never actually picked up.

The movie reportedly played the Pussycat Theater circuit in Los Angeles, and the world premiere may very well have been a topless bar in Glendale.

Ed Wood wrote the following excerpt in *Sensual Films* magazine:

A year ago I made my first film in the nudie market. It was called *Take It Out In Trade,* and although it might be classed with an X rating, I kept away from any sexual contacts simply so that I wouldn't be lying in faking such a scene. It is simply filled with pretty naked girls which any private eye might meet. But I was able to make it real, and filmed it in real localities. This one will not be turned away from at the box office."

1971
NECROMANIA
Cinema Classics Production.
Released by Stacey Films
Color, 16 mm, Approx. 60 min.
Written and Directed by Ed Wood
Camera: Hal Guthu (soft footage),
Ted Gorley (hard footage)
Sound: George Malley
Grip: John Andrews
Editor: Ed Wood
Cast: Rene Bond, Ric Lutze, Marie
Arnold, Ed Wood

1971
THE ONLY HOUSE
A Cinema Classics Production. Released by Stacey Films
Color, sound, 16 mm, approx. 60 min.
Written and Directed by Ed Wood
Camera: Ted Gorley

Notes: "Press material indicates the film concerns prostitutes, bootleggers, ghosts, rapes, lesbianism and orgies." This information from the American Film Institute's Volume on films released in the U.S. between 1960-1970 makes *The Only House in Town* (as they list it) sound suspiciously like *Necromania*. But the movie, made three months after *Necromania*, may also be known as *The Young Marrieds*. To add to the mystery, Wood's novel *The Only House* reads exactly like the plot to *Necromania*. But both *Necromania* and *The Only House* are listed in Wood's resumé. According to Ted Gorley, *The Only House* was inferior to *Necromania* and did not have supernatural elements. It was shot in three days, probably on a budget lower than *Necromania*.

1971
THE UNDERGRADUATE
Jacques Descent Productions
Screenplay: Ed Wood

1972
CLASS REUNION
SCA Distributors
Produced and Directed by A.C. Stephen (Steven Apostolof)
Screenplay by Edward D. Wood, Jr., and A. C. Stephen
Color, 85 min.
Cast: Marsha Jordan (Jeannie); Rene Bond (Thelma); Ric Lutze (Harry); Terry Johnson (Liza); Flora Weisel (Henrietta); Sandy Carey (Fluff); Forman Shane (Charlie); Starlyn Combe (Rosie).

Notes: *Class Reunion* is essentially one simulated sexual coupling after another with tidbits of Wood dialogue sandwiched in between. The high point of the film is Ric Lutze's dialogue at the conclusion: "It's the end of the year and you're so beautiful, you're so beautiful and life is so wonderful. Maybe that's the reason ... the only reason ... well ... there'll always be another class reunion."

1972
THE COCKTAIL HOSTESSES
SCA Distributors
Produced and Directed by A. C. Stephen
Screenplay by Edward D. Wood, Jr. and A. C. Stephen
Music: J. Mendozoff
Director of Photography: R. Ruben
Color, 80 min.
Cast: Rene Bond (Toni); Terry Johnson (Jackie); Lynn Harris (Millie); Kathy Hilton (Lorraine); Forman Shane (Larry); Douglas Frey (Tom); Duane Paulsen (Howard); Norman Field (Henderson).

1972
DROPOUT WIFE
SCA Distributors
Produced and Directed by A. C. Stephen
Screenplay by Edward D. Wood, Jr. and A. C. Stephen
Cast:Angela Canon, Forman Shane, Ric Lutze, Terry Johnson, Rick Cassidy

Ed as "Pops" in *Fugitive Girls,* which Wood also scripted.
[photo courtesy Steve Apostolof]

1974
FUGITIVE GIRLS (5 LOOSE WOMEN)
SCA Distributors
Produced and Directed by A. C. Stephen (Steve Apostolof)
Screenplay by Edward D. Wood, Jr.

Assistant Director: Dick Trent (Ed Wood)
Cameraman: Robert Birchall
Karate Supervisor: Jerry Morrey
Color, 90 min.
Cast: Jamie Abercrombie (Paula); René Bond (Toni); Talie Cochrane (Kat); Dona Desmond (Sheila); Margie Lanier (Dee); Forman Shane (Kyle); Nicole Riddell (Jan); Douglas Fray (Presser); Sunny Boyd (Tears); Gary Schneider (Bat); Flash Storm (Crack); Ed Wood (Pops).

Notes: In addition to playing Pops, the gas station attendant, Wood also doubles as the sheriff (wearing sunglasses and mustache).

1975
Sex Education Correspondence School
Pendulum Publications / SECS Productions
A series of twelve super 8 films, approx. 20 min. each, written and directed by Ed Wood and Charles Anderson.

1976
THE BEACH BUNNIES
SCA Distributors
Produced and Directed by A. C. Stephen
Screenplay by Edward D. Wood, Jr., and A. C. Stephen
Color, 90 min.
Cast: Wendy Cavanaugh (Bonnie); Brenda Fogerty (Elaine); Linda Gildersleeve (Sheila);

Mariwin Roberts (Laurie); Forman Shane (Chris) John Aquaboy (Dennis); Rick Cassidy (Dave); Marian Proctor (Rock).

Notes: Rather routine SCA entry with some amusing turns in Wood's script. Bodybuilder Rick Cassidy starred in hundreds of west coast X rated movies in the early 1970's.

OTHER WOOD SCRIPTS (According to his resumé.):

Escape From Time (Martha C. Brown Productions); *Portraits in Murder* (MacLachlan Brothers); *White Flash* (J. C. Productions); *Bed Time Talk* (Pete Perry Productions); *The Wicked West* (Capricorn Industries); *The Venus Fly Trap* (Japan); *Love Feast* (Capricorn Industries); *Talk Sexy Y'All* (Boris Petroff Productions — may be another title for *Shotgun Wedding)*. Wood also acted in Joe Robertson's *Mrs. Stone's Thing* (1970).

LOOPS

Wood made an unspecified number of hardcore 12 minute films in the 1970's for Swedish Erotica. Inasmuch as these films are uncredited, Wood's output in this area is unlikely to be documented. Some of the films he may have directed: *Massage Parlour; Girl Friday; The Jailer.*

TELEVISION FEATURE CREDITS

According to Wood's resume, he scripted the following tv movies: *Little Old Lady from Pasadena* (Westlake Productions, Inc.); *Morpheus Fiddles Nero* (Lea-Tuck Prod.); *The Showdown* (Sid R. Ross, Prod.); *Double Noose* (Sid R. Ross Prod.); *War Drums* (Sid R. Ross). Wood may well have directed segments of *The Sam Yorty Show* at KTTV Studios in 1964.

MISCELLANEOUS TELEVISION CREDITS

Wood directed *Thrills in Sports,* a live television show for KTLA, directed commercials for Story-Ad films (approx. 125 commercials), Play-Ad Films (approx. 30 commercials).

LIVE REVUES AND NIGHTCLUBS

Wood produced and headlined at The Dells, Woodstock, NY, and at The Kavockas Club in Washington, D.C. He wrote and directed The Bela Lugosi Review at the Silver Slipper, Las Vegas, and The Tom Keene Review, a Western Variety show.

UNREALIZED PROJECTS

1953
Bob Steele of the Border Patrol
Wood was to script a series of low budget westerns for Bob Steele at Commodore Productions.

1953
Dr. Acula
Wood was to have written and directed this proposed television series starring Bela Lugosi as Dr. Acula, a mysterious investigator of the supernatural. Ted Allan was to have produced. Lugosi announced the project on the television series, *You Asked For It.*

1954

The Vampire's Tomb

The Vampire's Tomb was first announced as a forthcoming production in the August 2, 1954 issue of the *Los Angeles Times*. According to the Sept. 9 edition of *The Hollywood Reporter,* the project was set to roll Oct. 1, with Wood flying to San Francisco to close financing. Wood did not shoot *The Vampire's Tomb* in October, but began *Bride of the Atom* instead. Bela Lugosi was to star as Dr. Acula, and the rest of the projected cast included Tom Keene, Loretta King, Bobby Jordan, Lyle Talbot, Dolores Fuller, Duke Moore and Devila, a Wood discovery modeled after Vampira.

1954

Doctor Voodoo

This transposed version of Ulmer's *The Black Cat* was to have been backed by financier Elliott Hyman, but Allied Artists president Steve Brody rejected the script. Lugosi and Karloff were to have starred.

1953 - 1955

The Phantom Ghoul

Also known as *The Ghoul Goes West,* this project was originally announced in 1953, and was to star Bela Lugosi, Lon Chaney Jr., Tor Johnson and John Carradine. When Lugosi checked himself into Norwalk State Hospital in April, 1955, he was studying the script, which was to be filmed upon his release. When Gene Autry, who was to play the hero sheriff, pulled out under suspicious circumstances, Wood tried to get Bob Steele or Ken Maynard to replace him. Harold Daniels *(Terror in the Haunted House, House of the Black Death)* was to direct, with Wood doubling as the producer-writer of the projected color / widescreen production.

1956

Rock and Roll Hell (Hellborn)

Wood's *Rebel Without a Cause* began shooting in July, 1956. After shooting 1200 feet of film, the project was abandoned by producer George Weiss, who later sold the footage to actor Conrad Brooks. Most of this footage was later incorporated into *The Sinister Urge* and *Night of the Ghouls.* Projected cast: Ed Wood, Conrad Brooks, Duke Moore, Tom Mason.

1957

Piranhas

Wood was to have directed this horror film, with music by *Bride of the Monster* composer Frank Worth.

1957

The Dead Never Die

Wood was to have directed this script by William Harlow and Kirk Kirkham from an original story by Criswell and Paul Marco. The projected cast: Criswell, Vampira, John Breckinridge, Paul Marco, Brad Jayson, Lynne Brighton, Lee Trant, Judy Parks and David De Mering.

1958

Trial By Terror

One of a series of horror films for Atomic Productions which Wood was to have directed.

1958
Ghouls of the Moon or The Undead Masses
This was to incorporate unused film of Bela Lugosi.

1959
Masquerade Into Eternity
Wood was to write and direct this "Melodrama about a Hollywood movie troupe trapped on a Cuban-type location." Ben Frommer was to play "The Colonel, the head of a military government," and was announced as participating in the project as an associate producer.

1960
House of Horrors
Commissioned by Kenne Duncan, who was to play the key role of Talya the mad artist. The part of Mario, a 400 pound giant could only have been written with Tor Johnson in mind. A revealing segment occurs as Talya paints captive girls in his dungeon studio.

1960
The Peeper
Originally titled *The Peeping Tom,* but changed no doubt in deference to Michael Powell's *Peeping Tom* (1960), *The Peeper* once again featured the detectives of *The Sinister Urge,* Lt. Matt Carson and Sgt. Randy Stone, as they attempt to crack a series of sexually motivated murders of attractive women. The culprit is a homicidal peeping tom.

1961
The Silent Night
This script later became *I Awoke Early the Day I Died.*

1963
Portraits in Terror
A trilogy consisting of Wood's *Final Curtain, The Night the Banshee Cried,* and the unfilmed *Into My Grave,* a premature burial-inspired story.

1963 - 1964
Attack of the Giant Salami
A science fiction spoof Wood tried to get off the ground, with a projected cast of Joe E. Brown, Boris Karloff and Valda Hansen, abandoned when Brown died. Known at various times as *Operation Salami* and *Invasion of the Gigantic Salami.*

1965
To Catch a Raw Indian
About a writer who wants to direct a motion picture about displaced cliff-dwelling Indian tribes.

1965
Joaquin Murieta
Wood was keen on making a movie about the reknown bandit of the old west. After he was captured, Murieta's head and the hand of a companion, Three-Fingered Jack, were pickled in alcohol and auctioned off at a sheriff's sale for $36.

1966
Rue Pigalle

Wood's script, from his novel *69 Rue Pigalle,* about a transvestite who solves a series of murders in Paris, was to have been made by SCA films, with A. C. Stephen directing, but financing was withdrawn. Lon Chaney was in the projected cast.

1966
Tangier

A proposed television series in the action-adventure crime-detective genre, from a story by A. C. Stephen. Teleplay by Edward D. Wood, Jr.

"Tangier — a bawdy-boisterous city where crime is a basic industry, life is cheap — murder, a common habit ..."

1966
Enchanted Isle

Unfilmed screenplay by Ed Wood concerns a mob princess in a south sea island, pagan sacrifice, imbroglios involving black pearls and unrealized sexual desires. Projected cast was to include Dana Andrews, John Ireland and Lon Chaney, Jr.

1967
Devil Girls

About a drug-smuggling teenage girl gang, adapted from the eponymous Wood novel. Tor Johnson was to play Chief, a giant who works for Jockey, a former racing car driver who runs a "low-class hamburger joint," which the girl gang frequents.

Snap Happy

Wood worked on a screenplay with stuntman Rodd Redwing about Matthew Brady, civil war era photographer.

The Life of Mickey Cohen

Paul Marco was to play the notorious Hollywood gangster. Cohen figured prominently in Liz Renay's autobiography, *My Face for the World to See.*

1973
Mice on a Cold Cellar Floor / Epitaph for the Town Drunk / To Kill a Saturday Night

Three dark and somber tales about poverty and the bleakness of life. Dialogue from *Mice on a Cold Cellar Floor:*

Harry: "We're nothing but mice ... just like them mice over there in the corner ... we're all just mice on a cold cellar floor."

In *Epitaph for the Village Drunk,* town drunk Harry Poole surprises the townspeople by saving the life of a young boy who falls under the ice in a creek. Having no other place to stay, Harry spends the night in jail where old timers bring him a couple bottles. Unable to keep warm, Harry burns his mattress and dies when the jail catches fire.

To Kill a Saturday Night was to have featured John Carradine and David Ward as two small-town winos.

1973
The Teachers
Unrealized Wood script in which attractive junior college students soon learn the best method to achieve high grades from their instructors.

1973
The Basketballers
Unfilmed screenplay by Ed Wood and Stephen Apostolof involves sex, sports and drugs on a small town college campus.

1973
The Airline Hostesses
Unfilmed Wood screenplay about the sexual preoccupations of airline pilots and stews.

1974
I Awoke Early the Day I Died
An original screenplay by Ed Wood, based upon his 1960 script, *Night of Silence* (or *The Silent Night*).

Synopsis: Overcoming a nurse and dressing in her clothes, a madman escapes from Hope Sanitarium. Stealing a gun and a sedan, the madman goes on a wild crime spree, robbing a loan office and killing the manager.

Coming upon an ancient cemetery, the madman witnesses a burial service. When the undertaker leaves, the madman opens the coffin and finds a skeleton dressed in cult-like robes, and the hammer and silver tuning fork employed during the funeral ceremony. The thief lays the briefcase stuffed with stolen money on the skeleton. He strikes the tuning fork, and the sound of bagpipe music fills the air. The thief goes into contortions, and the coffin lid closes with his money inside. The thief runs towards the sound of the bagpipe, falling into an open grave, knocking himself unconscious. Awakening the next day, the thief discovers that the coffin and his money are missing. He comes upon the caretaker and finds that the coffin has been moved. Angered, he smothers the old caretaker with a pillow.

He tracks down the coffin, and finds his briefcase empty. He finds names and addresses of the mourners at the funeral ceremony, and one by one these mourners meet their end at his hands, except for a carnival sharpshooter, who escapes death when the carnival midget, fat lady and human skeleton rush to his aid.

Stealing a cab, the thief once more returns to the old cemetery. He comes upon the corpse of the caretaker and, haunted by the dead man's staring eyes, carries him and his bagpipes to an open grave. The bagpipes drop and rip open, revealing the stolen money. The thief drops the body, and gust of wind carries the money off in every direction. Now hearing furious bagpipe music, the madman screams in a rage. Running after the money, he falls into an open grave, breaking his neck.

I Awoke Early the Day I Died is quintessential Ed Wood with its thematic obsession with death, graveyards, burlesque and the grotesque. In the tradition of the Russell Rouse-directed *The Thief* (1952), the movie was to have no dialogue, only incidental sounds, screams, laughter and music. Aldo Ray was set to play the madman-thief, John Carradine was to have been the undertaker, and John Agar and David Ward were slated to have played policemen. Of all his projects in Wood's last years, this was his personal favorite.

1974

Heads No Tails

Unfilmed script for producer Barry Elliott was inspired by the Tod Slaughter films of the '30's. It has four different endings.

1976

The Day the Mummies Danced

Wood's return to the horror genre was to have been filmed on location at the famous Guanajuato caves in Mexico, which feature twisted mummies as a tourist attraction. Projected cast: Aldo Ray, John Agar, and Dudley Manlove, who, according to Wood, was to have financed a good part of the production.

1976

Lugosi ... Post Mortem

Blue Dolphin Records contracted Wood to write a book and screenplay based on his own experiences with Bela Lugosi in the last five years of the actor's life. Wood wanted Peter Coe to play Lugosi. Karl Johnson was to have played the role of his father, Tor. The nearly completed script and book were left behind when Wood was evicted and is presumed to have been destroyed.

1977

Shoot 7

Wood wrote the book for this unproduced musical on the St. Valentine's Day massacre.

1977

Venus De Milo

A fantasy-adventure revolving around the mystery of the famous statue's missing arms. Wood wanted to film this in the Mediterranean and star his teenage neighbor/discovery Shannon Dolder.

Edward D. Wood, Jr. in *Glen or Glenda*

[photo courtesy Dolores Fuller]

How a man changed his sex soon will be rushed to the screen

By ALINE MOSBY
United Press Hollywood Correspondent

Hollywood never misses a bet on the headlines, so a movie company has rushed out with the inevitable—a picture about a man who's changed into a woman.

Films have been based on such news events as a little girl falling into a well, the Korean war and a guy who went into the Army with his lion.

Thus before the newsprint dried on the copy about Christine Jorgensen, the ex-GI turned glamour girl, Producer George Weiss of Screen Classics, Inc., and Director Edward Wood were shooting scene 5.

Behind locked doors, so MGM wouldn't find out, they filmed "I Changed My Sex."

GETTING WIND of this production scoop, I trailed them to a tiny rental studio on Santa Monica Blvd., called "Quality Pictures."

Director Wood, a sort of Orson Welles of low-budget pictures, wrote, directed and starred in the movie. He used to dance with famed Martha Graham, too, he added.

"There is no comparison to the Christine Jorgensen case," Wood insisted, examining his orange socks and black suede shoes.

Producer Weiss, who has given you such side-street theater movies as "Pin Down Girl" (lady wrestlers) and "Girl Gang" (teen-age narcotics users), says there is "nothing censorable whatsoever" in his new picture.

THIS FILM opens with scenes of Bela Lugosi sitting in his usual laboratory and pouring the usual evil potions into test tubes that smoke and crackle. Bela, Wood explained, plays an "all-powerful science-god figure. This is almost science-fiction."

Lugosi, with suitable eerie under-lighting, peers at the tiny people of the world. We then dissolve to investigate two earthly lives. One plot involves Wood, who plays a man who wants to wear woman's clothes. The other story involves musician Tommy Haines, who plays a man who by operations such as Miss Jorgensen's is turned into a woman. In real life Haines, or Miss Haines, actually is a woman, and Wood actually is a man who is going to marry his leading lady, Dolores Fuller, who in real life is a woman.

"It's documentary," exclaimed Wood. "We talked to hundreds of people and psychiatrists. We had doctors supervising the operation scene."

"We do exploitation pictures," boomed Producer Weiss.

Index

Acknowledgements

For their continued support and assistance in this venture, I am particularly grateful to: Chris Eckoff, Tomata du Plenty, Evelyn Bianca, Cole Gagne and John Black of Backtrack Video, Seattle.

For information, assistance and the use of valuable materials, I express gratitude to: John Andrews, Carl Anthony, Steve Apostolof, Lorraine Ashcroft, Buddy Barnett, Harold Bear, Henry Bederski, Alan Betrock, Paul Bianca, Richard Bojarski, Nick Bougas, Conrad Brooks, Louis R. Cafini, Eric Caidon, Tim Caldwell, Tony Cardoza, Tom Corrigan, Phil Chamberlin, Robert Cremer, Don Fellman, Irene Forrest, Dolores Fuller, Dave Friedman, Dale Gasteigger, Joseph Green, Valda Hansen, Ric Hardman, Larry Hardy, Maura Hefner, David J. Hogan, Mike Hornyak, Alexander Kogan, Alan Licht, Michael Lucas, Bill Mackleheny, Dudley Manlove, Paul Marco, Jimmy McDonough, Mona McKinnon, Candido Medina, Richard Meltzer, Ted V. Mikels, Dennis P. Mitchell, Fred Mollin, Titus Moody, Don Nagel, Maila Nurmi, Aldo Ray, Garydon Rhodes, Fred Robertson, Joseph Robertson, William Rotsler, Kregg Sanders, Ray Dennis Steckler, Harry Thomas, Stuart Timmons, John Tydings, Patty Wallace, David Ward, Tina Warren, Tom Weaver, Kathy Wood, Mildred and Frank Worth, and Scott Zimmerman.

Thanks also must go to: Paul Ambrose, Ives Arnold, Brian Bailey, Glen Branca, Sumner Crane, Paul Dyer, Jr., Michael Grimm, John Pierre Jackson, Donald Krieger, Mike Kuchar, Ron Lash, Johnny Legend, Petteri Laitinen, Michael Weldon, John White, John Wooley, and Rob D. Wray.

I regret that the following individuals did not live to see the publication of this book, which they all contributed to: Ron Ashcroft, Bernie Bloom, Timothy Farrell, Buddy Hyde, Aldo Ray, Roy Reid and Lillian Wood.

Special thanks to my editor, Adam Parfrey, who saw it right away.

For a complete Feral House catalogue
send SASE to

FERAL HOUSE
PO BOX 3466
PORTLAND, OR 97208

Feral House Puts The Lead
Back In Your Pencil

Kooks
A Guide to the Outer Limits of Human Belief
by Donna Kossy

Black messiahs, self-trepanation, soul-as-smell, devil is a
dinosaur, voluntary human extinction, flat earth, anti-grav-
ity, men can have babies, etc. ... all the news unfit to
print. Perfect toilet reading.
$16.95 • 8 1/2 x 11 • 254 pages • ISBN: 0-922915-19-9

Cult Rapture
Revelations of the Apocalyptic Mind
by Adam Parfrey

The true story of Walter and Margaret Keane, Christian
patriots do armed revolution, weird sex cults, brotherhood
of the snake, Elvis' most disgusting fan, underneath the
sheets with the Archangel Uriel, East Indian sleight-of-
hand artist becomes God; driving Highway 61 with James
Shelby Downard; SWAT team members unveil plans for
the future; mind control technology; much more. All
Parfrey, no filler. Available November, '94.
$14.95 • 6 x 9 • 340 pages • ISBN: 0-922915-22-9

CAD
A Handbook for Heels
Edited by Charles Schneider

All the forgotten lore of the red-blooded American males,
complete with two-fisted tales & pulchritudionous pictorials.
$14.95 • 8 1/2 x 11 • ISBN: 0-922915-09-1

To order, send cash, check, or money order for book plus $1.75
postage to Feral House, PO Box 3466, Portland, OR, 97208.